THE SOUNDS OF KOREAN
A Pronunciation Guide

Miho Choo
&
William O'Grady

University of Hawai'i Press
Honolulu

© 2003 University of Hawai'i Press
All rights reserved
Printed in the United States of America

08 07 06 05 04 03   6 5 4 3 2 1

Library of Congress Cataloging–in–Publication

Choo, Miho
    The sounds of Korean : a pronunciation guide / Miho Choo & William O'Grady.
      p. cm.
    Includes bibliographical references and index.
    ISBN 0-8248-2601-9 (pbk. : alk. paper)
    1. Korean language—Pronunciation by foreign speakers. 2. Korean
language—Pronunciation by foreign speakers—Problems, exercises, etc.
I. O'Grady, William D. (William Delaney), 1952– II. Title.

PL915.C466 2003
495.7'3421—dc21

                                     2003042690

Camera-ready copy has been provided by the authors.

University of Hawai'i Press books are printed on acid-free paper
and meet the guidelines for permanence and
durability of the Council on Library Resources.

Printed by Versa Press Inc.

This book is dedicated to the memory

of our friend Stan Starosta

Contents

Acknowledgments

We are grateful to a number of people who took the time to read earlier versions of *The Sounds of Korean* and to provide helpful comments. Special thanks are due to Dong-Jae Lee, Hae-Young Kim, Sang-Yee Cheon, and Youngkeun Lee for their detailed comments and suggestions. We also received helpful feedback and advice from Ned Shultz, Sunyoung Lee, S.-Y. Lee, Kyu-Seek Hwang, Sooyeon Tahk, Young-sook Shim, Hyun-ho Joo, and two anonymous referees for the University of Hawai'i Press. Eduardo Contreras provided valuable technical support, Victoria Anderson offered insightful advice on phonetic matters, and Peter Kobayashi assisted us with the artwork.

Shinwoong Lee played an indispensable role in the creation of the CD that accompanies this book. In addition to serving as the male voice on the CD during many long hours of studio work, he offered valuable advice on the recording material itself.

We also owe a special debt of gratitude to In-Sung Ko, for his assistance with the palatography and linguography studies that we drew upon in describing the place of articulation of various Korean consonants. Thanks are also due to the five native speakers of Korean who served as subjects for this study and to the Center for Korean Studies at the University of Hawai'i for funding this work.

We would also like to express our appreciation to the Liberal Arts Instructional Technology Services at the University of Texas at Austin for their technical and financial support during the preparation of the CD. Special thanks are due to our audio specialist Mike Heidenreich, who spent countless hours supervising the recording and preparing the final version of the CD. In addition, we are grateful to director Joe TenBarge, who played a major role in securing funding for the project.

Finally, we owe thanks to the editorial and production team at the University of Hawai'i Press who contributed to bringing this book into being—especially executive editor Pat Crosby, managing editor Ann Ludeman, production editor Lucille Aono, and copyeditor Nancy R. Woodington.

Part I

Pronunciation Guide

Chapter 1

Learning to Pronounce Korean

How many different speech sounds are there? Fifty? A hundred? The answer may surprise you: there are about eight hundred—six hundred consonant sounds and two hundred vowels.[1]

That's far more than any single language can use. To keep things manageable, individual languages typically make contrasts among no more than fifty sounds. And with about eight hundred sounds to choose from, it's unlikely that any two languages will end up with exactly the same sound system.

Herein lies one of the great challenges of second language learning. Although infants are able to hear even the subtlest differences among sounds in any language, this ability starts to diminish around the age of ten or twelve months. By the time children finish elementary school, they have to struggle to make and hear phonetic contrasts other than those in their native language.[2] And, of course, things don't get any easier for adolescents and adults.

That doesn't mean that you can't become fluent in another language, however. It *is* possible to master the pronunciation of a second language—but only if you go about it in a systematic way. You need to know precisely what sounds your new language has, how they are produced, and what changes they undergo in particular contexts. Then you have to practice—both by listening and by speaking.

The first goal of second language learning is to pass through what might be called the "threshold of intelligibility"—to reach the point where you can make yourself understood and can understand what others are saying.[3] To achieve that goal in Korean, three challenges must be met.

First, Korean has a number of speech sounds that have no direct counterpart in English—including three 'p'-like sounds, three 't'-like sounds, three 'k'-like sounds, three 'ch'-like sounds, and two 's'-like

---

[1]Ladefoged (1999).
[2]Eimas (1996:31), Werker et al. (1996).
[3]See, for example, Celce-Murcia, Brinton & Goodwin (1996).

sounds, in addition to several unfamiliar vowels. Mastering these contrasts is a necessary step toward becoming fluent in Korean.

Second, the pronunciation of particular Korean sounds can vary enormously depending on the context in which they occur. Take ㄱ, for instance. At the end of a word like 백 'hundred', its pronunciation resembles the 'k' sound in the English word *backbone*, but it is pronounced like a 'g' sound in 백일 'hundred days' and like a 'ng' sound in 백만 'million'. Learning how these adjustments work will dramatically improve your ability to speak and understand Korean.

Third, Korean uses pitch, loudness, and length (what linguists call *prosody*) in ways that give it a rhythm and a flow quite different from English. Learning these aspects of pronunciation is also vital to improving the naturalness of your Korean.

We will consider all of these things in this book. If you're a beginner, you'll find the information you need to cross the threshold of intelligibility in Korean. And if you're a more advanced student, you'll have an opportunity to fine-tune your pronunciation and improve your comprehension, so that both become more native-like.

1.1 The organization of this book

The Sounds of Korean is divided into two parts. Part I consists of five chapters, all focusing on the description of different aspects of Korean pronunciation. Chapter 2 presents the vowel sounds, while chapter 3 deals with consonants. Chapter 4 discusses the various adjustment processes that modify speech sounds in different positions within words and phrases, and chapter 5 tackles the role of prosody in expressing meaning and emotion. Through explanations and examples, we'll take you through the basic facts and contrasts that are needed to make your speech intelligible and natural-sounding.

Throughout our discussion, we will focus on the pronunciation of so-called standard Korean. This is the Korean which is spoken by educated people in the Seoul area and which is almost always taught in second language classrooms.

Figure 1.1 Map of Korea

Part II of *The Sounds of Korean* makes up the heart of the book. It consists of a large set of practice exercises specifically designed to complement the descriptions and explanations in Part I. These exercises, each with its own instructions, have been recorded on the accompanying CD by two native speakers of standard Korean, one male and one female.

In preparing the practice exercises, we were careful to employ natural colloquial speech that represents the way Korean is actually spoken. The goal of language learning is to become proficient in a new language—which means being able to communicate and to understand what others are saying. Attaining this goal is possible only if you are exposed to Korean as it is spoken in the real world. If Koreans pronounce 봐 'Look' as if it were 바, and if they sometimes pronounce 꽃이 'flower + subject marker' as if it were 꼬시, you need to know this. Otherwise, you'll never understand spoken Korean, and your own speech will never sound fluent.

Some of the practice exercises target the pronunciation of individual words, while others focus on full sentences. In constructing both types of practice exercise, we have made every effort to choose common vocabulary items and to use them in natural and colloquial sentences. In addition, we have made sure that the words and sentences on the CD are pronounced at a moderate speed. Even this may seem fast if you are a beginning student. Indeed, some of the subtler phonetic contrasts found in Korean are initially difficult to perceive at any speed. However, as you make progress, the sounds and rhythms that give Korean its phonetic identity will become increasingly familiar to you. It will be easier to make yourself understood, it will be easier to comprehend what Koreans are saying, and it will even be easier to read and write the language. With diligent and regular use of the practice exercises, you may be surprised at how quickly your pronunciation and comprehension improve—even a few weeks of faithful practice will make a difference.

1.2 Pronunciation and spelling

Before we go any further, a note of caution is in order. There is a natural temptation to pronounce words the way they are written, but this just won't work for Korean. (Or for English either, as you'll realize if you think about the pronunciation of words such as *Wednesday, comb,* and *knee.*)

Written languages differ in terms of how they capture the relationship between pronunciation and spelling. In a language such as Spanish, the writing system represents pronunciation quite directly, and there is nearly a one-to-one relationship between letters and sounds. In Chinese, on the other hand, written symbols represent entire words rather than individual sounds.

The Korean writing system, *hangul,* lies somewhere in the middle of the spectrum.[4] In general, the goal of hangul is to provide a single spelling for each root and each suffix, without regard for variations in their pronunciation. So 옷 'clothes' has a single spelling, regardless of how the final consonant is pronounced—as a 't'-like sound when the word stands alone, as an 's'-like sound in 옷을 (with the direct object marker), as a 'sh'-like

---

[4]For a general discussion of the history and workings of hangul, see Kim-Renaud (1997) and Sampson (1985).

sound in 옷이 (with the subject marker), or as an 'n'-like or even 'm'-like sound in 옷만 (with the suffix that means 'only'). English spelling often adopts a similar strategy, by the way. That's why the root in words like *creative* and *creation* is spelled *creat* even though the *t* has a 'sh'-like pronunciation in the second word.

As we'll see in more detail in the chapters that follow, Korean spelling follows the principle of one spelling per root or suffix with great regularity and efficiency. In fact, one of the advantages of studying the sound system of Korean is that you will also end up with a better understanding of how hangul works.

In describing and discussing the sounds of Korean, it is sometimes necessary to represent a word's pronunciation more directly than spelling permits. As you will see, for example, words such as 입력 'input' and 꽃잎 'petal' are pronounced very differently from the way they are spelled. Where spelling does not suffice, we use hangul inside square brackets to help indicate how the word is pronounced—[임녁] for 입력 and [꼰닙] for 꽃잎. This does not capture all the phonetic details, of course, but it is nonetheless helpful, especially when used in conjunction with the CD.

Syllables and consonant relinking

Another important feature of hangul has to do with the manner in which it represents syllables. A syllable is simply a chunk of speech built around a vowel—so you'll always have as many syllables in a word as there are vowel sounds. (The English word *bed* contains just one syllable, *ago* has two, *computer* has three, and so on.) As you have probably already noticed, hangul groups sounds together into syllable-sized chunks. In words such as 나무 'tree', 먹다 'eat', and 자동차 'automobile', these letter groupings correspond exactly to the syllables used in Korean speech. However, things work differently when one syllable ends in a consonant and the next syllable begins with a vowel sound—as happens in words such as 밥이 'cooked rice + subject marker', 언어 'language', 앞에 'in front', and so on. Under these circumstances, the consonant ends up being pronounced at the beginning of the second syllable, thanks to an adjustment process that we call *consonant relinking*.[5] As a result, 밥이 is pronounced [바비], 언어 is pronounced [어너], and so forth.

Consonant relinking is a far-reaching process in Korean and can even extend across word boundaries when two words are pronounced together as a group, with no intervening pauses. That's why 예쁜 우산 'pretty umbrella' is pronounced [예쁘누산], with the ㄴ of 예쁜 at the beginning of the second word rather than at the end of the first. Exactly the same thing happens with the ㄹ in 물 있어요 'There's water' and in many other cases.

Example		Pronounced
밥이	'cooked rice + subject marker'	[바비]
언어	'language'	[어너]
예쁜 우산	'pretty umbrella'	[예쁘누산]
물 있어요	'There's water'	[무리써요]

Hangul does not directly represent the effects of consonant relinking. However, it does provide a very good clue as to when consonant relinking takes place. Notice that the second syllable of 밥이, 언어, and other words that undergo consonant relinking begins with the so-called zero consonant ㅇ. This symbol marks an empty position at the beginning of the syllable—the very position in which the consonant from the preceding syllable is heard when the word is pronounced.[6]

밥＿이

You'll find practice exercises involving consonant relinking in section A-1 of the CD that accompanies this book.

With these preliminaries behind us, we are ready to have a look at how the individual sounds of Korean are pronounced. We'll begin with vowel sounds in the next chapter and then move on to consonants from there.

---

[5]The term *resyllabification* is also used for this phenomenon.

[6]It is important not to confuse the ㅇ that occurs at the beginning of a syllable with the one that occurs at the end. The former is a place holder with no pronunciation of its own, but the latter stands for the 'ng' sound (see section 3.7).

Chapter 2

Vowels

Vowel sounds in any language are made by modifying the position of the tongue, lips, and jaw. You can get a feel for this by comparing the 'ee' of *see* with the 'oo' of *Sue* in English. If you say these sounds one right after the other *(ee-oo, ee-oo),* you'll feel the tongue moving from a high front position in your mouth for the 'ee' to a more back position for 'oo'. You'll also notice that your lips are rounded for 'oo', but not for 'ee'.

The 'ah' sound in *father* is different again. Your tongue is in a low position, and your mouth is more open than for 'ee' or 'oo'. (You'll feel your jaw drop if you put your finger on your chin as you go from 'ee' to 'ah'.)

There are basically two ways to learn the Korean vowel sounds. One is to start with the vowels of English and try to make the changes that are needed to produce similar (and not-so-similar) Korean sounds. The other is to become aware of how your tongue, lips, and jaw work together to produce vowel sounds. We will use both techniques here so that you can pick and choose the pieces of information that are most helpful to you.

We'll begin in a relatively informal way by comparing the vowels of Korean with their nearest counterparts in English. Section 2.3 provides a more technical description for those who want to understand the mechanics of vowel production in more detail.

To make our discussion more manageable, we'll divide Korean vowels into two groups—simple vowels and diphthongs.

2.1 Simple vowels

There are eight simple vowels in Korean.[1] Because of similarities and differences in how they are produced, it makes sense to consider them in small groups rather than separately.

---

[1]Vowel length can be used to distinguish between words in Korean. For example, 눈 means 'eye' when it has a short vowel, but 'snow' when it has a long vowel; 새 means 'new' when it has a short vowel, but 'bird' when it has a long vowel; and 병 means

2.1.1 The vowels ㅣ, ㅜ, & ㅡ

The vowels ㅣ and ㅜ are very similar to sounds found in English and are therefore easy to produce and perceive. However, as we will see, ㅡ presents a bit more of a challenge.

The vowel ㅣ

The ㅣ sound has a pronunciation almost identical to the 'ee' sound in English words such as *bee,* except that the tongue is slightly higher in the mouth.

The vowel ㅜ

The vowel ㅜ is pronounced in virtually the same way as the 'oo' in *Sue,* although perhaps with the tongue slightly higher in the mouth and with the lips somewhat more rounded and protruded. It too creates little or no problem for English speakers.

The vowel ㅡ

The vowel ㅡ requires more attention, since English has nothing quite like it. One way to learn how to pronounce it is to start with the more familiar ㅣ sound. As you pronounce ㅣ, move your tongue slightly back in your mouth while keeping your lips relaxed and unrounded. The resulting sound is Korean ㅡ .

Many beginning students have trouble hearing the difference between ㅡ and ㅜ, and therefore miss important distinctions, such as the one between 그 'that' and 구 'nine', or between 들 'field' and 둘 'two'. It may help to remember that ㅜ is produced with the tongue further back in the mouth and that it has strong lip rounding. In contrast, ㅡ is produced with the tongue more forward and without lip rounding.

'bottle' when it has a short vowel, but 'illness' when it has a long vowel. Except for some older speakers, however, most Koreans no longer make these contrasts.

You will find practice exercises for the vowels ㅡ and ㅜ in section V-1 of the CD.

2.1.2 The vowels ㅔ, ㅐ, ㅗ, & ㅓ

None of these four vowels is exactly like any of the vowels of English. Let us consider each one in turn.

The vowel ㅔ

The ㅔ sound is similar to the vowel in English words such as *bay* and *bait*, but with one important difference: the English vowel is followed by a 'y' sound. If you pronounce *bay* slowly, you'll probably be able to feel your tongue rising for the 'y'. And if you put a finger on your jaw, you may feel it closing slightly near the end of the word as the 'y' is pronounced. The Korean ㅔ sound does not include this extra component, so your tongue and jaw should remain stable throughout the entire vowel.

The vowel ㅐ

The vowel ㅐ is produced with the tongue slightly lower and the mouth slightly more open than for the ㅔ sound. If you put a finger or two on your chin, you should feel it drop slightly for ㅐ, compared to ㅔ. The end result should be a sound somewhere between the 'e' of *bet* and the 'a' of *bat*.

The contrast between ㅔ and ㅐ

The contrast between ㅔ and ㅐ has all but disappeared in contemporary Korean, and most speakers pronounce the two sounds alike, more or less as ㅔ. Nonetheless, the distinction is still maintained in initial syllables by a few speakers, especially in careful speech, as in 게 'crab' versus 개 'dog', 세 집 'three houses' versus 새 집 'new house', or 제 'my' versus 재 'ash'. The contrast has been largely lost in other positions,[2] though, and

---

[2]Martin (1992:28), Sohn (1994:433).

words such as 모레 'the day after tomorrow' and 모래 'sand' are pronounced identically by virtually all speakers of Korean.

Even when a distinction is made in initial syllables between ㅔ and ㅐ, it is very subtle—so subtle that even native speakers of Korean have trouble perceiving it when there is no context[3] and may have to ask each other, "Is it 'ㅓ ㅣ' (ㅔ) or 'ㅏ ㅣ' (ㅐ)?" Indeed, the pronunciation of one common word has changed because of the difficulty of the ㅔ/ㅐ contrast. In colloquial Korean, the word 네 'your' is pronounced [니], so as to better distinguish it from 내 'my'. (Remember that we use square brackets to indicate a word's pronunciation when the spelling does not suffice.)

Although it has been largely lost in pronunciation, the ㅔ/ㅐ distinction is still alive and well in the spelling of words, including words that are borrowed into Korean from English. As the following examples help show, ㅔ is consistently used for the English vowel sounds in words such as *bell* and *table*, while ㅐ is employed for the vowel sound in *apple*.

The spelling of some English loan words

벨	'bell'	애플	'apple'
테이블	'table'	로맨스	'romance'
멕시코	'Mexico'	샌드위치	'sandwich'
레스토랑	'restaurant'	캘리포니아	'California'

The vowel ㅗ

The ㅗ sound of Korean is very similar to the 'o' in English words such as *low*—with one significant difference. English 'o' is accompanied by a following 'w' sound, which you can hear if you pronounce *low* slowly. (You'll feel your lips become tighter and rounder as you say the 'w'.) In contrast, the Korean vowel stands by itself, with no accompanying 'w' sound, so your tongue and jaw should remain stable throughout the entire sound.

---

[3]Lee (1995).

The vowel ㅓ

Perhaps the most difficult vowel of all for second language learners is ㅓ. There are two techniques that you might find helpful in learning how to pronounce it. One is to start with the 'uh' sound that occurs in words such as *up* and *pub*. As you produce this vowel, try moving your tongue to a more back position without rounding your lips. The resulting sound is ㅓ. (You can watch for lip rounding by looking in the mirror as you practice.)

Another technique is to begin by pronouncing ㅗ. Then, gradually relax your lips so that they are no longer rounded and open your mouth a bit more by lowering your jaw slightly. (If you place your finger just beneath your chin, you should feel it drop a little for ㅓ compared to ㅗ.) The resulting sound, with a tongue position a bit lower than for ㅗ and with no lip rounding, is ㅓ.[4] An advantage of this technique is that it allows you to practice the ㅗ/ㅓ contrast, which is difficult for English speakers but crucial for distinguishing between words such as 돌 'stone' and 덜 'less', 고기 'meat' and 거기 'there', and many others.

Sections V-2 through V-4 of the CD contain practice exercises involving the vowels ㅔ, ㅐ, ㅗ, and ㅓ.

2.1.3 The vowel ㅏ

The vowel ㅏ is quite similar to the 'ah' sound in the pronunciation of words such as *father* and *cot* in most parts of the United States and Canada. It is produced with the tongue more forward and a little lower in the mouth than for ㅓ. You should therefore feel your jaw drop slightly when you go from ㅓ to ㅏ.

The contrast between ㅏ and ㅓ is an important one, and is used to distinguish between many words, including 발 'foot' versus 벌 'bee', and 다 'all' versus 더 'more'. Section V-5 of the CD contains practice exercises that will help you master the contrast between these two vowels.

---

[4]Some Koreans seem to pronounce ㅓ in a more forward position than ㅗ, without perceptibly lowering the tongue.

2.2 Diphthongs

Diphthongs are two-part sounds consisting of a *glide* and a vowel. (The 'y' sound in *yes* and the 'w' sound in *we* are glides.)

2.2.1 The 'y' diphthongs: ㅑ, ㅕ, ㅒ, ㅖ, ㅛ, ㅠ, & ㅢ

Korean has six diphthongs in which the glide 'y' precedes the vowel: ㅑ, ㅕ, ㅒ, ㅖ, ㅛ, and ㅠ, all of which are produced by combining 'y' with the appropriate following vowel. Thus ㅑ consists of 'y' plus ㅏ, ㅕ consists of 'y' plus ㅓ, and so on. In addition, there is one diphthong in which the 'y' sound comes after the vowel—namely ㅢ, whose pronunciation we will discuss shortly.

The 'y' diphthongs of Korean

Diphthong	Example	
ㅑ	약	'medicine'
ㅕ	역	'train station'
ㅒ	애기	'story'
ㅖ	예	'example'
ㅛ	욕	'abusive language'
ㅠ	육	'six'
ㅢ	의사	'doctor'

Two sorts of contrasts are especially worthy of note. The first involves the distinction between simple vowels and diphthongs such as ㅔ and ㅖ. Because the 'y' sound is often weakly pronounced (see section 4.3), diphthongs may be difficult to identify in some cases.

A second important contrast involves certain pairs of diphthongs themselves. Because English speakers sometimes find it difficult to distinguish ㅏ from ㅓ and ㅓ from ㅗ, they may also have trouble with the contrast between ㅑ and ㅕ, as in 약 'medicine' versus 역 'train station', and with the contrast between ㅕ and ㅛ, as in 역 'train station' versus 욕 'abusive language'.

Because the distinction between ㅖ and ㅒ has been largely lost (section 2.1.2), there is typically no contrast between ㅖ and ㅒ either. Where the contrast is maintained (primarily at the beginning of words), ㅐ is pronounced with the tongue slightly lower and the mouth slightly more open than for ㅔ, parallel to ㅒ and ㅖ.

The diphthong ㅢ also requires special attention, because it can be pronounced in three different ways. At the beginning of words such as 의사 'doctor' and 의자 'chair', it has the expected diphthongal pronunciation in careful speech: the vowel ㅡ followed by a 'y'. (There are some speakers, though, who pronounce the glide very weakly or not at all in this position, saying [으사] for 의사 .)

A different pronunciation occurs when 의 is used to represent the possessive suffix, as in 미국의 수도 'America's capital'. Here it is pronounced as the simple vowel ㅔ, just like the suffix 에 'to'.

When ㅢ is neither word-initial nor the possessive suffix, it is pronounced as the simple vowel ㅣ. So 희망 'hope' and 거의 'almost' are pronounced [히망] and [거이], respectively.

Three pronunciations for ㅢ		
Position/Use	Pronunciation	Examples
• at the beginning of a word	ㅢ (or ㅡ)	의사, 의자
• as the possessive suffix	ㅔ	미국의 수도
• elsewhere	ㅣ	희망, 거의

For practice involving the 'y' diphthongs of Korean, go to sections V-6 and V-7 of the CD.

2.2.2 The 'w' diphthongs: ㅟ, ㅘ, ㅝ, ㅙ, ㅞ, & ㅚ

Korean has six 'w' diphthongs: ㅟ, ㅘ, ㅝ, ㅙ, ㅞ, and ㅚ. The first five are produced with an initial 'w' sound followed by the appropriate vowel. Thus ㅟ is 'w' plus ㅣ, ㅘ is 'w' plus ㅏ, and so on. The sixth diphthong, ㅚ, cannot be broken down in this way; instead, it has essentially the same pronunciation as ㅞ ('w' plus ㅔ).

The 'w' diphthongs of Korean

Diphthong	Example	
ㅟ	위기	'crisis'
ㅘ	왕	'king'
ㅝ	월급	'monthly salary'
ㅙ	왜	'why'
ㅞ	웬일이야?	'What's up?'
ㅚ	외국	'foreign country'

As we'll see in section 4.3, the 'w' glide tends to be pronounced very weakly in colloquial Korean when it does not occur at the beginning of a word.

At least three contrasts involving 'w' diphthongs can be difficult for second language learners. The first involves the distinction between ㅟ and ㅢ, as in 위기 'crisis' versus 의기 'spirits/vigor'. The first diphthong consists of the 'w' glide followed by the vowel ㅣ, while the second one consists of the vowel ㅡ followed by the 'y' glide.

A second contrast that many students find difficult involves ㅘ and ㅝ, as in 완만하다 'be gradually sloped' versus 원만하다 'be well rounded'. This contrast presupposes the distinction between the vowels ㅏ and ㅓ discussed in section 2.1.3.

The third contrast worth mentioning involves ㅙ, ㅞ, and ㅚ, all three of which are routinely pronounced alike. As noted in section 2.1, the contrast between ㅐ and ㅔ is usually lost, making it necessary to rely on context to determine which vowel is intended. The same is true for the contrast between the diphthongs ㅙ and ㅞ, as well as ㅚ, whose pronunciation is essentially that of ㅞ. For those who make the contrast in careful speech, the tongue is slightly lower and the mouth is slightly more open for the pronunciation of ㅙ than for ㅞ or ㅚ.

There are few opportunities for these contrasts to be made. Although ㅚ occurs frequently (as in 외국 'foreign country', 외식 'eating out', and 회사 'company'), relatively few words contain the ㅙ diphthong. (The most common is 왜 'why'.) Even fewer items contain ㅞ, the most common being 웬일이야? 'What's up?'

Section V-8 of the CD contains practice exercises for the 'w' diphthongs of Korean.

2.3 Appendix: The mechanics of vowels

This section discusses some technical details relating to how Korean vowel sounds are produced. This information is not required to make use of the practice exercises.

The details of vowel production

We can understand how any vowel is produced by answering three questions.

1. Is the tongue in a high, mid, or low position in the mouth?

2. Is the tongue in the front, central, or back region of the mouth?

3. Are the lips rounded or not?

Phoneticians often make use of drawings such as the one in figure 2.1 to depict the position of the tongue and lips during the production of vowel sounds.[5]

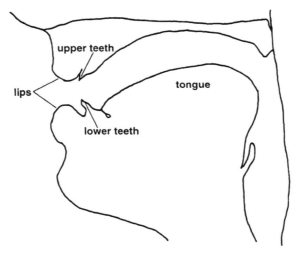

Figure 2.1 The inside of the mouth (side view)

---

[5]The vocal tract diagrams used in this book were prepared with the help of the *Draw Vocal Tract* software developed at UCLA by Peter Ladefoged and the assistance of Peter Kobayashi.

In order to understand how Korean vowels are pronounced, it helps to divide the mouth into four vertical regions, as shown in figure 2.2.

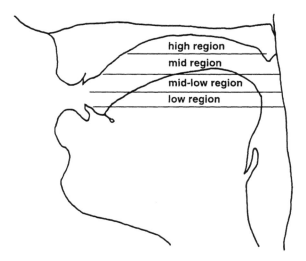

Figure 2.2 The four vertical regions

In addition, there are three horizontal regions:

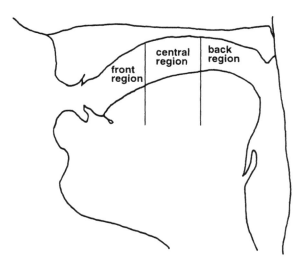

Figure 2.3 The three horizontal regions

Linguists commonly employ a *vowel quadrangle* to represent the position of the tongue in the mouth during the pronunciation of simple vowel sounds. The Korean vowel quadrangle looks like this.

	Front	Central	Back
High	ㅣ	—	ㅜ
Mid	ㅔ		ㅗ
Mid-Low	ㅐ		ㅓ
Low		ㅏ	

Figure 2.4 The Korean vowel quadrangle[6]

The key to mastering the Korean vowel system lies in recognizing that the tongue operates in the two dimensions depicted here—one horizontal (front, central, and back) and the other vertical (high, mid, mid-low, and low).

The vowels on the left side of the quadrangle are pronounced with the tongue in the front region of the mouth, while those on the right side of the quadrangle are pronounced with the tongue in the back region of the mouth. You should be able to feel your tongue move from front to back in your mouth as you go from ㅣ to ㅜ, from ㅔ to ㅗ, or from ㅐ to ㅓ.

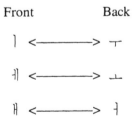

Front   Back

ㅣ <———————> ㅜ

ㅔ <———————> ㅗ

ㅐ <———————> ㅓ

Figure 2.5 Front-back distinctions

---

[6]Yang (1996).

The vowels in the top row of the quadrangle are produced with the tongue at a high position in the mouth, while those in lower rows are pronounced with the tongue in lower positions. Since the jaw tends to be more open for the lower vowels, you can keep track of tongue height to some extent simply by placing a finger on your jaw. Begin with ㅣ, ㅔ, ㅐ, and ㅏ, and then go to ㅜ, ㅗ, ㅓ, and ㅏ. Within each series you should be able to feel your jaw in four different positions—almost closed for ㅣ and ㅜ, slightly more open for ㅔ and ㅗ, still more open for ㅐ and ㅓ, and very open for ㅏ. (Remember that ㅜ and ㅗ also have lip rounding.)

Jaw position	Tongue position	Vowels		
Almost closed	High	ㅣ	—	ㅜ
Slightly more open	Mid	ㅔ		ㅗ
Still more open	Mid-Low	ㅐ		ㅓ
Very open	Low		ㅏ	

Figure 2.6 High-low distinctions

Once you feel comfortable with these four vertical positions, you can begin to concentrate on the one horizontal contrast that can be difficult for English speakers, namely, — versus ㅜ. As noted in our earlier discussion, the tongue is high for both vowels but is positioned much more toward the front of the mouth for — than it is for ㅜ, which is a back vowel. Moreover, unlike —, ㅜ is pronounced with lip rounding.

Chapter 3

Consonants

All consonant sounds are made by narrowing or closing some part of the mouth or throat. When phoneticians talk about how consonants are pronounced, they always ask three questions.

1. The *where* question: Where in the mouth or throat does the narrowing or closure take place?[1]

2. The *how* question: What actions are necessary to bring this about? (For example, do the lips come together, or does the tongue move up and touch the roof of the mouth?)

3. The *what else* question: Are there any accompanying actions elsewhere in the mouth or throat? (For example, do the vocal cords vibrate? Is the sound pronounced with extra forcefulness?)

By answering these three questions, it is possible to understand exactly how any consonant in any language is pronounced.

In order to understand the pronunciation of Korean consonants, as well as their relationship to similar-sounding English consonants, it is necessary to pay special attention to the "what else" question. Two factors are particularly important—*aspiration* and *voicing*. These terms may be new to you, but the concepts behind them are very simple.

Aspiration

If you hold the palm of your hand slightly below your mouth when you say the English word *pie* or *tie*, you'll notice a puff of air at the end of the consonant sound. This puff of air is aspiration. Section 3.9 describes more precisely how aspiration is produced. For the most part, though, you

---

[1]The answers that we give to this question here are based on palatographic and linguographic studies that we conducted on five native speakers of Korean with the help of In-Sung Ko and Victoria Anderson.

should be able to figure out how aspiration works just by reading the description of the different consonant sounds and by doing the practice exercises on the CD.

Voicing

If you touch a finger to your neck right above your larynx (voice box) as you slowly say the word *so*, you'll notice that the vocal cords are inactive during the 's' but that they vibrate as you say the 'o'. Sounds that are produced without vocal cord vibrations are said to be *voiceless;* sounds produced with accompanying vocal cord vibrations are called *voiced*. Here are some sample voiceless and voiced consonants in English—you should be able to hear the difference by pronouncing the relevant words slowly as you hold a finger or two above your larynx. (All vowels are voiced, so you'll always hear vocal cord vibrations for them.)

Voiceless	Voiced
p as in *pie*	*b* as in *bye*
t as in *to*	*d* as in *do*
k as in *Kate*	*g* as in *gate*
ch as in *chill*	*j* as in *Jill*
s as in *Sue*	*z* as in *zoo*
	l as in *low*
	m as in *my*
	n as in *no*
	ng as in *sing*

Voicing in Korean consonants is usually the result of an adjustment process rather than an inherent feature of the sounds themselves. However, because the process is so common and widespread, we will deal with it in this chapter as well as in the chapter on adjustments.

What counts as a word

One more thing is very important for understanding the pronunciation of Korean consonants—the concept of a *word*. The simplest type of word consists of a root and any associated suffixes—like the subject marker

-이/가, the direct object marker -을/를, the location particles -에 and -에서, the tense marker -았/었, sentence enders such as -요 and -습니다, and even the copula verb -이다 (which cannot stand alone as a separate word). Thus each boxed element in the following sentences is a word.

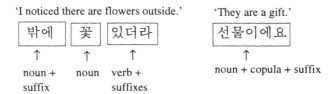

'I noticed there are flowers outside.' 'They are a gift.'

A noun can consist of just a root or of a root and one or more suffixes. However, a verb root cannot stand alone; it must be accompanied by at least one suffix.

Some words, called *compounds,* consist of two or more smaller words. Like their English counterparts, Korean compounds are sometimes written with a space between their component parts and sometimes with no space.

겉옷	(겉 + 옷)	'outer garment'
꽃집	(꽃 + 집)	'flower shop'
부엌 바닥	(부엌 + 바닥)	'kitchen floor'

As you will see shortly, various pronunciation rules in Korean treat words that occur inside compounds just like words that stand alone, regardless of whether they are written with a space.

3.1 ㅍ, ㅂ, & ㅃ

The basic pronunciations of ㅍ, ㅂ, and ㅃ are heard at the beginning of a word. As we will see shortly, somewhat different pronunciations occur in other positions.

3.1.1 Basic pronunciation

The ㅍ, ㅂ, and ㅃ sounds all involve complete closure of the lips. In this respect, they are just like the English 'p' and 'b' sounds. This is where the similarity ends, however. In order to understand the difference among the three Korean sounds as well as their relationship to English 'p' and 'b', it is necessary to focus on aspiration. (Voicing is not relevant to the basic pronunciation of ㅍ, ㅂ, and ㅃ, which are all voiceless at the beginning of a word.)

If you hold the palm of your hand slightly below your mouth when you say the English word *pay*, you'll feel aspiration right after you finish the 'p' sound. Korean ㅍ is aspirated too, but more strongly than English 'p', so you should feel a more noticeable puff of air when you pronounce it.

In contrast, ㅂ is produced with much less force than ㅍ and with very little aspiration—far less than English 'p'. At times, the aspiration is so slight that ㅂ may even sound a bit like English 'b'. (Remember though that 'b' is voiced, whereas the basic pronunciation of ㅂ is not.) Because of its relatively unforceful pronunciation, ㅂ is often called *lax*.

The sound ㅃ is different again. Not only does it have no aspiration at all, it is *tense*. This means that it is pronounced with extra muscular effort, which translates into extra firm closure of the lips and extra quick opening of the lips at the end of the sound. English speakers may think it sounds like 'b', because both sounds are completely unaspirated. However, ㅃ is different from English 'b' in two ways—it is pronounced with more intensity, and it is voiceless.

One way to tell that you are pronouncing the ㅃ correctly is to listen to the pitch on the vowel that follows it. If your pronunciation is right, the pitch should be slightly higher than after ㅂ .[2]

Korean versus English at the beginning of a word			
Sound	Aspiration	Voicing	Other
ㅍ (풀 'glue')	heavy	no	
'p' (pool)	moderate	no	
ㅂ (불 'fire')	very light	no	lax
'b' (bull)	none	yes	
ㅃ (뿔 'horn')	none	no	tense

---

[2]Kim (1965), Han & Weitzman (1970), and Silva (1998).

The ㅍ-ㅂ-ㅃ contrast is a challenging one for English speakers, but it is also extremely important. Without it, you won't be able to make distinctions such as the following.

ㅍ versus ㅂ			ㅂ versus ㅃ		
팔 'arm'	발 'foot'		방 'room'	빵 'bread'	
피 'blood'	비 'rain'		빈 'empty'	삔 'sprained'	

The table below summarizes the key properties of ㅍ, ㅂ, and ㅃ at the beginning of a word.

ㅍ, ㅂ, & ㅃ at the beginning of a word		
Sound	Where and how	What else
ㅍ (aspirated)	lips closed	heavy aspiration
ㅂ (lax)	" "	very light aspiration
ㅃ (tense)	" "	no aspiration; extra strong closure; quick, crisp release of the closure; slightly higher pitch on the following vowel

You can find practice exercises involving these sounds in sections C-1 through C-3.1 of the CD.

3.1.2 ㅍ, ㅂ, & ㅃ before a consonant or at the end of a word

As we have just seen, the consonants ㅍ, ㅂ, and ㅃ are all produced by completely closing off the air flow at the lips. As we have also seen, the difference in the basic pronunciation of these three sounds depends on how this closure is released—with heavy aspiration in the case of ㅍ, with very light aspiration in the case of ㅂ, and with no aspiration but extra crispness in the case of ㅃ. If for some reason the closure were not released, there would be no way to distinguish among the three sounds.

This is just what happens when a consonant occurs in front of another consonant or at the end of a word in Korean—it must have full closure throughout its articulation, with no release. This results in the loss of aspiration and tenseness, leading to the cancellation of the usual phonetic contrasts.

The consonant ㅃ happens not to occur in front of another consonant or at the end of a word, but ㅍ and ㅂ do. And when they do, they both sound like an unreleased ㅂ. Thus 깊다 'be deep', with ㅍ in front of a consonant, is pronounced [깁따]. And 잎 'leaf', with ㅍ at the end of the word, is pronounced [입], just like 입 'mouth'. (As in the preceding chapter, the items in square brackets are pronunciations rather than spellings. You can ignore details that are not relevant to the point at hand; they will be discussed in due course.)

The unreleased pronunciation is found at the end of a word even when the next word begins with a vowel. Thus the ㅍ that occurs at the end of the word 잎 'leaf' is pronounced as if it were ㅂ in 잎 있어요 'There's a leaf' and 맨앞 아니야 'It's not the very front', as well as in the two-word compound 잎안 'the inside of the leaf'. (안 is a noun meaning 'inside', so 잎안 is a compound in Korean.)

Example (two words)		Pronounced
잎 있어요	'There's a leaf'	[이비써요]
맨앞 아니야	'It's not the very front'	[매나바니야]
잎안	'the inside of the leaf'	[이반]

On the other hand, the usual aspiration is retained in 앞이 'front + subject marker', 잎에 'on the leaf', and 깊어요 'It's deep', where ㅍ occurs in front of a suffix that begins with a vowel.

Example (single word)		Pronounced
앞이	'front + subject marker'	[아피]
잎에	'on the leaf'	[이페]
깊어요	'It's deep'	[기퍼요]

ㅍ & ㅂ before a consonant or at the end of a word

What happens	Examples
ㅍ & ㅂ are pronounced as unreleased ㅂ	깊다, 깁다, 잎, 입, 잎안

Section C-3.2 of the CD contains practice exercises involving full closure.

3.1.3 ㅍ, ㅂ, & ㅃ between voiced sounds

As mentioned at the beginning of this chapter, sounds produced with accompanying vocal cord vibrations are called *voiced*; sounds produced without vocal cord vibrations are said to be *voiceless*. As already noted and as you can see for yourself by slowly saying the English words *bye* and *pie*, 'b' is voiced, but 'p' is voiceless. If you touch a finger to your neck right above your larynx, you should be able to feel the vocal cords vibrate as you say the 'b' but not the 'p'. (The vowel is voiced in both words.)

The lax consonant ㅂ is voiceless except when it occurs between voiced sounds (that is, vowels or the consonants ㅁ, ㄴ, ㅇ, and ㄹ). In that position, it "catches" the vocal cord vibrations of its neighbors and is fully voiced and completely unaspirated, taking on a very 'b'-like pronunciation.

The effects of this change can be heard by comparing the pronunciation of the ㅂ in 불 'fire' and 이불 'comforter'—it's voiceless in the first word, but fully voiced in the second word. You can hear the same contrast in 바지 'pants' and in 내 바지 'my pants', where the voicing process can extend over a word boundary (see section 5.2).

The basic pronunciation of ㅍ and ㅃ is always voiceless.[3] As long as you pronounce ㅍ with appropriate aspiration and ㅃ with appropriate tenseness, you don't need to worry about whether there are vocal cord vibrations—that part will automatically come out right.

Remember, though, that when ㅍ or ㅂ occurs at the end of a word (ㅃ does not occur in this position), they are pronounced as an unreleased, fully closed ㅂ. When this happens, voicing takes place if the following word begins with a vowel sound. So the final consonant of 잎 'leaf' is voiceless

---

[3]Kagaya (1974:162).

when the word stands alone, but voiced in 잎안 'the inside of the leaf' and in 잎 없어요 'There are no leaves'. Similarly, ㅂ is voiceless in 입 'mouth', but voiced in 입안 'the inside of the mouth' and in 입 아파요 'My mouth hurts'.

Example		Pronounced
잎안	'the inside of the leaf'	[이 반], with a 'b'-like ㅂ
입안	'the inside of the mouth'	[이 반], with a 'b'-like ㅂ

Voicing	
Where it happens	What happens
between voiced sounds (vowels, ㅁ, ㄴ, ㅇ, or ㄹ)	a consonant with a ㅂ pronunciation becomes fully voiced ('b'-like)

You can practice voicing with the help of the examples in section C-1 and A-2 of the CD.

3.1.4 Some helpful hints

As you seek to improve your mastery of the ㅍ-ㅂ-ㅃ contrast, you may find the following additional information helpful.

• In terms of aspiration, Korean ㅂ falls closer to English unaspirated 'b' than to moderately aspirated 'p'. But in terms of voicing, it is closer to 'p' since both are voiceless. As a result, there is confusion when Korean words are written in English. As you may have noted, the family name 박 is written as *Park* (or *Pak*) by some and as *Bak* by others. Some Korean restaurants write 불고기 as *pulgogi*, and others spell it *bulgogi*. The current official romanization system writes ㅂ as *b* at the beginning of a word.

- ㅃ is quite close to the 'p' sound in English words such as *spy* and *spot*. It might also help you to know that it sounds a lot like the 'p' of Spanish (in a word like *padre* 'father') and French (as in *pomme* 'apple').[4]

- The voiced version of ㅂ that occurs between voiced sounds in examples such as 왼발 'left foot' is pronounced in a more relaxed way than the English 'b' in *eyeball*. In contrast, ㅃ is pronounced with more intensity (and is voiceless too). This may help you hear the difference between 이 방 'this room' and 이 빵 'this bread'.

- Like ㅂ, English 'p' is not released when it occurs in front of a consonant (as in *cupcake*). However, it is released when it occurs at the end of a word (as in *cup*). Care must be taken not to release the ㅂ sound at the end of a Korean word such as 입 'mouth' or 잎 'leaf'.

3.2   ㅌ, ㄷ, & ㄸ

The basic pronunciation of ㅌ, ㄷ, and ㄸ is found at the beginning of a word. Somewhat different pronunciations show up in other positions.

3.2.1 Basic pronunciation

The ㅌ, ㄷ, and ㄸ sounds of Korean are all made by using the tongue to close off the flow of air through the mouth just behind the upper front teeth. They differ from English 't' and 'd' in various ways.

First, whereas English speakers use the tip of the tongue to produce 't' and 'd' sounds, Koreans typically use the blade, which is just behind the tip, for ㅌ, ㄷ, and ㄸ.[5] Second, the tongue makes contact with the central part of the bony dental ridge behind the upper front teeth in English, but it typically touches against the front part of this ridge and even the back of the teeth in Korean. These differences are illustrated in figure 3.1.

---

[4]Martin (1992:27).
[5]Sohn (1994:432), Kim (1999).

blade of the tongue makes contact
with front part of dental ridge

tip of the tongue makes contact
with central part of dental ridge

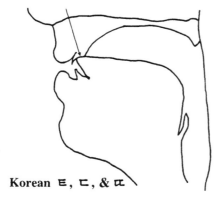
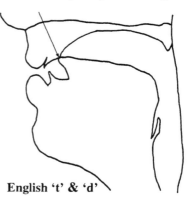

Korean ㅌ, ㄷ, & ㄸ

English 't' & 'd'

Figure 3.1   Korean ㅌ, ㄷ, & ㄸ versus English 't' & 'd'

A third and even more important difference has to do with the existence in Korean of a three-way aspirated-lax-tense contrast parallel to the one associated with ㅍ, ㅂ, and ㅃ. (Voicing is not relevant to the basic pronunciation of ㅌ, ㄷ, and ㄸ, which are all voiceless at the beginning of a word.)

Korean ㅌ is more strongly aspirated than English 't', while lax ㄷ has very little aspiration—far less than English 't'. At times the aspiration is so slight that ㄷ may even sound a bit like English 'd'. (Remember, though, that 'd' is voiced, whereas the basic pronunciation of ㄷ is not.)

In contrast, ㄸ has no aspiration at all. However, like ㅃ, it is tense. This means that it is pronounced with extra firm pressure of the tongue against the dental ridge and extra crisp release of that closure at the end of the sound. Listen for the pitch on the vowel that follows the ㄸ; if you're producing the consonant correctly, the pitch should be higher than on the vowel that comes after a ㄷ.

Korean ㄸ sometimes sounds like 'd' to the English ear, perhaps because both are totally unaspirated. The two sounds are actually quite different, however. Not only is ㄸ voiceless, it is pronounced with more intensity than 'd'.

Korean versus English at the beginning of a word			
Sound	Aspiration	Voicing	Other
ㅌ (탄 'burnt')	heavy	no	
't' (tan)	moderate	no	
ㄷ (단 'sweet')	very light	no	lax
'd' (Dan)	none	yes	
ㄸ (딴 'different')	none	no	tense

The ㅌ-ㄷ-ㄸ contrast is a subtle one for English speakers, but it is also important. Without it, you won't be able to distinguish among words such as the following.

ㅌ versus ㄷ				ㄷ versus ㄸ			
탑 'tower'	답 'an answer'			달 'moon'	딸 'daughter'		
통 'a can'	동 'east'			덕 'virtue'	떡 'rice cake'		

The following table summarizes the key properties of ㅌ, ㄷ, and ㄸ.

ㅌ, ㄷ, & ㄸ at the beginning of a word		
Sound	How and where	What else
ㅌ (aspirated)	the blade of the tongue presses against the dental ridge and/or the back of the upper front teeth	heavy aspiration
ㄷ (lax)	" "	very light aspiration
ㄸ (tense)	" "	no aspiration; extra strong closure; quick, crisp release of the closure; slightly higher pitch on the following vowel

You will find helpful practice exercises for these sounds in sections C-5 through C-8.1 of the CD.

3.2.2 ㅌ, ㄷ, & ㄸ before a consonant or at the end of a word

As noted in section 3.1.2, consonants must have full closure throughout their articulation when they occur in front of another consonant or at the end of a word. In the case of ㅌ, ㄷ, and ㄸ, this means that the blade of the tongue must maintain its pressure against the dental ridge throughout, nullifying the usual aspirated-lax-tense contrast. ㄸ happens not to occur in front of another consonant or at the end of a word, but ㅌ and ㄷ do. When this happens, they both end up being pronounced as an unreleased ㄷ. Thus 밭다 'be very close/soon' and 받다 'receive' have the same pronunciation, [받따]. Similarly, 밑 'bottom' is pronounced [믿], with no aspiration.

The unreleased pronunciation is used at the end of a word even when the next word begins with a vowel, as in 솥 없어요 'There's no kettle' or 밥솥 있어요 'There's a rice cooker'. The same is true for the ㅌ at the end of 솥 in the two-word compound 솥안 'the inside of the kettle'. (Recall that 안 is a noun in Korean, so 솥안 is a compound, not a simple word.)

Example (two words)		Pronounced
솥 없어요	'There's no kettle'	[소덥써요]
밥솥 있어요	'There's a rice cooker'	[밥쏘디써요]
솥안	'the inside of the kettle'	[소단]

In 솥에 'in the kettle', 밑에 'at the bottom', and 같아요 'They're the same', in contrast, ㅌ has the usual aspiration because it occurs in front of a suffix that begins with a vowel.

Example (single word)		Pronounced
솥에	'in the kettle'	[소테]
밑에	'at the bottom'	[미테]
같아요	'They're the same'	[가타요]

ㅌ & ㄷ before a consonant or at the end of a word

What happens	Examples
ㅌ & ㄷ are pronounced as unreleased ㄷ	같다, 곧다, 밑, 곧, 솥안

You can find practice exercises for this in section C-8.2 of the CD.

3.2.3 ㅌ, ㄷ, & ㄸ between voiced sounds

The lax consonant ㄷ is normally voiceless. However, like ㅂ, it is fully voiced, and therefore has a 'd'-like pronunciation when it occurs between voiced sounds (vowels or the consonants ㅁ, ㄴ, ㅇ, and ㄹ). You can hear this for yourself by comparing 도 'province' and 포도 'grape', 다 'all' and 길다 'It's long', or 돌 'stone' and 큰 돌 'big stone' (in which the voicing can extend over a word boundary—see section 5.2).

The basic pronunciation of aspirated ㅌ and tense ㄸ is always voiceless—they are automatically produced without vocal cord vibrations. As noted above, though, ㅌ loses its aspiration and has the pronunciation of an unreleased ㄷ when it occurs at the end of a word. (ㄸ does not occur at all in this position.) Under these circumstances, voicing takes place if the following word begins with a vowel sound. So, the final consonant of 솥 'kettle' is voiceless when the word stands alone, but it is voiced and has a 'd'-like pronunciation in 솥 없어요 'There's no kettle' and in 솥안 'the inside of the kettle'. Similarly, ㄷ is voiceless in 맏- 'eldest', but has a voiced 'd'-like pronunciation in 맏아들 'eldest son'.

Example		Pronounced
솥 없어요	'There's no kettle'	[소덥써요],* with a 'd'-like ㄷ
맏아들	'eldest son'	[마다들], with two 'd'-like ㄷs

*For a discussion of why ㅅ and other lax consonants become tense after another consonant, see section 4.12.

	Voicing
Where it happens	What happens
between voiced sounds (vowels, ㅁ, ㄴ, ㅇ, or ㄹ)	a consonant with a ㄷ pronunciation becomes fully voiced ('d'-like)

Sections C-5 and A-2 of the CD give you a chance to practice this.

3.2.4 Some helpful hints

As you seek to improve your mastery of the ㅌ-ㄷ-ㄸ contrast, you may find the following additional information helpful.

- In terms of aspiration, Korean ㄷ falls closer to English unaspirated 'd' than to moderately aspirated 't'. But in terms of voicing, it is closer to 't' since both are voiceless. As a result, there is confusion when Korean words are written in English. You may have noticed, for example, that the Korean city 대구 is sometimes spelled *Taegu* and sometimes *Daegu*. The current official romanization system writes ㄷ as *d* at the beginning of a word.

- ㄸ is similar to the 't' sound in the English words *style* and *steak*. It also strongly resembles the 't' of Spanish (as in *todo* 'all') and French (as in *ton* 'tone').

- The voiced version of ㄷ that occurs between voiced sounds in words such as 구두 'dress shoes' is pronounced in a more relaxed way than the 'd' in *voodoo*. In contrast, ㄸ is pronounced with more intensity (and is voiceless). This may help you hear the difference between 진담 'serious talk' and 진땀 'sweat from anxiety'.

- Like ㄷ, English 't' is not released when it occurs in front of a consonant (as in *batboy*). However, it is released when it occurs at the end of a word (as in *bat*). Care must be taken not to release the ㄷ sound at the end of a Korean word such as 밑 'bottom' or 곧 'soon'.

3.3 ㅋ, ㄱ, & ㄲ

The basic pronunciation of ㅋ, ㄱ, and ㄲ is heard at the beginning of a word. However, somewhat different pronunciations show up in other positions.

3.3.1 Basic pronunciation

The ㅋ, ㄱ, and ㄲ sounds all involve closing off the flow of air through the mouth by pressing the body of the tongue firmly against the soft back part of the roof of the mouth—just like the 'k' and 'g' sounds of English in words such as *key* and *gear*. However, none of the Korean sounds is equivalent to English 'k' or 'g' because of the three-way contrast in Korean involving aspiration and tenseness, parallel to what we find for ㅍ, ㅂ, and ㅃ and for ㅌ, ㄷ, and ㄸ. (Voicing is not relevant to the basic pronunciation of ㅋ, ㄱ, and ㄲ, which are all voiceless at the beginning of a word.)

Korean ㅋ is more strongly aspirated than English 'k', while lax ㄱ has very little aspiration—far less than English 'k'. At times, the aspiration is so slight that ㄱ may sound like English 'g'. (Remember, though, that 'g' is voiced, whereas the basic pronunciation of ㄱ is not.)

In contrast, ㄲ has no aspiration at all, and it is tense. It is pronounced with extra muscular effort, which translates into extra firm pressure of the tongue against the roof of the mouth and extra quick release of that closure at the end of the sound. A higher pitch on the following vowel provides a good indication that you have made the consonant tense enough for it to sound like ㄲ and to be distinguished from ㄱ.

English speakers may hear a strong similarity between Korean ㄲ and English 'g', as both sounds are completely unaspirated. However, ㄲ is different from English 'g' in two ways—it is pronounced with more intensity, and it is voiceless.

Korean versus English at the beginning of a word			
Sound	Aspiration	Voicing	Other
ㅋ (키 'height')	heavy	no	
'k' (key)	moderate	no	
ㄱ (기 'spirit; energy')	very light	no	lax
'g' (gear)	none	yes	
ㄲ (끼 'risqué spirit')	none	no	tense

The ㅋ - ㄱ - ㄲ contrast is difficult for English speakers, but without it you won't be able to hear or make differences such as the following.

ㅋ versus ㄱ			ㄱ versus ㄲ		
콩	'bean'	공 'ball'	개	'dog'	깨 'sesame'
큰	'big'	근 'approximately'	굴	'oyster'	꿀 'honey'

The following table summarizes the most important properties of ㅋ, ㄱ, and ㄲ.

ㅋ, ㄱ, & ㄲ at the beginning of a word		
Sound	How and where	What else
ㅋ (aspirated)	the body of the tongue presses against the back part of the roof of the mouth	heavy aspiration
ㄱ (lax)	" "	very light aspiration
ㄲ (tense)	" "	no aspiration; extra strong closure; quick, crisp release of the closure; slightly higher pitch on the following vowel

Sections C-9 through C-12.1 of the CD contain practice exercises involving these sounds.

3.3.2 ㅋ, ㄱ, & ㄲ before a consonant or at the end of a word

Like the other contrasts we have considered, ㅋ, ㄱ, and ㄲ must have full closure throughout their articulation when they occur in front of a consonant or at the end of a word. This means that the back of the tongue must maintain contact with the roof of the mouth, precluding the usual aspirated-lax-tense contrast. As a result, ㅋ, ㄱ, and ㄲ are all pronounced as an unreleased ㄱ. Thus 박 'gourd' and 밖 'outside' are both pronounced [박], 섞다 'mix' is pronounced [석따], and 부엌 'kitchen' is pronounced [부억], with no aspiration.

The unreleased pronunciation is found in word-final position even when the next word begins with a vowel, as you can hear in 밖 어두워요 'The outside is dark' and 부엌 있어요 'There's a kitchen'. The same thing happens in two-word compounds such as 부엌안 'the inside of the kitchen'.

Example (two words)		Pronounced
밖 어두워요	'The outside is dark'	[바거두워요]
부엌 있어요	'There's a kitchen'	[부어기써요]
부엌안	'the inside of the kitchen'	[부어간]

ㄲ keeps its basic pronunciation in 밖에 'on the outside' and 섞어요 'Mix it', where it occurs in front of a suffix that begins with a vowel. And ㅋ can retain its usual aspirated pronunciation in 부엌에 'in the kitchen', where it too occurs in front of a suffix that begins with a vowel. (However, most Koreans pronounce ㅋ as if it were ㄱ in this word as a result of the consonant weakening process discussed in section 4.15.)

Example (single word)		Pronounced
밖에	'on the outside'	[바께]
섞어요	'Mix it'	[서꺼요]
부엌에	'in the kitchen'	[부어케] (or [부어게])

ㅋ, ㄱ, & ㄲ before a consonant or at the end of a word	
What happens	Examples
ㅋ, ㄱ, and ㄲ are pronounced as unreleased ㄱ	부엌칼, 약다, 섞다, 부엌, 박, 밖, 부엌안

You'll find helpful practice exercises for these contrasts in section C-12.2 of the CD.

3.3.3 ㅋ, ㄱ, & ㄲ between voiced sounds

The lax consonant ㄱ is normally voiceless, but when it occurs between voiced sounds (vowels or the consonants ㅁ, ㄴ, ㅇ, and ㄹ), it is fully voiced and ends up with a 'g'-like pronunciation. To hear this difference, listen carefully to the pronunciation of ㄱ in 금 'gold' versus 지금 'now', 구 'nine' versus 친구 'friend', and 가방 'bag' versus 작은 가방 'small bag' (where the voicing can extend over a word boundary—see section 5.2).

When they have their basic pronunciation, aspirated ㅋ and tense ㄲ are voiceless. However, when they occur at the end of a word, they are pronounced as unreleased ㄱ. They become voiced in this position if the next word begins with a vowel. So the final consonant of 부엌 'kitchen' and 밖 'outside' is voiceless when these words stand alone, but voiced in 부엌안 'the inside of the kitchen' and 밖 안 보여요 'I can't see the outside'. Similarly, ㄱ is voiceless in 백 'one hundred', but voiced with a 'g'-like pronunciation in 백원 'one hundred won'.

Example		Pronounced
부엌안	'the inside of the kitchen'	[부어간], with a 'g'-like ㄱ
백원	'one hundred won'	[배권], with a 'g'-like ㄱ
밖 안 보여	'I can't see the outside'	[바간보여], with a 'g'-like ㄱ

	Voicing
Where it happens	What happens
between voiced	a consonant with a ㄱ pronunciation
sounds (vowels,	becomes fully voiced ('g'-like)
ㅁ, ㄴ, ㅇ, or ㄹ)	

You'll find practice exercises in sections C-9 and A-2 of the CD.

3.3.4 Some helpful hints

As you seek to improve your mastery of the ㅋ-ㄱ-ㄲ contrast, you may find the following additional bits of information helpful.

- In terms of aspiration, Korean ㄱ falls closer to English unaspirated 'g' than to moderately aspirated 'k'. But in terms of voicing, it is closer to 'k' since both are voiceless. As a result, there is confusion when Korean words are written in English, which is why there is uncertainty over how to spell 김치, which is sometimes written as *kimchi* and sometimes as *gimchi*. The current official romanization system writes ㄱ as *g* at the beginning of a word.

- ㄲ sounds a lot like the 'k' sound in English words such as *sky* and *skate* as well as like the 'k' sound of Spanish *con* 'with' and French *cou* 'neck'.

- The voiced version of ㄱ that occurs between voiced sounds in words such as 한글 'Korean alphabet' is pronounced in a more relaxed way than the 'g' in *angle*. In contrast, ㄲ is pronounced with more intensity (and is voiceless). This may help you hear the difference between 토기 'earthenware' and 토끼 'rabbit'.

- Like ㄱ, 'k' is not released when it occurs in front of a consonant (as in *backdrop*). However, it is released when it occurs at the end of a word (as in *back*). Care must be taken not to release the ㄱ sound at the end of a Korean word such as 부엌 'kitchen', 박 'gourd', or 밖 'outside'.

3.4 ㅊ, ㅈ, & ㅉ

As with the other sounds we have been examining, the basic pronunciation of ㅊ, ㅈ, and ㅉ is found at the beginning of a word. Other pronunciations show up in other positions.

3.4.1 Basic pronunciation

Like all the consonants we have described so far, ㅊ, ㅈ, and ㅉ are produced by completely closing off the flow of air through the mouth. But unlike these other consonants, ㅊ, ㅈ, and ㅉ include a brief period near their conclusion when the closure is released just enough to create a narrow passage. Air from the lungs then rushes out through that passage, creating friction. You can hear this effect clearly in the English 'ch' sound at the beginning of the word *chin* or in the 'j' sound at the beginning of *jig*. Say the words slowly, and you should be able to feel a period of closure at the beginning of the sound followed by a period of friction.

The ㅊ, ㅈ, and ㅉ sounds are produced in roughly the same place as ㅌ, ㄷ, and ㄸ. The blade of the tongue makes contact with the front part of the dental ridge (or a little further back for some speakers).[6] This point of contact is somewhat more forward in the mouth than for English 'ch' and 'j'.

Even more important, Korean makes a three-way aspirated-lax-tense contrast. (Voicing is not relevant for the basic pronunciation of ㅊ, ㅈ, and ㅉ, which are all voiceless at the beginning of a word.)

Korean ㅊ is more strongly aspirated than English 'ch', which results in a longer period of 'sh'-like friction.[7] In contrast, the lax ㅈ sound has very little aspiration—far less than English 'ch'. At times the aspiration is so slight that ㅈ may sound a bit like English 'j'. (Remember, though, that 'j' is voiced, and ㅈ is not.)

Korean ㅉ has absolutely no aspiration, but it is tense—which gives it a quick, crisp articulation. It differs from English 'j' in being voiceless and in being pronounced with more intensity. You may also find it helpful to know that a vowel following ㅉ has a slightly higher pitch than one following ㅈ.

---

[6]Kim (1999).
[7]Shin & Hayward (1997:14).

Korean versus English at the beginning of a word			
Sound	Aspiration	Voicing	Other
ㅊ (침 'saliva')	heavy	no	
'ch' (chin)	moderate	no	
ㅈ (짐 'luggage')	very light	no	lax
'j' (jig)	none	yes	
ㅉ (찜 'steamed food')	none	no	tense

These are challenging contrasts, but mastering them is crucial for differentiating among many important words, including the following.

ㅊ versus ㅈ		ㅈ versus ㅉ	
찬 'cold'	잔 'small'	잠 'a sleep'	짬 'spare time'
총 'gun'	종 'bell'	족 '(beef) hock'	쪽 'piece; side'

The following table summarizes the key properties of ㅊ, ㅈ, and ㅉ.

ㅊ, ㅈ, & ㅉ at the beginning of a word		
Sound	How and where	What else
ㅊ (aspirated)	the blade of the tongue presses against the dental ridge and then pulls back to create a narrow opening	heavy aspiration
ㅈ (lax)	" "	very light aspiration
ㅉ (tense)	" "	no aspiration; extra strong closure; quick, crisp release of the closure; slightly higher pitch on the following vowel

The practice exercises in sections C-13 through C-16.1 of the CD will help you master these distinctions.

3.4.2 ㅊ, ㅈ, & ㅉ before a consonant or at the end of a word

When ㅊ and ㅈ occur in front of another consonant or at the end of a word, they must be fully closed throughout their articulation. (ㅉ does not occur in these positions.) This blocks the period of friction that normally occurs at the end of these consonants, resulting in an unreleased ㄷ sound. Thus 낯 'face' and 낮 'daytime' are pronounced alike, as [낟]. Similarly, 빛 'light' and 빚 'debt' are pronounced with a final ㄷ both when they stand alone and when they occur in front of a consonant, as in 빛깔 'color' and 빚장이 'creditor'.

The unreleased pronunciation is found in word-final position even when the next word begins with a vowel, as in 빛 안나요 'It doesn't shine' and 빚 안져요 'I'm not getting into debt'. The same is true at the end of the first word inside a two-word compound, which is why 꽃안 'the inside of the flower' is pronounced [꼬단] and 몇월 'what month' is pronounced [며뒬].

Example (two words)		Pronounced
몇월	'what month'	[며뒬]
꽃안	'the inside of the flower'	[꼬단]
빛 안 나요	'It doesn't shine'	[비단나요]
빚 안 져요	'I'm not getting into debt'	[비단져요]

In contrast, there is no full closure in 꽃이 'flower + subject marker', 낮에 'in the daytime', or 잊어요 'Forget about it', where ㅈ and ㅊ occur in front of a suffix beginning with a vowel, and are therefore released in the usual way.

Example (single word)		Pronounced
꽃이	'flower + subject marker'	[꼬치]
낮에	'in the daytime'	[나제]
잊어요	'Forget about it'	[이저요]

An interesting exception here is 며칠 'what day' (from 몇 'what' and 일 'day'), in which ㅊ retains its basic aspirated pronunciation. This happens because Koreans treat 며칠 as a single unanalyzable word rather than as 몇 plus 일. This is reflected in the spelling (며칠), where 몇 is not even written as a unit.

ㅊ & ㅈ before a consonant or at the end of a word	
What happens	Examples
ㅊ and ㅈ are pronounced as unreleased ㄷ	빛깔, 빛쟁이, 낮, 낮, 몇월, 빚 안져

You can find practice exercises involving full closure of ㅊ and ㅈ in section C-16.2 of the CD.

3.4.3 ㅊ, ㅈ, & ㅉ between voiced sounds

Although normally voiceless, ㅈ—and to some extent ㅉ as well—are fully voiced between voiced sounds (vowels or the consonants ㅁ, ㄴ, ㅇ, and ㄹ), where they end up with a 'j'-like pronunciation. You can hear the effects of voicing by comparing the pronunciation of 제 'my' with 어제 'yesterday', 장 'sauce' with 간장 'soy sauce', 짜 'It's salty' with 가짜 'a fake', or 자리 'seat' with 친구 자리 'my friend's seat' (where the voicing can extend over a word boundary—see section 5.2).

Aspirated ㅊ is always voiceless when it has its basic pronunciation. Remember, though, that both ㅊ and ㅈ are pronounced as unreleased ㄷ when they occur at the end of a word. (ㅉ does not occur in this position.) If the following word begins with a vowel, voicing occurs, giving a 'd'-like pronunciation. You will therefore hear a voiceless ㄷ sound at the end of 빚 'debt' and 몇 'what; how many' when these words stand alone, but a voiced 'd'-like pronunciation in 빚 없어요 'I have no debts' and 몇월 'what month'.

Example		Pronounced
어제	'yesterday'	[어제], with a 'j'-like ㅈ
빛 없어요	'I have no debts'	[비덥써요], with a 'd'-like ㄷ
몇월	'what month'	[며뒬], with a 'd'-like ㄷ

Voicing	
Where it happens	**What happens**
between voiced sounds (vowels, ㅁ, ㄴ, ㅇ, or ㄹ)	a consonant with a ㅈ pronunciation becomes fully voiced ('j'-like)
	a consonant with a ㄷ pronunciation becomes fully voiced ('d'-like)

3.4.4 Some helpful hints

As you seek to improve your mastery of the ㅊ-ㅈ-ㅉ contrast, you may find the following additional information helpful.

- In terms of aspiration, Korean ㅈ falls closer to English unaspirated 'j' than to moderately aspirated 'ch'. But in terms of voicing, it is closer to 'ch' since both are voiceless. As a result, there is confusion when Korean words are written in English, which is why the family name 정, for instance, is spelled *Chung* by some and *Jung* by others. The current official romanization system writes ㅈ as *j* at the beginning of a word.

- The voiced version of ㅈ that occurs in words such as 모직 'woolen fabric' is pronounced in a more relaxed way than the English 'j' sound in a word such as *magic*. In contrast, ㅉ is pronounced with more intensity. This may help you make and hear the difference between 공자 'Confucius' and 공짜 'free of charge'.

- Unlike ㅊ and ㅈ, English 'ch' is released both when it occurs in front of a consonant (as in *enrichment*) and when it occurs at the end of a word (as in *rich*). Care must be taken to pronounce ㅊ and ㅈ as an unreleased ㄷ in these contexts in Korean words such as 빛깔 'color' and 빚 'debt'.

3.5 ㅅ & ㅆ

The consonants ㅅ and ㅆ each have three pronunciations, depending on the following vowel and on their position in the word. The first two pronunciations are found in front of a vowel in the same word; the third occurs in front of a consonant or at the end of a word.

3.5.1 Basic pronunciation

In front of a vowel in the same word, both ㅅ and ㅆ are produced by creating a narrow opening between the blade of the tongue and the front part of the dental ridge and/or the upper front teeth. Differentiating between the two sounds is one of the most difficult challenges facing students of Korean, who struggle to make contrasts such as the following.

살	'flesh; skin'	쌀	'uncooked rice'
삼	'ginseng'	쌈	'lettuce wrap'
가서	'Go and . . .'	갔어	'She went'

In fact, not all native speakers of Korean hear or make this distinction: speakers of the 경상도 dialect in the southeastern part of Korea pronounce ㅅ and ㅆ alike, as ㅅ. But speakers of standard Korean have both sounds, so it's important to learn to distinguish between them. The contrast has been described as follows:

To an American ear, the best description might be this: ㅅ is something less than what you expect of an 's', and ㅆ is something more. There is fuzzy 'lisp'-like quality to the lax ㅅ. If you hear a clearcut 's', it is probably ㅆ. If you hear an 's' that you can't make up your mind about, an 's' that seems to have something missing, it is probably ㅅ.[8]

---

[8]Martin (1992:28).

Both ㅅ and ㅆ are voiceless in all positions. ㅅ is lax and should therefore be pronounced in a relaxed way, without creating an overly narrow passage between the tongue and the dental ridge behind the teeth. It may also help to know that ㅅ is very lightly aspirated, with a slight release of air at its conclusion.[9]

In contrast, ㅆ is tense. It should be pronounced forcefully with a very narrow passage for the air to flow through. As with other tense sounds, a higher pitch on the following vowel is a good indication that you have pronounced it correctly.

Basic pronunciation of ㅅ & ㅆ		
Sound	How and where	What else
ㅅ (lax)	the blade of the tongue is positioned behind the upper front teeth, leaving a narrow opening	very light aspiration
ㅆ (tense)	the blade of the tongue is positioned behind the upper front teeth, creating a very narrow opening	no aspiration

Section C-17.1 of the CD contains practice exercises that will help familiarize you with this contrast.

3.5.2   ㅅ & ㅆ with a 'sh'-like pronunciation

When ㅅ or ㅆ occurs inside a word and in front of any of the vowels listed below, they end up with a 'sh'-like pronunciation, lax in the case of ㅅ and tense in the case of ㅆ.

---

[9]Kagaya (1974:171ff.), Iverson (1983:193), Sohn (1994:434), Lee & Ramsey (2000:63).

in front of the vowel ㅣ	시 'poem', 다시 'again'
	맛이 'taste + subject marker'
	씨 'seed', 포도씨 'grape seed'
in front of a 'y' diphthong	셔요 'It's sour', 마셔요 'Drink it'
	샤워 'shower'
in front of ㅟ[10]	쉬워요 'It's easy'

Although the term *'sh'-like* is often used to describe these pronunciations, it is important to realize that neither 시 nor 씨 is identical to the English word *she*. Not only do ㅅ and ㅆ have to respect the lax-tense contrast, they are pronounced more toward the front of the mouth than English 'sh', with the blade of the tongue on the front part of the dental ridge.

3.5.3 ㅅ & ㅆ before a consonant or at the end of a word

Like the other consonants we have considered in this chapter, ㅅ and ㅆ must be fully closed when they occur in front of a consonant or at the end of a word. The flow of air associated with ㅅ and ㅆ is therefore blocked in these positions, resulting in an unreleased ㄷ. Thus 낫다 'It's better' and 났다 'It came out' are pronounced identically, as [낟따]. And 옷 'clothes' is pronounced with a final ㄷ sound, both when it stands alone and when it occurs in front of a consonant, as in 옷도 'clothes too'.

The unreleased (fully closed) pronunciation is found in word-final position even when the next word begins with a vowel, as in 옷 있어요 'There are the clothes' and 붓 아니에요 'It's not a brush'. The same is true inside two-word compounds, as in 옷안 'the inside of the clothes'.

Example (two words)		Pronounced
옷 있어요	'There are the clothes'	[오디써요]
붓 아니에요	'It's not a brush'	[부다니에요]
옷안	'the inside of the clothes'	[오단]

---

[10]The English words *(milk)shake* and *Sheraton*, which are often written as 쉐이크 and 쉐라톤, are pronounced with an initial 'sh'-like consonant, despite their spelling.

Of course, ㅅ and ㅆ retain their usual pronunciation in 옷은 'clothes +
topic marker', 빗어요 'Comb it', and 갔어요 'He went', where they occur
in front of a suffix beginning with a vowel.

Example (single word)		Pronounced
옷은	'clothes + topic marker'	[오슨]
빗어요	'Comb it'	[비서요]
갔어요	'He went'	[가써요]

ㅅ and ㅆ before a consonant or at the end of a word

What happens	Examples
ㅅ and ㅆ are pronounced	낫다 , 났다,
as unreleased ㄷ	옷, 옷안

One contrast that is especially worthy of note involves 옷이에요 'They
are the clothes' and 옷 있어요 'There are the clothes'. Because -이다 'be'
cannot stand alone as a separate word in speech or writing, 옷이에요
counts as a single word, and ㅅ therefore has a 'sh'-like pronunciation.
However, we find the fully closed ㄷ pronunciation in 옷 있어요, where
ㅅ occurs at the end of the first of two separate words. A similar contrast is
found for 빗이에요 'It's a comb' and 빗 있어요 'There's a comb'.

Example		Pronounced
Single word		
옷이에요	'They are the clothes'	[오시에요]
빗이에요	'It's a comb'	[비시에요]
Two words		
옷 있어요	'There are the clothes'	[오디써요]
빗 있어요	'There's a comb'	[비디써요]

An interesting special case involves the contrast between 맛없다 'to
taste bad' and 맛있다 'to taste good'. In the first phrase, the ㅅ at the end

of the word 맛 has a fully closed ㄷ pronunciation, as expected. Thus 맛없다 is pronounced [마덥따].

However, most Koreans pronounce 맛있다 as [마싣따], with a lax 'sh'-like pronunciation for the ㅅ.[11] This is usually explained by saying that 맛있다 has become a single word in Korean, perhaps because it is so commonly used. Since a ㅅ that occurs in front of a vowel inside the same word is not subject to full closure, the apparent exception turns out not to be an exception after all.

Frequency seems to be the key to creating exceptions like these. The ㅅ in the infrequent expression 입맛 있다 'to have an appetite' is pronounced with full closure, yielding [임마딛따]. The same is true for the relatively uncommon 멋없다 'to look unstylish', which is pronounced [머덥따]. On the other hand, the very common expression 멋있다 'to look cool and stylish' behaves as if it were a single word, just like 맛있다. It is therefore pronounced [머싣따], with a lax 'sh-like' pronunciation for the ㅅ.

Example		Pronounced
Treated as a single word		
맛있다	'to taste good'	[마싣따]
멋있다	'to look cool and stylish'	[머싣따]
Treated as two words		
맛없다	'to taste bad'	[마덥따]
멋없다	'to look unstylish'	[머덥따]

As first noted in chapter 1, Korean writing does not always provide a reliable indication of where word boundaries are. You can see this here too, as both 맛있다 and 맛없다 are written without a space, even though 맛없다 is really two words.

You will find practice exercises that further illustrate full closure of ㅅ and ㅆ in section C-17.2 of the CD.

---

[11]This is in spite of the fact that for many years the Korean Ministry of Education tried to impose the pronunciation [마딛따]. This effort was not entirely unsuccessful, and you may find some speakers who use this pronunciation.

3.6 ㅎ

The basic pronunciation of ㅎ is the one heard at the beginning of a word. As you will see below, very different pronunciations are found in other positions.

3.6.1 Basic pronunciation

The ㅎ sound of Korean is produced in essentially the same manner as the 'h' of English. The vocal cords are partially closed, creating a narrow passage through which air from the lungs must pass. The resulting friction in the throat corresponds to the 'h' sound.

When pronounced forcefully, ㅎ may be accompanied by additional friction behind the dental ridge if it occurs in front of ㅣ (as in 힘 'energy') and at the lips if it occurs in front of ㅜ (as in 후추 'black pepper').

Basic pronunciation of ㅎ	
Sound	How and where
ㅎ	the vocal cords close part-way, creating a narrow passage through which air from the lungs passes

Section C-18.1 of the CD offers opportunities to hear and practice ㅎ.

3.6.2 ㅎ before a consonant or at the end of a word

No Korean words end in ㅎ,[12] but ㅎ can occur in front of another consonant. When this happens, the second consonant generally takes on an

---

[12]The word 히읗, the name of the letter ㅎ, appears to end with this consonant, but there is reason to think that this is just an idiosyncrasy of Korean spelling and that the word really ends in the ㅅ sound. That explains why the final consonant is pronounced as if it were ㄷ when the word stands alone, but as ㅅ in front of a subject or direct object marker, as in 히읗이 or 히읗을. It also explains why the first consonant in the suffix 도 'too' has a tense rather than aspirated pronunciation in 히읗도 'ㅎ too'.

aspirated pronunciation—as in 좋다 'It's good', which is pronounced [조타]. This is discussed in detail in section 4.7.

However, when ㅎ occurs in front of ㅅ, it must have full closure—just like the consonants in the preceding sections. This is achieved by pronouncing it as if it were ㄷ. The effects of this can be heard in 파랗습니다 'It is blue', which is pronounced [파랃씀니다], and 그렇습니다 'It is so', which is pronounced [그럳씀니다].

ㅎ in front of ㅅ	
What happens	Examples
ㅎ is pronounced as unreleased ㄷ	파랗습니다, 그렇습니다

Summary of the effects of full closure

In sum, ㅎ is somewhat special in that it shows the effects of full closure only in front of ㅅ. In contrast, the other consonants we have been considering show the effects of full closure summarized below, both in front of any other consonant and at the end of a word.

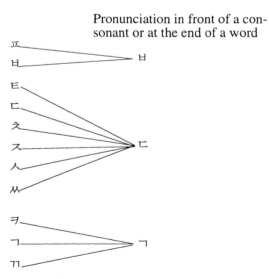

Figure 3.2 The effects of full closure

Section C-18.2 of the CD presents practice exercises that will help you better understand the modifications brought about by the position in which a consonant occurs.

3.6.3 ㅎ between voiced sounds

When ㅎ occurs between voiced sounds, one of two things can happen. In some words, such as 좋아요 'It's good', it is simply dropped—giving the pronunciation [조아요]. But in other words, such as 전화 'telephone', it can be either dropped or pronounced weakly. This is discussed in much more detail in section 4.6.

3.7 ㅁ, ㄴ, & ㅇ

The pronunciation of the consonants ㅁ, ㄴ, and ㅇ does not vary in the way that the pronunciation of other consonants does. However, there are other factors to watch for, especially for ㄴ. As we will see in the next chapter, the pronunciation of this sound can be modified by a neighboring consonant (sections 4.8 and 4.10). In addition, ㅇ is special in that it occurs only at the end of a syllable. (Remember that the ㅇ that occurs in words such as 우유 'milk' is just a place holder with no pronunciation of its own.)

3.7.1 Basic pronunciation

Like their English counterparts 'm', 'n', and 'ng', Korean ㅁ, ㄴ, and ㅇ are *nasal* sounds, which simply means that vibrating air escapes through the nose instead of the mouth as they are pronounced. (You can feel these vibrations by placing your finger on your nose as you say the sounds.) The consonants ㅁ, ㄴ, and ㅇ are pronounced in essentially the same manner as English 'm', 'n', and 'ng', respectively, except that ㄴ is produced with the blade of the tongue rather than the tip. English speakers should therefore have little or no difficulty pronouncing or hearing these sounds.

ㅁ , ㄴ , & ㅇ		
Sound	How and where	What else
ㅁ	the lips are pressed firmly together	nasal
ㄴ	the blade of the tongue presses against the bony ridge behind the upper front teeth	"
ㅇ	the body of the tongue makes contact with the back part of the roof of the mouth	"

3.7.2 Double ㄴ & ㅁ

One thing to watch for with both ㄴ and ㅁ is a subtle length contrast. An example of this contrast involving ㄴ can be heard in 많아요 'There is a lot' versus 만나요 'We meet'. The key to perceiving and producing this distinction is to realize that the second word contains two ㄴ sounds that have been run together—one at the end of the first syllable and the second at the beginning of the second syllable. In contrast, 많아요 is pronounced [마나요]; it contains a single ㄴ, which ends up at the beginning of the second syllable because of the consonant relinking process discussed in the first chapter. (ㅎ is not pronounced at all here.)

A similar contrast occurs with ㅁ, as you can see by comparing 그물 'fish net' with 금물 'forbidden thing'.

In order to hear and practice the nasal sounds of Korean, including the contrast between single and double consonants, go to section C-19 of the CD.

3.8 ㄹ

Korean ㄹ has two pronunciations. Both involve the tip and/or blade of the tongue making contact with the dental ridge and/or the back of the upper front teeth, but in other respects they are very different.

3.8.1 ㄹ between vowels

When ㄹ occurs between vowel sounds, as in 노래 'song', 얼음 'ice', and 물 있어요 'There's water', the tip and/or blade of the tongue flaps quickly against the dental ridge. The resulting sound is quite similar to the 'r' found in Spanish words such as *caro* 'dear' or Japanese words such as *haru* 'spring'.[13] It is very different from English 'r', which is pronounced with the tip of the tongue curled back and away from the dental ridge.

Although primarily found between vowels, the flapped 'r' pronunciation is also heard at the beginning of 리을, the name for the letter ㄹ itself and the only native Korean word to begin with this sound. It is also used at the beginning of various borrowed words, such as 레스토랑 'restaurant' and 리본 'ribbon'.

3.8.2 ㄹ in other positions

When ㄹ occurs in front of a consonant, as in 날씨 'weather', or at the end of a word that stands alone, as in 불 'fire', it is pronounced with the tongue touching against the dental ridge just behind the teeth. The end result is a sound very much like the 'clear l' that occurs at the beginning of English words such as *leg* and *lip* rather than the 'dark l' found after vowels in words such as *milk* and *pull*.

When two ㄹs occur together, as they do in the word 빨래 'laundry', each has the 'l' pronunciation. As the spelling indicates, the first ㄹ is pronounced at the end of the first syllable and the second one at the beginning of the second syllable. (As we will see in section 4.9.2, ㄹ has a different fate when it occurs after other consonants.) This leads to contrasts such as the one between 다리 'leg; bridge' and 달리 'differently'. The first word has a single ㄹ, with the flapped 'r' pronunciation discussed in the preceding section, while the second word has a double ㄹ, with a double 'l' pronunciation.

You may also hear the 'l' pronunciation of ㄹ at the beginning of various borrowed words, such as 렌즈 'lens' and 립스틱 'lipstick', although some speakers may use the flapped 'r' here.

---

[13]Sohn (1994:435).

Sound	How and where
ㄹ between vowels or at the beginning of a word	the tip and/or blade of the tongue flaps quickly against the dental ridge
ㄹ in front of a consonant, at the end of a word that stands alone, or after another ㄹ	the tip and/or blade of the tongue touches against the dental ridge

Section C-20 of the CD contains practice exercises that will help you become familiar with these sounds.

3.9 Appendix: The details of aspiration

This section discusses some technical details relating to how Korean consonant sounds are produced. This information is not required to make use of the practice exercises.

As we have seen, the degree of aspiration is crucial for distinguishing among Korean consonant sounds at the beginning of a word and for understanding how they differ from English consonants. The pronunciation of any consonant that involves closure can be broken down into three steps when it occurs in front of a vowel:

1. Firm closure at some point in the mouth (e.g., at the lips, at the dental ridge behind the upper front teeth, or on the roof of the mouth).

2. Accumulation of air pressure behind the closure as air continues to flow into the mouth from the lungs.

3. Release of the closure at the end of the consonant and the beginning of vocal cord vibrations associated with the vowel.

The third step is the crucial one, as the precise timing of the vocal cord vibrations determines how much aspiration there will be (that is, how strong a puff of air there will be). That's because vocal cord vibrations interfere with the flow of air from the lungs through the larynx. If the vocal cords start vibrating as soon as the closure is released, there won't be any aspiration at all. On the other hand, if there is a delay between the point at which the closure is released and the point at which the vocal cords begin to vibrate, there will be aspiration.

This is all very subtle, but you should be able to notice it for yourself by comparing the pronunciation of the English words *bay* and *pay*. Hold one hand (or a slip of paper) in front of your mouth and the other hand on your larynx, and then say each word very slowly. You should notice that the vocal cord vibrations in *bay* (represented in figure 3.3 as *xxx*) start a little before the lips open and that there is therefore no aspiration.

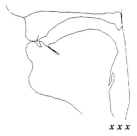
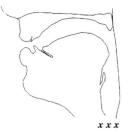

xxx   *xxx*

Step 1: lip closure; vocal cord vibrations begin while the lips are still closed   Step 2: opening of the lips and continuation of vocal cord vibrations

Figure 3.3 Two steps in the pronunciation of the 'b' sound in *bay*

Compare this with what happens when you say the word *pay*. The vocal cord vibrations in this word don't start until an instant after the lips open—so there will be a puff of air. In fact, you'll find that you can increase the amount of aspiration by delaying the onset of the vocal cord vibrations. To see this, draw out your pronunciation of *pay* by saying it very slowly: you'll notice that the slightly longer interval between the time when the lips open and the beginning of vocal cord vibrations translates into a more noticeable aspiration.

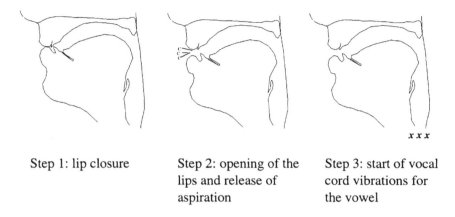

xxx

Step 1: lip closure   Step 2: opening of the   Step 3: start of vocal
                             lips and release of   cord vibrations for
                             aspiration   the vowel

Figure 3.4 Three steps in the pronunciation of the 'p' sound in *pay*

Korean ㅍ involves a longer delay before the start of vocal cord vibrations than does English 'p' and therefore has more aspiration. In contrast, ㅂ is pronounced with a much shorter delay and hence has only very light aspiration. And ㅃ has no delay at all—the vocal cords always start vibrating as soon as the lips open, preventing any aspiration. As depicted in figure 3.3, English 'b' is different again: because it is voiced, there are vocal cord vibrations even *before* the lips open.

The other series of aspirated, lax, and tense consonants (ㅌ-ㄷ-ㄸ, ㅋ-ㄱ-ㄲ, and ㅊ-ㅈ-ㅉ) work the same way. That is, the aspirated sounds ㅌ, ㅋ, and ㅊ have a longer delay before the beginning of vocal cord vibrations than their English counterparts 't', 'k', and 'ch', and therefore have more aspiration. The lax consonant sounds ㄷ, ㄱ, and ㅈ are pronounced with a much shorter delay before the onset of vocal cord vibrations and therefore have only very light aspiration. And the tense consonant sounds ㄸ, ㄲ, and ㅉ have no delay at all between the release of the closure and the beginning of vocal cord vibrations. All these sounds differ from English 'd', 'g', and 'j', which are voiced and therefore have vocal cord vibrations *before* the closure is released.

Chapter 4

Adjustments

The sounds making up a word are not like beads on a string, unaffected and unchanged by their surroundings. Rather, they interact with their neighbors in many ways, sometimes undergoing major modifications to accommodate each other's presence.

All languages make adjustments of this sort. In English, for instance, *want to* is often contracted to *wanna* in casual speech. The 'h' in *her* can be dropped, giving the colloquial pronunciation heard in *I see 'er*. The 'n' of *income* can be pronounced as 'ng' because of the 'k' sound that immediately follows it. And so forth.

Korean too has adjustment processes, some of which have quite drastic effects. We'll look at fifteen important adjustment processes in this chapter and at the changes that they bring about. We'll explain exactly what each change involves and give you a chance to hear and practice it with the help of the CD that accompanies this book. By learning these adjustments, you'll not only improve your pronunciation and your comprehension, you'll come to have a better understanding of how Korean spelling works.

4.1 Consonant relinking

The single most basic and common adjustment process in Korean involves syllable structure. As explained in chapter 1, a consonant that occurs at the end of one syllable is pushed into the next syllable when the second syllable starts with a vowel sound. Thus, 밥이 'rice + subject marker' is pronounced [바비], with the last consonant 'relinked' to the vowel of the second syllable. (As in other chapters, square brackets indicate pronunciations, not spellings.)

밥ᅩ이

Here are some other examples.

Word	Pronounced
믿음 'belief'	[미듬]
악어 'crocodile'	[아거]
밖에 'outside'	[바께]
음악 'music'	[으막]

A consonant may even be relinked over a word boundary within a group of words pronounced in the same breath. That is why 예쁜 우산 'pretty umbrella' is pronounced [예쁘누산] and 꼭 오세요 'Please come by for sure' is pronounced [꼬고세요].

Remember that relinking also applies to consonants whose pronunciation is affected by the full closure that takes place at the end of a word in Korean. Thus the sentence 옷 안 사요 'I'm not buying clothes' is pronounced [오단사요] and 꽃 아니에요 'It's not a flower' is pronounced [꼬다니에요].

Consonant relinking	
(can apply across word boundaries)	
Where it happens	**What happens**
if the next syllable begins with a vowel sound	the consonant is pronounced at the beginning of the next syllable

---

In some cases, consonant relinking permits the pronunciation of a consonant that otherwise would go unpronounced. For instance, ㅂ is not heard in 넓다 'be wide', because Korean allows no more than one consonant to be pronounced at the end of a syllable. However, it is heard in 넓어요, where relinking places it at the beginning of the second syllable. Similarly, ㅅ is not pronounced in 값 'price', but it is heard in 값이 'price + subject marker', where relinking places it at the beginning of the second syllable.[1] And ㄹ is not pronounced in 젊다 'be young', but it is in 젊어요, where relinking pushes ㅁ into the second syllable.

---

[1] However, 값어치 'worth' is always pronounced [가버치], and 밥값은 'the price of a meal + topic marker' is often pronounced [밥까븐]—both without the ㅅ. Moreover, 닭이 'chicken + subject marker' and 흙이 'earth + subject marker' are almost always pronounced [다기] and [흐기], respectively, without the ㄹ.

Without relinking			With relinking	
넓다	[널따]	'It's wide'	넓어요	[널버요]
값	[갑]	'price'	값이	[갑씨]
젊다	[점따]	'She's young'	젊어요	[절머요]

Section A-1 of the CD provides helpful practice exercises for consonant relinking.

4.2 Voicing

As explained in detail in chapter 3, the lax consonant sounds ㅂ, ㄷ, ㄱ, and ㅈ become fully voiced when they occur between voiced sounds (that is, vowels or the consonants ㅁ, ㄴ, ㅇ, and ㄹ). As a result, ㅂ ends up with a 'b'-like pronunciation, ㄷ with a 'd'-like pronunciation, ㄱ with a 'g'-like pronunciation, and ㅈ with a 'j'-like pronunciation.

Voiceless		Fully voiced		
비	'rain'	준비	'preparation'	(ㅂ is 'b'-like)
다	'all'	멀다	'It's far'	(ㄷ is 'd'-like)
개	'dog'	조개	'clam'	(ㄱ is 'g'-like)
자	'ruler'	상자	'box'	(ㅈ is 'j'-like)

Voicing can also affect a consonant that occurs at the end of a word if the next word begins with a vowel. Thus, the ㅂ at the end of 입 'mouth' in 입안 'the inside of the mouth' has a 'b'-like pronunciation because of its position between vowel sounds. Similarly, the ㄱ at the end of 백 'one hundred' in 백원 'one hundred *won*' has a 'g'-like pronunciation.

Voicing can also apply across a word boundary, as in 내 바지 'my pants', where it affects ㅂ, or 큰 가방 'big bag', where it affects ㄱ. However, as we will see in section 5.2 of the next chapter, voicing in these cases is blocked when the second word carries high pitch.

As explained in detail in the preceding chapter, consonants that occur at the end of a word have a fully closed (unreleased) pronunciation.

Consonant   Fully closed pronunciation

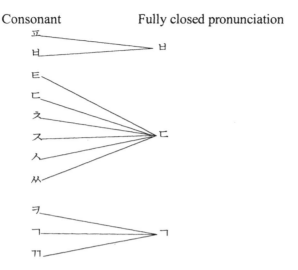

Figure 4.1 The effects of full closure at the end of a word

When any of these consonants occurs at the end of a word that is followed by a word beginning with a vowel, they too end up being voiced. Here are some examples.

Example		With closure	After voicing
잎안	'the inside of the leaf'	[입]안	ㅂ is 'b'-like
솥 없어요	'There's no kettle'	[솓] 없어요	ㄷ is 'd'-like
꽃 아니야	'It's not a flower'	[꼳] 아니야	ㄷ is 'd'-like
빚 안 져요	'I'm not going into debt'	[빋] 안 져요	ㄷ is 'd'-like
맛 없어요	'It has no taste'	[맏] 없어요	ㄷ is 'd'-like
부엌안	'the inside of the kitchen'	[부억]안	ㄱ is 'g'-like
밖 어두워	'The outside is dark'	[박] 어두워	ㄱ is 'g'-like

> ### Voicing
> *(can apply across a word boundary)*
>
> | Where it happens | What happens |
> | --- | --- |
> | between voiced sounds (vowels, ㅁ, ㄴ, ㅇ, or ㄹ) | consonants with the pronunciation of ㅂ, ㄷ, ㄱ, or ㅈ become fully voiced (ㅂ is 'b'-like, ㄷ is 'd'-like, ㄱ is 'g'-like, ㅈ is 'j'-like) |

The CD contains practice exercises for voicing in section A-2, as well as in sections C-1 (for ㅂ), C-5 (for ㄷ), C-9 (for ㄱ), and C-13 (for ㅈ).

4.3 Diphthong reduction

In colloquial speech, the glide portion of a diphthong (the 'w' or 'y') can be weakened or even dropped. The most frequently affected diphthongs are those beginning with the glide 'w', which is reduced and often completely dropped in faster speech, except when it occurs at the beginning of a word. You can hear the effects of this adjustment in words such as 가위 'scissors' and 사과 'apple', which can be pronounced [가이] and [사가], respectively.

Example		Pronounced
가위 있어요?	'Do you have scissors?'	[가이이써요]
사과 먹어요	'Eat the apple'	[사가머거요]
추워요	'It's cold'	[추어요]
귀 아파요	'My ear hurts'	[기아파요]

Remember that 'w' is retained when the diphthong occurs at the beginning of a word, as in 위 'top', 왕 'king', or 월요일 'Monday'.

Among the diphthongs beginning with the glide 'y', ㅒ and ㅖ are particularly susceptible to reduction. The 'y' is maintained at the beginning of a word, as in 얘 'this kid' and 예습 'preview', but it is commonly dropped in other positions, as in the following examples.

Example		Pronounced
개	'the kid'	[개]
폐	'lung'	[페]
시계	'watch'	[시게]
얼마예요?	'How much is it?'	[얼마에요]

The other 'y' diphthongs (ㅑ, ㅕ, ㅛ, and ㅠ) maintain their full pronunciation in all contexts.

A general word of warning here: the effects of diphthong reduction are not reflected in the spelling, which therefore differs from the pronunciation that we write inside square brackets. In the long run, though, an understanding of how adjustment processes affect a word's pronunciation will help you remember not only how to pronounce it but also how to spell it.

Diphthong reduction		
Affected sounds	Where it happens	What happens
'w' diphthongs; the 'y' diphthongs ㅒ and ㅖ	positions other than the beginning of a word	the 'w' and 'y' sounds are weakened or even dropped in colloquial speech

The diphthong ㅢ, with the 'y' glide at the end, requires special comment. As mentioned in section 2.2.1, ㅢ retains its full diphthongal pronunciation at the beginning of words such as 의사 'doctor' and 의자 'chair' in careful speech. In faster speech, however, the glide is pronounced very weakly or not at all.

In other positions, ㅢ has a different fate. When used to represent the possessive suffix, as in 미국의 수도 'America's capital', it is pronounced as the simple vowel ㅔ. And when it is neither word-initial nor the possessive suffix, it is pronounced as the simple vowel ㅣ, as in 희망 'hope' and 거의 'almost', which are pronounced [히망] and [거이], respectively.

You can find practice exercises illustrating diphthong reduction in section A-3 of the CD.

4.4 Contraction

Contraction is a process that shortens a word by reducing the number of syllables that it contains. There are many different types of contraction in Korean, a number of which occur with great frequency. Becoming familiar with the particular contraction processes described below will dramatically improve both your comprehension and the naturalness of your speech.

Reduction of ㅗ and ㅜ to the glide 'w'

One very common type of contraction reduces the vowels ㅗ and ㅜ to the glide 'w' in faster speech when they precede a suffix that begins with a vowel. Thus the three-syllable word 보아요 'Look' can be pronounced [봐요], with the diphthong ㅘ created from the vowels ㅗ and ㅏ. And 주어요 'Give it to me' can be pronounced as two-syllable [줘요], with the vowels ㅜ and ㅓ merged into the diphthong ㅝ.

Without contraction		With contraction
보아요	'Look'	[봐요]
주어요	'Give it to me'	[줘요]

The effects of this type of contraction can be reflected in the spelling: 보아요 is sometimes written as 봐요, 주어요 is sometimes written as 줘요, and 오 + 아 + 요 'Come' is *always* written as 와요, perhaps because reduction of ㅗ to 'w' is obligatory in this word.

It is even possible to go one step further by dropping the glide entirely if it doesn't occur at the beginning of a word (see section 4.3 above), leaving just the vowel ㅏ in the case of ㅘ and just ㅓ[2] in the case of ㅝ. Thus 봐 'Look' can be pronounced [바] and 뭐 'what' can be pronounced [머], although they are never spelled this way.

---

[2] Or even ㅗ, so that 뭐에요? 'What is it?' can be pronounced [머에요] or [모에요]. In some words, deletion of the glide can only result in ㅗ. For example, the reduced form of 주어 'Give it to me' can only be [조].

Without glide deletion		With glide deletion
여기 봐요	'Look here'	[여기바요]
뭐예요?	'What is it?'	[머에요]

Reduction of ㅣ to the glide 'y'

Contraction also affects the vowel ㅣ, changing it into the glide 'y' when it occurs in front of a suffix that begins with a vowel. Thus, 시어요 'It's sour' can be pronounced [셔요], and 기어요 'It's crawling' can be pronounced [겨요].

Without contraction		With contraction
시어요	'It's sour'	[셔요]
기어요	'It's crawling'	[겨요]
피어요	'It's blooming'	[펴요]

This sort of contraction is obligatory in some words, as in 마시 + 어 + 요 'Drink it', which is always pronounced [마셔요]—and is written that way too. (There seems to be no general rule about when contracted spellings are possible, by the way, so you'll have to learn the conventions on a case-by-case basis.)

Contraction of the direct object and topic markers

Another very common type of contraction affects 를, the version of the direct object marker that attaches to nouns that end in a vowel. As the following examples show, 를 can be shortened to ㄹ in colloquial speech.

Without contraction		With contraction
나를	'I + direct object marker'	[날]
차를	'car + direct object marker'	[찰]
코를	'nose + direct object marker'	[콜]
누구를	'who + direct object marker'	[누굴]

An equally general contraction process affects 는, the version of the topic marker that attaches to words that end in a vowel, reducing it to ㄴ.

Without contraction		With contraction
나는	'I + topic marker'	[난]
차는	'car + topic marker'	[찬]
사과는	'apple + topic marker'	[사관]
누구는	'someone + topic marker'	[누군]

In the case of both processes, pronouns may have contracted spellings, but nouns may not.

Contraction of the copula verb -이다

The first vowel of copula verb forms such as -입니다 or -인데요 can be deleted after a vowel. Thus 가수입니다 'I am a singer' is contracted to [가숩니다] and 저입니다 'It's me' is contracted to [접니다]. (In general, pronoun + copula combinations may have contracted spellings, but nouns may not.)

Without contraction		With contraction
가수입니다	'I am a singer'	[가숩니다]
저인데요	'It's me ...'	[전데요]

In cases where the -이세요 or -이다 form of the copula is called for, contraction after a vowel is obligatory in both pronunciation and spelling, as in 누구세요 'Who is it?' and 전화다 'It's a phone call'.

Contraction of specific words

Less general types of contraction apply to specific words, including the following frequently used items.

Without contraction		With contraction
나의	'I + possessive marker'	[내]
저의	'I (formal) + possessive marker'	[제]
무엇	'what'	[뭐]
무엇을	'what + direct object marker'	[무얼]/[뭘]
이것을	'this + direct object marker'	[이걸]
이것은	'this + topic marker'	[이건]
이것이	'this + subject marker'	[이게]
그런데	'by the way, but'	[근데]
그러면	'if that is so'	[그럼]
그렇지	'right?'	[그치]
-때문에	'because'	[때메]
다음	'next'	[담]
처음	'first'	[첨]

The pronouns 내 and 제 are almost always written as they are pronounced, but the situation varies for the other words. Except for the last four items, most can be spelled as they are pronounced, at least in less formal writing.

Contraction of identical vowels

One final contraction process is worth mentioning. When identical vowels occur next to each other, they are contracted into a single vowel. You can hear the effects of this in 재미있어요 'It's fun' and 어디 있어요? 'Where is it?', where the two consecutive ㅣ sounds are pronounced as if they were a single vowel. (In casual writing, you may even see these expressions spelled as 재밌어요 and 어딨어요.)

Without contraction		With contraction
재미있어요	'It's fun'	[재미써요]
어디 있어요?	'Where is it?'	[어디써요]

The exercises in section A-4 of the CD will give you a chance to practice contraction.

4.5 Special changes to the pronunciation of vowels

Two vowels—the diphthong that occurs in the honorific sentence ender -요 and the ㅗ that is used in various grammatical endings—undergo changes to their pronunciation that you need to be familiar with.[3]

Pronunciation of ㅛ as if it were ㅕ

In casual speech, the pronunciation of the listener-honorific ending 요 is modified to the point where it closely resembles ㅕ. Thus 가요 'Go' is pronounced [가여] and 보세요 'Please look' is pronounced [보세여]. (This change in pronunciation is not reflected in the spelling, however.)

Example		Pronounced
가요	'Go'	[가여]
보세요	'Please look'	[보세여]
우표요	'a postage stamp, please'	[우표여]

Remember that this change affects only the *suffix* 요. The noun 가요 'pop song' is therefore unaffected by this adjustment, even though it has the same spelling as the verb 가요 'Go'.

Pronunciation of ㅗ as if it were ㅜ

The vowel ㅗ in the grammatical endings -하고 'and', -고 'and/that', -로 'to, by means of', and -도 'too' is often pronounced as if it were ㅜ in colloquial speech. You can hear the effects of this change on 고 in 사과하고 배 'apple and pear' and in 뭐라고? 'What did you say?'. Examples involving -로 and -도 include 어디로? 'to where?', 차로 'by car', and 빵도 'bread too'.

---

[3]A less systematic change, not discussed here, involves the pronunciation of ㅕ as if it were ㅡ. Thus 먹던 'that I was eating' is often pronounced [먹든], 언제 'when' is often pronounced [은제], and 덜 'less' is often pronounced [들].

Example		Pronounced
사과하고 배	'apple and pear'	[사과하구배]
뭐라고?	'What did you say?'	[뭐라구]
어디로	'to where'	[어디루]
차로	'by car'	[차루]
빵도	'bread too'	[빵두]

There are two important things to remember about this change. First, it affects only the pronunciation; the spelling is not modified except in advertisements, in informal letters, and in novels that try to convey the flavor of colloquial speech. Second, only grammatical endings, not content words, are affected. Thus, the 고 that means 'storage place' in words such as 냉장고 'refrigerator' and 차고 'garage' must have its usual pronunciation, as must the 도 that means 'drawing' in words such as 지도 'map' and 괘도 'wall chart'. Similarly, there is no change to the pronunciation of the 로 that means 'toil' in words such as 피로 'fatigue' and 과로 'over-exertion'.

Practice exercises involving this change can be found in section A-5 of the CD.

4.6 ㅎ reduction

When ㅎ occurs between voiced sounds (vowels or the consonants ㅁ, ㄴ, ㅇ, and ㄹ) in colloquial speech, it is always weakly pronounced and may be lost entirely in faster speech. The effects of this process can be heard in examples such as the following, in which ㅎ is lightly pronounced, if at all.

Example		Pronounced
영화	'movie'	[영와]
여행	'travel'	[여앵]
죄송합니다	'I am sorry'	[죄송암니다]
전화	'telephone'	[저놔]

Notice, by the way, that the loss of ㅎ in an example such as 전화 'telephone' opens up the consonant position at the beginning of the second syllable. This results in relinking of the ㄴ, which takes over the position formerly occupied by ㅎ.

ㅎ reduction can even take place across word boundaries when two words are pronounced together as a group. This leads to the weakening and possible loss of ㅎ in phrases such as 언제 해요? 'When do we do it?' in faster speech. We will return to this in section 5.2.

Example		Can be pronounced
언제 해요?	'When do we do it?'	[언제애요]
다시 해요	'Do it again'	[다시애요]
파란 하늘	'blue sky'	[파라나늘]

Full deletion of ㅎ is obligatory when it occurs at the end of a verb root in front of a vowel sound. This happens in words such as 좋아요 'It's good' and 많아요 'There's a lot', where the ㅎ is never pronounced.

Example		Pronounced
좋아요	'It's good'	[조아요]
많아요	'There's a lot'	[마나요]

ㅎ reduction
(can apply across a word boundary)

Where it happens	What happens
between voiced sounds (vowels, ㅁ, ㄴ, ㅇ, ㄹ)	ㅎ is obligatorily deleted at the end of a verb root; elsewhere it is weakened and may be dropped

You can find practice exercises involving ㅎ reduction in section A-6 of the CD.

4.7 Aspiration

When ㅎ occurs next to certain consonants, it has a special fate. Instead of being weakened or deleted, it is absorbed into the neighboring sound, causing aspiration. There are two subpatterns here—those in which ㅎ precedes the consonant and those in which it follows it.

4.7.1 ㅎ precedes the other consonant

The following examples illustrate what happens when ㅎ occurs in front of a lax consonant other than ㅅ (which is discussed in section 3.6.2). Combination with ㄷ yields a ㅌ sound, combination with ㄱ yields a ㅋ sound, and combination with ㅈ results in a ㅊ sound. (There happen not to be any words in which ㅎ precedes ㅂ.)

Example		Pronounced	
좋다	'It's good'	[조타]	ㅎ + ㄷ > ㅌ
그렇게	'so; like that'	[그러케]	ㅎ + ㄱ > ㅋ
그렇지만	'but'	[그러치만]	ㅎ + ㅈ > ㅊ

4.7.2 ㅎ follows the other consonant

When ㅎ comes after a lax consonant, aspiration also takes place.

Example		Pronounced	
급히	'hurriedly'	[그피]	ㅂ + ㅎ > ㅍ
맏형	'eldest brother'	[마텽]	ㄷ + ㅎ > ㅌ
백화점	'department store'	[배콰점]	ㄱ + ㅎ > ㅋ

A total of eleven different consonants can precede ㅎ and undergo aspiration. However, if we think in terms of pronunciation, only three consonant sounds are involved—because of the effects of full closure. This is summarized in figure 4.2.

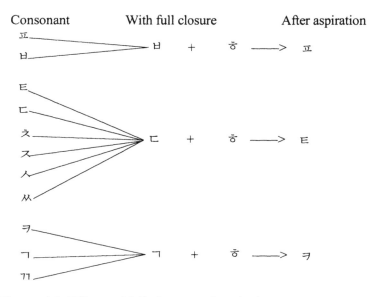

Figure 4.2 Effects of full closure and aspiration

Here are two examples of how aspiration affects a consonant with a fully closed pronunciation.

Example		With closure	After aspiration
옷하고	'clothes and ...'	[옫]하고	[오타고]
낮하고	'day and ...'	[낟]하고	[나타고]

It is important not to be fooled by the spelling here. The final consonant of 옷 'clothes' is written as ㅅ but is pronounced as an unreleased (fully closed) ㄷ. When there is a following ㅎ, as there is in 옷하고 'clothes and...', aspiration takes place, giving the pronunciation [오타고]. The same type of thing happens in 낮하고 'day and...', where ㅈ (pronounced as if it were ㄷ) is followed by ㅎ. Aspiration gives the pronunciation [나타고].

Aspiration applies not only within words, as in the examples above, but also across word boundaries if the two words are pronounced as a group. You can hear the effects of this sort of aspiration in phrases such as 밥 해요 'I am making a rice meal' and 꼭 할게요 'I'll do it for sure', in which

ㅂ and ㄱ take on an aspirated pronunciation because of the ㅎ at the beginning of the next word.

Example		Pronounced
밥 해요	'I am making a rice meal'	[바패요]
꼭 할게요	'I'll do it for sure'	[꼬칼께요]
옷 한벌	'a suit of clothes'	[오탄벌]
솥 하나	'one kettle'	[소타나]
꽃 한송이	'one stem of a flower'	[꼬탄송이]

Here again, it is important not to be fooled by the spelling. In 옷 한벌 'a suit of clothes', for instance, the ㅅ that occurs at the end of the first word has to be pronounced with full closure, yielding a ㄷ sound. Aspiration then gives the pronunciation [오탄벌].

Aspiration
(can apply across a word boundary)

Where it happens	What happens
next to ㅎ	consonants with the pronunciation of ㅂ, ㄷ, ㄱ, or ㅈ become aspirated: ㅂ > ㅍ, ㄷ > ㅌ, ㄱ > ㅋ, ㅈ > ㅊ

Section A-7 of the CD contains several practice exercises involving aspiration.

4.8 Pronunciation of ㄴ as if it were ㄹ

When ㄴ and ㄹ occur next to each other, ㄴ is routinely pronounced as if it were ㄹ.[4] There are two patterns to consider here—the ㄹ + ㄴ pattern and the ㄴ + ㄹ pattern.

---

[4]This should not be confused with another phenomenon—the alternation between ㄴ and ㄹ that is found in Sino-Korean roots, depending on their position in a word. For example, the root meaning 'chaos' is 난 at the beginning of a word, as in 난리 'uproar', but 란 inside a word, as in 소란 'commotion'.

4.8.1 The ㄹ + ㄴ pattern

When ㄹ occurs in front of ㄴ, the ㄴ is pronounced as if it were ㄹ.

ㄹ + ㄴ
　　↑
pronounced as if it were ㄹ

The effects of this change can be heard in 월남 'Vietnam' and 일년 'one year', among many other words. The process can even apply across word boundaries, as in 늘 늦어요 'He is always late' and 설탕을 넣어요 'Put in sugar', both of which are pronounced with a double 'l' sound in connected speech.

Example		Pronounced
월남	'Vietnam'	[월람]
일년	'one year'	[일런]
늘 늦어요	'He is always late'	[늘르저요]
설탕을 넣어요	'Put in sugar'	[설탕을러어요]

Notice that English does not have this particular adjustment process; if it did, we would have to pronounce the word *walnut* as *wallut* and the phrase *will not* as *will lot.*

Pronunciation of ㄴ as if it were ㄹ: part 1
(can apply across word boundaries)

Where it happens	What happens
after ㄹ	ㄴ is pronounced as if it were ㄹ

4.8.2 The ㄴ + ㄹ pattern

When ㄴ occurs before ㄹ, it too is pronounced as if it were ㄹ.

ㄴ + ㄹ
↑
pronounced as if it were ㄹ

The effects of this change can be heard in 전력 'electric power', 선로 'railroad', and many similar examples.

Example		Pronounced
전력	'electric power'	[절력]
선로	'railroad'	[설로]
신라	'Shilla (dynasty)'	[실라]
편리	'convenience'	[펄리]
전례	'precedent'	[절례]

Notice, by the way, that English does not have an adjustment process of this type; if it did, we'd have to pronounce *evenly* as *evelly*.

The pronunciation of ㄴ as if it were ㄹ is somewhat more restricted in the ㄴ + ㄹ pattern than in the reverse pattern. In particular, the change happens only when the ㄹ is in a syllable that combines directly with the syllable containing the ㄴ. (Advanced students may be interested to know that these syllables all happen to be roots of Chinese origin.) Consider in this regard the pronunciation of 정신력 'mental strength' and 신문로 'Shinmun street', in which the first two syllables form a semantic unit.

정신 + 력 'mental strength'　　　　[정신녁]
'mind + strength'

신문 + 로 'Shinmun street'　　　　[신문노]
'Shinmun + street'

ㄴ is not pronounced as ㄹ here, because the syllable containing ㄴ combines first with the syllable to its left rather than with the syllable containing ㄹ.[5] In such cases, the ㄴ + ㄹ sequence is pronounced as a double ㄴ.[6] Here are some additional examples, with angled brackets indicating which syllables combine directly with each other, in accordance with the expression's meaning.

Example		Pronounced
<판단>력	'discernment'	[판단녀]
<한인>록	'Korean-American directory'	[하닌녹]
<철산>리	'Cheolsan-li'	[철싼니]
신<라면>	'Shin ramen'	[신나면]
예쁜 <리본>	'pretty ribbon'	[예쁜니본]

Pronunciation of ㄴ as if it were ㄹ: part 2	
Where it happens	**What happens**
when a syllable ending in ㄴ combines directly with a syllable beginning with ㄹ	ㄴ is pronounced as if it were ㄹ

You'll find opportunities to practice this adjustment process in section A-8 of the CD.

4.9 Nasalization

Nasalization is a process that converts an ordinary consonant into one of the three nasal consonants in Korean—ㅁ, ㄴ, or ㅇ. This happens in two separate situations.

---

[5]Contrary to what might be expected, 선릉 'the Sun royal tomb' may be pronounced [선능], even though the two syllables combine directly with each other. This may be because the root meaning 'royal tomb' has an alternate form 능 that is used when it is an independent word.

[6]An interesting special case here is 삼천리, which is used to mean 'Korea' but whose literal meaning is '3000 *li*'. (The *li* is a traditional unit of distance.) If 삼천리 were to be used literally, it would be pronounced [삼천니] because it would have the structure 삼천 + 리. When it is used to mean 'Korea', on the other hand, it is pronounced [삼철리], apparently because it no longer has the internal structure associated with the literal meaning.

4.9.1 Before ㅁ or ㄴ

When ordinary consonants are followed by the nasal consonant ㅁ or ㄴ, they take on a nasal pronunciation themselves.

Example		Pronounced	
십만	'100,000'	[심만]	ㅂ > ㅁ
믿는다	'I believe it'	[민는다]	ㄷ > ㄴ
작년	'last year'	[장년]	ㄱ > ㅇ

Notice that English does not have this type of nasalization. If it did, we'd pronounce *atmosphere* as *anmosphere* and *picnic* as *pingnic*.

Remember that consonant sounds must be fully closed when they occur in front of another consonant or at the end of a word. Because of this, many different consonants have the same pronunciation in these positions. Indeed, as the following summary helps show, eleven different consonants come down to just three sounds, each of which then takes on a nasal pronunciation when followed by a nasal sound.

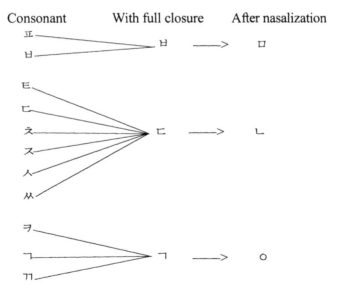

Figure 4.3 The effects of full closure and nasalization

Here are some examples that illustrate the interaction of full closure and nasalization.

Example		With closure	After nasalization
앞문	'front door'	[압]문	[암문]
몇년	'how many years'	[멷]년	[면년]
맞네요	'Oh, it fits'	[맏]네요	[만네요]
옛날	'old days'	[옏]날	[옌날]
갔나요?	'Is she gone?'	[갇]나요	[간나요]
부엌문	'kitchen door'	[부억]문	[부엉문]

The effects of nasalization in Korean can also be heard across word boundaries. In 밥 먹어요 'I am eating a meal', for instance, the final ㅂ of 밥 is nasalized because of the ㅁ at the beginning of 먹어요. Similarly, the ㅅ in 옷, with its fully closed ㄷ sound, is nasalized in 옷 많아요 'There are many clothes' because of the ㅁ in the following word.

Example	Pronounced
밥 먹어요 'I am eating a meal'	[밤머거요]
옷 많아요 'There are many clothes'	[온마나요]

Nasalization of consonants before ㅁ or ㄴ
(can apply across a word boundary)

Where it happens	What happens
before ㅁ or ㄴ	consonants with the pronunciation of ㅂ, ㄷ, or ㄱ become nasalized: ㅂ > ㅁ, ㄷ > ㄴ, ㄱ > ㅇ

You will find practice exercises for this type of nasalization in section A-9.1 of the CD.

4.9.2 Nasalization of ㄹ after a consonant other than ㄴ or ㄹ

A different sort of nasalization takes place *after* a consonant other than ㄴ or ㄹ. In such situations, ㄹ is pronounced as if it were ㄴ.

Consonant other   +   ㄹ
than ㄴ or ㄹ   ↑
                pronounced as if it were ㄴ

You can hear the effects of this change in 심리 'psychology', 공룡 'dinosaur', and the other examples below, in which ㄹ is pronounced ㄴ because of the preceding consonant.

Example		Pronounced
공룡	'dinosaur'	[공뇽]
심리	'psychology'	[심니]
음력	'lunar calendar'	[음녁]
양력	'solar calendar'	[양녁]
종류	'a kind, a sort'	[종뉴]

    This type of nasalization can also take place across a word boundary. Thus the ㄹ at the beginning of 라면 'ramen' is pronounced as if it were ㄴ in a sentence such as 나랑 라면 먹어요 'Eat ramen with me'. The same is true of the ㄹ at the beginning of 라디오 in 지금 라디오 들어요 'Now I'm listening to the radio'.

    An additional change occurs in words such as 입력 'power input', where ㄹ is nasalized and then triggers nasalization of ㅂ, giving the pronunciation [임녁].

Starting point: 입력 'power input'
                  ↓
             nasalization of ㄹ (입[녁])
                  ↓
             nasalization of ㅂ
                  ↓
Pronounced: [임녁]

A similar thing happens in 식량 'provisions', which is pronounced [싱냥] following nasalization of ㄹ and then of ㄱ.

Starting point: 식량 'provisions'
                         ↓
                    nasalization of ㄹ (식[냥])
                         ↓
                    nasalization of ㄱ
                         ↓
Pronounced: [싱냥]

Here are some other examples.

Example		Pronounced
압력	'pressure'	[암녁]
답례	'return favor'	[담녜]
확률	'probability'	[황뉼]
독립	'independence'	[동닙]
기억력	'memory power'	[기엉녁]

You might be amused to know that exactly the same changes take place when a Korean speaker says the name of the actress Meg Ryan, which is therefore pronounced 'Meng Nyan'!

Nasalization of ㄹ
(can apply across word boundaries)

Where it happens	What happens
after a consonant other than ㄴ or ㄹ	ㄹ is nasalized and pronounced as if it were ㄴ

Practice exercises for this type of nasalization can be found in section A-9.2 of the CD.

As noted in section 4.8.2, a ㄹ that follows a ㄴ undergoes nasalization when the syllables containing the two sounds do not combine directly. You can hear the effects of this change in 정신력 'mental strength' (with the structure 정신 + 력), which is pronounced [정신녁], and 예쁜 리본 'pretty ribbon', which is pronounced [예쁜니본]. This may be a broader implementation of the nasalization process that we are considering here.

4.10 Pronunciation of ㄴ as if it were ㅁ or ㅇ

The sound ㄴ can undergo a change in pronunciation under the influence of a neighboring consonant in the same word or even in the next word in the same group. Two distinct changes can take place:

• When followed by ㅍ, ㅂ, ㅃ, or ㅁ, ㄴ can be pronounced as if it were ㅁ.

Example		Can be pronounced
준비	'preparation'	[줌비]
뜨거운 물	'hot water'	[뜨거움물]

• When followed by ㅋ, ㄱ, or ㄲ , ㄴ can be pronounced as if it were ㅇ .

Example		Can be pronounced
한국	'Korea'	[항국]
큰 칼	'big knife'	[킁칼]
좋은 꿈	'happy dream'	[조응꿈]

Something similar happens in English. The 'n' in *input* can be pronounced 'm' because of the following 'p' sound and the 'n' in *incorrect* can be pronounced 'ng' because of the following 'k' sound.

It is important to look past the spelling when pronouncing Korean words. In 꽃무늬 'floral design', for instance, the final consonant of 꽃 'flower' is written ㅊ and would normally have the unreleased ㄷ pronunciation. However, nasalization takes place in this case because of the following ㅁ (see section 4.9.1). If nothing else happens, we get the pronunciation [꼰무늬]. But further modification is also possible—with the result that ㅊ ends up being pronounced as if it were ㅁ!

Starting point: 꽃무늬 'floral design'
                        ↓
                     nasalization ([꼰]무늬)
                        ↓
                     pronunciation of ㄴ as ㅁ
                        ↓
Pronounced: [꼼무니]

Here are some other examples.

Example	Pronounced
몇 명 'how many people'	[면명] or [몀명]
빗물 'rainwater'	[빈물] or [빔물]
낱말 'word'	[난말] or [남말]

Pronunciation of ㄴ as if it were ㅁ or ㅇ
(can apply across a word boundary)

Where it happens	What happens
in front of ㅍ, ㅂ, ㅃ, or ㅁ	a consonant that would normally be pronounced ㄴ is pronounced ㅁ
in front of ㅋ, ㄱ, or ㄲ	a consonant that would normally be pronounced ㄴ is pronounced ㅇ

Although this type of change is common in fast speech, its effects are easy to miss. Fortunately, though, there is nothing wrong with retaining a ㄴ sound in 준비 and 한국 in careful speech—or with pronouncing an 'n' in *input* or *incorrect*. Nonetheless, being familiar with this modification will help you fine-tune your pronunciation and improve your comprehension of the speech of others.

You can become more familiar with modifications to the pronunciation of ㄴ by doing the practice exercises in section A-10 of the CD.

4.11 Addition of ㄴ

In certain types of phrases and compounds, especially those consisting of independent words, a ㄴ sound is added at the beginning of an item that starts with ㅣ or a 'y'-initial diphthong (ㅑ, ㅕ, ㅒ, ㅖ, ㅛ, or ㅠ) when the previous item ends in a consonant. This added ㄴ is sometimes written, as in 앞니 'front tooth' (이 is the word for 'tooth' when it stands alone), but usually it is not. Nonetheless, it can be heard at the beginning of the second syllable in words such as 담요 'blanket', 한여름 'midsummer', and 면양말 'cotton socks', among others.

Example		Pronounced
담요	'blanket'	[담뇨]
한여름	'midsummer'	[한녀름]
면양말	'cotton socks'	[면냥말]

Once added, the ㄴ can be involved in further adjustments. In the expression 막일 'manual labor', for instance, the ㄴ that is added at the beginning of the second syllable triggers nasalization of the ㄱ (see section 4.9.1), resulting in the pronunciation [망닐].

Starting point: 막일 'manual labor'
                     ↓
               addition of ㄴ to 일 (막[닐])
                     ↓
               nasalization of ㄱ
                     ↓
Pronounced: [망닐]

In 집 열쇠 'house key', the ㅂ undergoes nasalization because of the ㄴ that has been added to the beginning of 열쇠, yielding the pronunciation [짐널쐬].

Starting point: 집 열쇠 'house key'
                           ↓
                    addition of ㄴ to 열쇠 (집[널]쇠)
                           ↓
                    nasalization of ㅂ
                           ↓
Pronounced: [짐널쐬]

Here are some other examples.

Example		Pronounced
십육	'sixteen'	[심뉵]
앞일	'future matter'	[암닐]
꽃잎	'petal'	[꼰닙]
색연필	'color pencil'	[생년필]
부엌일	'kitchen work'	[부엉닐]

In cases where the first item ends in ㄹ, the added ㄴ takes on a ㄹ pronunciation as well, consistent with the adjustment process discussed in section 4.8.1. Thus 틀니 'denture' is pronounced [틀리], with a ㄹ pronunciation for the added ㄴ. (This is one of the few cases where the added ㄴ is represented in the spelling.)

Example		Pronounced
전철역	'subway station'	[전철력]
올여름	'this summer'	[올려름]
휘발유	'volatile oil'	[휘발류]

Three types of complex words

In order to understand where ㄴ is most likely to be added, it is necessary to distinguish among three different types of multipart words in Korean—classic compounds, which consist of independent words, semi-compounds, which consist of an independent word and a *bound root* (an item that has a wordlike meaning but cannot stand alone as an independent word), and words that consist just of bound roots. As we will see, addition of ㄴ typically takes place in the first two types of words, but not in the third type.

The following examples—like most of the examples we have considered so far—are all phrases and compounds that consist of two independent words. When the first word in these expressions ends in a consonant and the second word begins with ㅣ or a 'y'-initial diphthong, a ㄴ sound is almost always added.

Example		Pronounced
한 일	'work that I did'	[한닐]
무슨 요일	'what day of the week'	[무슨뇨일]
태양열	'solar energy'	[태양녈]
구급약	'first-aid medication'	[구금냑]
염색약	'hair dye'	[염생냑]

There are some exceptions, however. One such case is 독약 'poisonous drug', which is pronounced [도갹]—with no ㄴ, even though it is a compound consisting of two independent words. Moreover, ㄴ is never added to the verb 있다. So, 빗 있어요 'I have a comb' can only be pronounced [비디써요] and never [빈니써요].

In certain phrases, addition of ㄴ is optional. For example, 옷 입어요 'I am putting on clothes' can be pronounced either [오디버요] or [온니버요], and 못 일어나요 'I can't get up' can be pronounced either [모디러나요] or [몬니러나요].

The next set of examples are all semi-compounds that consist of one independent word and one bound root. (The final syllable in each example has a wordlike meaning—양 means 'ocean', 욕 means 'bath', 용 means 'use', and so forth, but it cannot be used as a word on its own.) Most words of this type have an added ㄴ when the first item ends in a consonant and the second item begins with ㅣ or a 'y'-initial diphthong.

Example		Pronounced
태평양	'Pacific Ocean'	[태평냥]
일광욕	'sunbathing'	[일광뇩]
여행용	'for travel use'	[여행뇽]
영업용	'for business use'	[영엄뇽]
도시락용	'for use in a lunchbox'	[도시랑뇽]

However, as the following examples show, some semi-compounds fail to undergo this adjustment.

Example		Pronounced
한약	'Chinese medicine'	[하냑]
육일	'the sixth day'	[유길]
외국인	'foreigner'	[외구긴]

Finally, we come to words that consist of two bound roots. As the next set of examples illustrates, ㄴ is not added to such words at all.

Example		Pronounced
선약	'previous engagement'	[서냑]
금연	'No smoking'	[그면]
흡연	'smoking'	[흐변]
낙엽	'fallen leaf'	[나겹]
경영	'management'	[경영]
경유	'gasoline'	[경유]
할인	'discount'	[하린]

Addition of ㄴ
(applies across word boundaries)

Where it happens	What happens
at the beginning of the second item in various multipart words and phrases if (i) the first item ends in a consonant, and (ii) the second one begins with ㅣ or a 'y'-initial diphthong	a ㄴ sound is added

4.12 Tensing

Under certain circumstances, a lax consonant can be given a tense
pronunciation.

Lax consonant	Pronounced
ㅂ	ㅃ
ㄷ	ㄸ
ㄱ	ㄲ
ㅈ	ㅉ
ㅅ	ㅆ

It is necessary to distinguish between two subtypes of tensing—one that
applies with complete regularity and one that must be learned on a case-by-
case basis.

4.12.1 Predictable tensing

Tensing applies with complete regularity when a lax consonant occurs
right after a consonant other than ㄹ or a nasal (ㅁ, ㄴ, or ㅇ). Notice
how the first consonant of the second syllable receives a tense pronunciation
in the following examples.

Word		Pronounced	
겁보	'coward'	[겁뽀]	ㅂ > ㅃ
덥다	'It's hot'	[덥따]	ㄷ > ㄸ
학기	'semester'	[학끼]	ㄱ > ㄲ
곧장	'straight'	[곧짱]	ㅈ > ㅉ
학생	'student'	[학쌩]	ㅅ > ㅆ
앞길	'road ahead'	[압낄]	ㄱ > ㄲ
같다	'to be the same'	[갇따]	ㄷ > ㄸ
낮잠	'nap'	[낟짬]	ㅈ > ㅉ
맛살	'crab/clam meat'	[맏쌀]	ㅅ > ㅆ

Tensing after ㅎ is somewhat more restricted. There, ㅅ is tensed—as in 좋습니다 'It is good', which is pronounced [졷씀니다]. However, as we saw in section 4.7.1, other lax consonants are aspirated after ㅎ.

Like many other adjustment processes in Korean, tensing can apply across a word boundary. You can hear the effects of this type of tensing by listening carefully to the pronunciation of the ㅂ in 책 보세요 'Look at the book, please'—it becomes tense because of the consonant at the end of the preceding word. For more on this, see section 5.2.

Predictable tensing
(can apply across a word boundary)

Affected sounds	Where it happens	What happens
lax consonants:	after a consonant other than ㄹ or a nasal (ㅁ, ㄴ, or ㅇ) (after ㅎ, only ㅅ is tensed)	the lax consonant is tensed
ㅂ		ㅂ > ㅃ
ㄷ		ㄷ > ㄸ
ㄱ		ㄱ > ㄲ
ㅈ		ㅈ > ㅉ
ㅅ		ㅅ > ㅆ

Tensing in these cases is a very natural phonetic process, and you will probably find that you do it subconsciously without the need for much instruction or practice. You can find exercises involving predictable tensing in section A-12.1 of the CD.

A side-effect of tensing in some cases is that the consonant that precedes the tensed consonant may be dropped. Thus 입구 'entrance' can be pronounced [이꾸] in faster speech. Here are some other examples.

Example		Pronounced
밥값	'price of a meal'	[밥깝] or [바깝]
앞길	'road ahead'	[압낄] or [아낄]
숯불	'charcoal fire'	[숟뿔] or [수뿔]
같다	'to be the same'	[갇따] or [가따]
곧장	'straight'	[곧짱] or [고짱]
낮잠	'nap'	[낟짬] or [나짬]
맛살	'crab/clam meat'	[맏쌀] or [마쌀]

4.12.2 Nonpredictable tensing

In some words, such as 여권 'passport', 치과 'dentist's office', and 한자 'Chinese character', tensing occurs after a vowel or after the consonants ㅁ, ㄴ, ㅇ, or ㄹ.

Example		Pronounced
시가	'market price'	[시까]
치과	'dentist's office'	[치꽈]
잠보	'sleepyhead'	[잠뽀]
인기	'popularity'	[인끼] or [잉끼]
한자	'Chinese character'	[한짜]
용돈	'spending money'	[용똔]
출장	'business trip'	[출짱]

This type of tensing does not follow a general rule. For example, it occurs in the 시가 that means 'market price' and in the 한자 that means 'Chinese character' (see above), but not in the 시가 that means 'city streets' or in the 한 자 that means 'one character/word'. Similarly, there is tensing in the word 장기 that means 'special talent', which is pronounced [장끼], but not in the word 장기 that means 'chess'. Examples such as these underline the need to learn words with nonpredictable tensing on a case-by-case basis.[7]

Another thing to watch for is optional tensing of the initial consonant in the suffix -밖에 'except', as well as in a few native Korean words and borrowed English words.

---

[7]There are subregularities that are perhaps worth noting, however. For example, the consonant in 거 (a shortened version of 것 'thing' that cannot stand alone) is tensed when preceded by a future tense modifier such as 먹을, but not when preceded by a present tense modifier such as 먹는 or a past tense modifier such as 먹은.

Example		Pronounced
먹을 거	'things to eat'	[머글꺼]
먹는 거	'things that I eat; edible things'	[멍는거]
먹은 거	'things that I ate'	[머근거]

Korean word		Pronounced		
나밖에	'except me'	[나빠께]	or	[나바께]
세다	'It's strong'	[쎄다]	or	[세다]
작다	'It's small'	[짝따]	or	[작따]
좁다	'It's narrow'	[쫍따]	or	[좁따]
잘라요	'Cut it'	[짤라요]	or	[잘라요]
닦아요	'Clean/wipe it'	[따까요]	or	[다까요]

Borrowed word		Pronounced		
버스	'bus'	[뻐쓰]	or	[버스]
바나나	'banana'	[빠나나]	or	[바나나]
달러	'dollar'	[딸러]	or	[달러]
게임	'game'	[께임]	or	[게임]
잼	'jam'	[쨈]	or	[잼]

Although tensing in these words is usually not obligatory, it does happen frequently (especially in the borrowed words).

Optional tensing in native Korean words, especially adjectives, typically signals intensity—with a tense initial consonant, 세다 means 'It's very strong', 작아요 means 'It's very small', and so on.

You will find practice exercises for nonpredictable tensing in section A-12.2 of the CD.

4.13 ㅅ insertion

A special type of insertion process occurs in compound words that contain at least one native Korean component. When the first word in these compounds ends in a vowel, ㅅ is inserted both in the pronunciation and in the spelling. This so-called 사이 시옷, literally 'in-between ㅅ', shows up in 찻집 'teahouse', from 차 'tea' and 집 'house', in 바닷가 'seaside', from 바다 'sea' and 가 'side', and in many other compounds.

Example	After insertion	
차 + 집	찻집	'teahouse'
바다 + 가	바닷가	'seaside'

Like other instances of ㅅ at the end of a word, an inserted ㅅ is pronounced as if it were ㄷ. Moreover, like other consonants in this position, it causes tensing of the following consonant (section 4.12.1). As a result, 바닷가 ends up being pronounced [바닫까] or [바다까].

Starting point: 바다 + 가 'sea + side'
                    ↓
                    ㅅ insertion (바닷가)
                    ↓
                    tensing of ㄱ
                    ↓
Pronounced: [바닫까] (or [바다까])

When the second word in the compound begins with a nasal consonant, the inserted ㅅ, with its unreleased pronunciation, undergoes the usual nasalization process (section 4.9.1). That is why you hear a ㄴ sound at the end of the second syllable in 바닷물 'seawater' (from 바다 'sea' and 물 'water').

Starting point: 바다 + 물 'sea + water'
                    ↓
                    ㅅ insertion (바닷물)
                    ↓
                    nasalization
                    ↓
Pronounced: [바단물]

In fact, a further adjustment can occur here too, resulting in the pronunciation of ㄴ as if it were ㅁ (section 4.10) and yielding [바담물].

An especially intriguing example involves the compound 나뭇잎, which is formed from the words 나무 'tree' and 잎 'leaf'. Its pronunciation, [나문닙], reflects both the insertion of ㅅ and the addition of ㄴ (section 4.11).

Starting point: 나무 + 잎 'tree + leaf'
                        ↓
                   insertion of ㅅ (나뭇잎)
                        ↓
                   addition of ㄴ to 잎 (나뭇[닙])
                        ↓
                   nasalization
                        ↓
Pronounced: [나문닙]

The compound 깻잎, formed from 깨 'sesame' and 잎 'leaf', works the same way and therefore ends up with the pronunciation [깬닙].

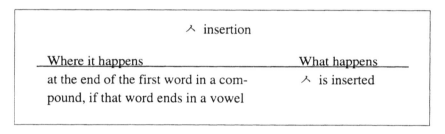

ㅅ insertion	
Where it happens	What happens
at the end of the first word in a compound, if that word ends in a vowel	ㅅ is inserted

Section A-13 of the CD contains practice exercises involving ㅅ insertion.

The current official spelling system requires 사이 시옷 in compounds that contain at least one native Korean component. However, you may find it useful to know that there is some variation in terms of whether 사이 시옷 is written. For example, the word for 'last night' is written 어제밤 by some and 어젯밤 by others, even though its pronunciation always reflects the presence of an inserted ㅅ.

4.14 Modifications to the pronunciation of ㄷ and ㅌ

In front of a suffix that begins with ㅣ or the 'y' diphthong ㅕ, ㄷ is pronounced as if it were ㅈ, and ㅌ is pronounced as if it were ㅊ. (The consonants ㄷ and ㅌ happen not to occur in front of diphthongs other than ㅕ.)

Example		Pronounced
맏이	'the eldest + person marker'	[마지]
같이	'together (be the same + adverb marker)'	[가치]
끝이	'the end + subject marker'	[끄치]
붙여요	'Paste it'	[부처요]

Remember that this change occurs only in front of a suffix. That's why it happens in 맏이, but not in 마디 'knuckle', where the ㅣ is part of the root and not a suffix. For the same reason, there is no change in the pronunciation of 어디 'where' or 티 'speck'. And there is also no change in words such as 같아요 'It's the same', in which the suffix does not begin with ㅣ or 'y'.

This adjustment process sometimes results in the same pronunciation for words with different spellings. A simple example of this involves 같이 'together' and 가치 'value', both of which are pronounced [가치].

A more complicated case involves 닫혀요 'It's being closed', which ends up with the same pronunciation as 다쳐요 'You're going to be hurt'. Two things happen here. First, the combination of ㄷ with ㅎ in 닫혀요 yields aspiration, resulting in a ㅌ (see section 4.7). Second, this ㅌ is pronounced as if it were ㅊ because of the following ㅕ, yielding the pronunciation [쳐]. As a result, 닫혀요 has exactly the same pronunciation as 다쳐요.

Starting point: 닫혀요 'It's being closed'
                          ↓
               aspiration (ㄷ + ㅎ > ㅌ)
                          ↓
               pronunciation of ㅌ as if it were ㅊ
                          ↓
Pronounced: [다쳐요]

Modifications to the pronunciation of ㄷ and ㅌ

Where it happens	What happens
in front of a suffix beginning with ㅣ or ㅕ	ㄷ is pronounced as if it were ㅈ ㅌ is pronounced as if it were ㅊ

Section A-14 of the CD contains several practice exercises involving these adjustments.

4.15 Consonant weakening

Two types of consonant weakening are common in Korean noun roots, one involving ㅍ and ㅋ and the other affecting ㅌ and ㅊ.

4.15.1 Weakening of ㅍ and ㅋ

When ㅍ and ㅋ occur at the end of a noun root in front of a suffix that begins with a vowel, we expect them to have their usual aspirated pronunciation. In fact, though, their pronunciation is often weakened. As a result, they lose their aspiration and are pronounced as if they were ㅂ and ㄱ, respectively. The effects of this change can be observed in words such as 무릎이 'knee + subject marker', in which the ㅍ can be pronounced as if it were ㅂ, and 부엌에 'in the kitchen', in which the ㅋ can be pronounced as if it were ㄱ. Both consonants also become voiced because they occur between vowels, so the ㅍ ends up with a 'b'-like pronunciation and the ㅋ with a 'g'-like pronunciation (section 4.2).

Example	Without weakening (uncommon)	With weakening (common)
무릎이 'knee + subject marker'	[무르피]	[무르비]
부엌에 'in the kitchen'	[부어케]	[부어게]

Note, though, that two common nouns—앞 'front' and 옆 'side'—escape the weakening process. Thus ㅍ retains its usual aspirated pronunciation in 앞에서 'in the front' and in 옆에 'next to'. The noun 잎 'leaf' also tends to resist weakening (as in 잎이 'leaf + subject particle'), perhaps to avoid homonymy with 입 'mouth'. However, weakening is frequent in compounds such as 깻잎 'sesame leaf' when there is a suffix that begins with a vowel.

Finally, it is important to note that weakening takes place only in nouns. So ㅍ has its usual aspirated pronunciation in 깊어요 'It's deep', 깊은 'deep', and 깊이 'deeply'.

4.15.2 Weakening of ㅌ and ㅊ

A second type of consonant weakening affects ㅌ and ㅊ when they occur at the end of a noun root in front of a suffix that begins with a vowel. Although these sounds are expected to have their basic pronunciation in these contexts, this does not always happen. As the examples below help illustrate, ㅌ can be pronounced as if it were ㅊ or ㅅ, and ㅊ can be pronounced as if it were ㅅ.

Example		Without weakening	With weakening
끝은	'end + topic marker'	[끄튼]	[끄츤] or [끄슨]
솥에	'in the kettle'	[소테]	[소세]
꽃을	'flower + object marker'	[꼬츨]	[꼬슬]

And in words such as 솥이 'kettle + subject marker' and 끝이 'end + subject marker', where ㅌ is normally pronounced as if it were ㅊ (see section 4.14), weakening can result in a ㅅ pronunciation.

Example		Without weakening	With weakening
끝이	'end + subject marker'	[끄치]	[끄시]
솥이	'kettle + subject marker'	[소치]	[소시]
밭이	'farm field + subject marker'	[바치]	[바시]

Remember that weakening takes place only in nouns, so ㅌ retains its usual pronunciation in 같아요 'It's the same' and 같은 'same', which are pronounced [가타요] and [가튼], respectively.

Consonant weakening		
Affected sounds	Where it happens	What happens
ㅍ	at the end of a noun root	ㅍ can be pronounced ㅂ
ㅋ	in front of a suffix that	ㅋ can be pronounced ㄱ
ㅌ	begins with a vowel	ㅌ can be pronounced ㅊ
ㅊ		or ㅅ
		ㅊ can be pronounced ㅅ

Section A-15 of the CD provides practice exercises for consonant weakening.

Weakening is not yet a fully established adjustment process in Korean and there may be some minor variation in its use from speaker to speaker. Although you don't have to weaken consonants in your own speech, this is a very common process in Korean, and a familiarity with it will help you understand the speech of others.

This completes our discussion of the adjustment processes that affect the pronunciation of Korean in connected speech. By paying close attention to the effects of these processes, you will improve the intelligibility and naturalness of your speech while enhancing your comprehension skills. Moreover, by understanding the systematic ways in which a word's pronunciation can differ from its written form, you should also be able to improve your spelling.

Chapter 5

Prosody

Previous chapters have concentrated on the manner in which individual sounds and words are pronounced—on the difference between ㅏ and ㅓ, on how to distinguish among ㅍ, ㅂ, and ㅃ, on the fact that 앞 'front' is pronounced [압] in the compound 앞문 'front door', and so forth. So far, though, we have said nothing about prosody—the rhythmic contour that is created through the interaction of pitch, loudness, and length.

Languages sound the way they do not just because of the manner in which individual syllables and words are pronounced, but also because of the prosodic patterns in which they occur. These patterns determine a language's phonetic terrain—its peaks, valleys, and plateaus. The purpose of this chapter is to give you an overall picture of how Korean prosody works.

5.1 Pitch, loudness, and length

The prosodic patterns of Korean and English are fundamentally different. A defining feature of the English system is the occurrence at regular intervals of syllables that are pronounced more loudly than their neighbors.

> The MAN will WASH the WINdow.

This loudness, which linguists call *stress*, tends to occur on content words such as the noun *man* and the verb *wash* rather than on function words such as *the* or *will*. It can even be used to help distinguish between words—such as the noun *REcord* and the verb *reCORD*.

Korean does not have English-type stress. Except for purposes of emphasis and contrast, all the syllables in a Korean sentence are pronounced with roughly equal loudness. However, there is a difference involving pitch. (You may already be familiar with the concept of pitch from music, where it is used to distinguish high notes from low notes.) In particular, the first syllable of a word tends to carry slightly higher pitch. So, despite the differences in the length of the following words, the first syllable is prominent in each case.[1]

Ⓚ적   'dramatic'

Ⓑ수적   'conservative'

Ⓒ자연적   'supernatural'

Notice how different this is from English, in which the second or third syllable from the end tends to be stressed and therefore more prominent in longer words.

draMAtic

conSERvative

superNAtural

Because of this, English speakers tend to mispronounce longer Korean words by incorrectly highlighting one of the middle syllables and pronouncing the remaining syllables too weakly.

A second important feature of Korean is that the final syllable of a phrase or a sentence is longer and therefore more audible than any of the others.

소파에서 일어 나   'Get off the sofa.'

하얀 코끼리 봐 요   'Look at the white elephant.'

In English, in contrast, sentences often end in a short, weak syllable, with stress falling on the second- or even the third-to-last syllable.

Get off the SOfa.

Look at the white ELephant.

---

[1] Sohn (1994:455), Jun (1993:42ff.).

Because of this, English-speaking students often give the final syllable of Korean sentences a short, weak pronunciation. This is a problem; your Korean will not sound natural if it is pronounced with an English stress pattern.

Length is also used to express emphasis and emotional involvement. For instance, with the first syllable lengthened and pronounced forcefully, 멀어요 means 'It's very far' and 하얗다 means 'It's very white'.

Section P-1 of the CD provides examples of words, phrases, and sentences that illustrate the basic features of Korean prosody.

5.2 Focus

When a word carries new information or is otherwise especially important, it is highlighted with the help of higher pitch, especially on the first syllable. This is called *focus*. In the following exchange, for instance, A asks B whether she did her homework, and B responds by placing the focus on 했어 'did' to indicate that she did in fact complete her homework, which is new information for the listener.

    A: 숙제했어?   'Did you do the homework?'
    B: 응, 숙제 *했어*.   'Yes, I *did* the homework.'

On the other hand, if A asks B what she did, B will respond by placing the focus on 숙제 'homework' since that word carries the new information.

    A: 뭐 했어?   'What did you do?'
    B: *숙제*했어.   'I did *homework*.'

For the most part, English and Korean work the same way in this respect, but there are at least two important differences. First, unlike English *be*, Korean -이다 cannot be focused by itself, since it cannot stand alone as a separate word in either speech or writing. Where there is a need to emphasize this item, the word to which it attaches (학생 in the example below) must be focused instead.

    A: 학생 아니죠?   'You're not a student, are you?'
    B: *학생*이에요.   'I *am* a student.'

A second important difference between English and Korean focus has to do with so-called *wh* words such as *who*, *what*, *where*, and so forth. As shown below, the Korean equivalents of these words can also function as indefinite pronouns, with meanings such as 'someone' and 'something'.

Korean word	As question words	As indefinite pronouns
누구/누가	'who'	'someone'
뭐	'what'	'something'
어디	'where'	'somewhere'
어떻게	'how'	'somehow'
어느	'which'	'some/certain'
어떤	'which/what type of'	'some/certain'
몇	'what/how many'	'several'

When they are used as question words, these elements are focused and therefore have higher pitch. However, when they function as indefinite pronouns, the high pitch is placed elsewhere. For example, 몇 (with the meaning 'how many') is focused in the question 친구가 몇 명 왔어요? 'How many friends came?'.

친구가 몇 명 왔어요?   'How many friends came?'
↑
focus is here

But when it means 'several', as in the sentence 친구가 몇 명 왔어요 'Several friends came', the focus is on either 친구가 or 왔어요.

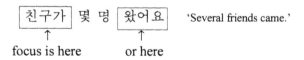

친구가 몇 명 왔어요   'Several friends came.'
↑   ↑
focus is here   or here

The location of focus can also distinguish between different types of questions. Take 어디 가?, for instance. With the focus on 어디, the sentence means 'Where are you going?', which requires an answer such as 학교에 'to school'. On the other hand, with the focus on 가, the sentence is a simple *yes-no* question meaning 'Are you going somewhere?'.

어디 가? 'Where are you going?'   어디 가 ? 'Are you going somewhere?'
  ↑   ↑
focus on this item signals   focus on this item signals
a *where* question   a *yes-no* question

Likewise, 누가 와요 means 'Who is coming?' when 누가 is focused, but 'Is someone coming?' when the focus in on 와요.

누가 와요? 'Who is coming?'   누가 와요 ? 'Is someone coming?'
  ↑   ↑
focus on this item signals   focus on this item signals
a *who* question   a *yes-no* question

You can find practice exercises that illustrate the use of focus in section P-2 of the CD.

The effect of pitch on adjustments

Pitch has an important effect on certain of the adjustment processes considered in the previous chapter. As you may recall, we noted there that a number of adjustment processes can apply across a word boundary, provided that the two words are pronounced together as a group. As we'll see next, though, the occurrence of a high pitch on the second word creates a sort of 'break' with the preceding word, blocking the adjustment process. At least three adjustment processes are affected in this way— ㅎ reduction, tensing, and voicing. Let us consider each process in turn.

As noted in section 4.6, the ㅎ sound is weakened or even entirely dropped when it occurs between voiced sounds. Thus, 영화 'movie' can be pronounced [영와]. The ㅎ sound can also be dropped in 뭐 해요?, but only if 뭐 means 'what' and therefore has high pitch (see above), in which case the sentence means 'What are you doing?'. However, if the sentence means 'Are you doing something?', with high pitch on 해요, the ㅎ is fully pronounced.

A similar contrast is found with tensing. As noted in section 4.12.1, a lax consonant receives a tense pronunciation when it follows a consonant other than ㄹ, ㅁ, ㄴ, or ㅇ. Thus, 책방 'bookstore' is pronounced

[책 빵]. The same thing happens in 책 받았어요 'I received a book', but only if the focus is on 책 (as in, 'I received a book, not clothes'). But ㅂ retains its lax pronunciation if the high pitch falls on the first syllable of 받았어요, as it would if you were saying 'Yes, I *received* the book' in answer to the question 'Did you get the book?'.

Finally, let us consider voicing. As discussed at various places in chapter 3 as well as in section 4.2 of the previous chapter, a lax consonant can be voiced when it occurs between voiced sounds—which is why ㄱ takes on a 'g'-like pronunciation in 시간 'time'. Voicing can also happen across a word boundary, but not when there is high pitch on the second word. Thus, the ㄱ of 가 'go' remains voiceless in the *yes-no* question 어디 가? 'Are you going somewhere', where the high pitch falls on the verb. However, it is voiced in the *where* question 어디 가? 'Where are you going', which has high pitch on 어디 rather than 가 .

Or take the sentence 다 자요 'They are all sleeping'. If it's uttered in answer to the question 'What are they doing?', the verb 자요 carries information new to the listener and therefore has high pitch on the first syllable. This in turn creates a break that blocks voicing of the ㅈ, even though it occurs between vowels. On the other hand, if the sentence is uttered in response to the question 'Who's sleeping?', 다 'all' carries the new information. There is therefore no high pitch on 자요 and the ㅈ is voiced.[2]

5.3 Intonation

Both Korean and English use intonation or pitch contour to distinguish among sentence types. Take the simple two-word sentence *He left* in English. Pronounced with falling intonation, it is a simple statement. But pronounced with a rising pitch contour, it is a question-like expression of disbelief.

He left.   He left?!
(statement)   (question expressing surprise)

---

[2]Interestingly, however, a relinked consonant is always voiced, regardless of pitch. Thus ㄱ has a 'g'-like pronunciation in 책 없어요 'There aren't any books', pronounced [채겁써요], even if the first syllable of the verb has high pitch.

Intonation is especially important in Korean, where statements and questions typically have an identical structure. Thus, only the intonation tells us whether 학생이 떠났어요 means 'The student left' or 'Did the student leave?'. In English, of course, the difference is usually signaled structurally as well, by placing an auxiliary verb such as *did* at the beginning of the sentence.

As in English, though, there is variation in Korean from speaker to speaker (especially between men and women) in the use of intonation. Moreover, as we will see in the next section, intonation can also be sensitive to the speaker's emotion, which makes it impossible to state any simple rule for its use. For basic cases, however, the following generalizations about the relationship between sentence type and intonation are worth noting.

• Neutral statements—falling or flat intonation

| 한국에 갑니다. | 'I am going to Korea.' |
| 한국말 잘 해요. | 'He speaks Korean well.' |

Flat intonation is especially noticeable when the final syllable of the sentence is prolonged, as it often is in Korean (see section 5.1).

•*Yes-no* questions—rising intonation

한국에 갑니까?	'Are you going to Korea?'
한국말 잘 해요?	'Do you speak Korean well?'
누가 와요?	'Is someone coming?'
어디 가요?	'Are you going somewhere?'

• *Wh* questions—rising or falling intonation

얼마예요?	'How much is it?'
몇 시예요?	'What time is it?'
누가 와요?	'Who is coming?'
어디 가요?	'Where are you going?'

Rising intonation in *wh* questions is more common and has a friendlier sound. Falling intonation in such patterns may sound curt and may give the question a demanding tone.

- Soft-sounding, nondemanding *wh* questions—rising intonation

얼마죠?   'How much is it?'

몇 시죠?   'What time is it?'

- Commands—falling or prolonged rising intonation

꼭 와.   'Make sure to come.'

전화하세요.   'Please call.'

A prolonged rising intonation creates a gentler command, roughly equivalent to English, 'Please call, okay?'. It tends to be used more by women than by men.

Section P-3 of the CD provides practice exercises involving the use of intonation to mark sentence types.

5.4 Intonation and the expression of emotion

Different emotions call for different intonations. Virtually identical sentences can mean totally different things depending on the emotion conveyed by their pitch contour. Think of how you can vary the intonation in a sentence like 'You're right' to indicate admiration, surprise, sarcasm, resentment, and so on.

Here are some examples from Korean. Bear in mind, though, that there are many other possibilities, reflecting the various types and degrees of human emotion—anger, frustration, shock, disbelief, joy, and sadness, to name just a few.

- Gentle suggestion—gently rising intonation

저쪽으로 가시죠?   'Why don't you go over to that side?'

좀 앉지?   'Why don't you have a seat?'

- Regret—falling intonation

좀 앉지.   'I wish he would sit down.'

파티에 갈걸.   'I wish I had gone to the party.'

• Strong conjecture—rising intonation

파티에 갈걸.   'I bet she is going to the party.'

아닐걸, 안 갈걸.   'I bet she is not; I don't think she is going.'

• Exclamation/surprise—dramatic tone

정말 맛있다!   'It's really delicious!'

와, 멋있네요!   'Wow, it looks fantastic!'

정말 잘 하는데요!   'She does it really well!'

• Boastfully providing some significant new information when using the -다 ending that is common among close friends—rising intonation

나 여자/남자 친구 생겼다.   'I've got a girl/boyfriend.'

나 다음주에 하와이 간다.   'I am going to Hawaii next week.'

In general, intonation mirrors emotion naturally in both English and Korean. But the above examples show how important intonation can be for distinguishing among sentences with different meanings in Korean. Notice, for instance, that the same -지 ending can be used for a gentle suggestion or an expression of regret, and that the same -걸 ending can be used to express regret or strong conjecture. In these and many other cases, listeners have to rely on intonation to get at the speaker's intended meaning.

Section P-4 of the CD contains practice exercises illustrating the use of intonation to mark emotion.

5.5 Thought groups

The words and suffixes that make up a longer sentence are often divided into smaller thought groups, each of which expresses part of the sentence's meaning. In the following sentence, for example, 월요일 밤에 'on Monday night' forms one thought group and 극장에 갔어 'I went to the theater' forms another—just as they do in the corresponding English sentence.

월요일 밤에 극장에 갔어   'On Monday night, I went to the theater.'

Prosody has a crucial role to play in this, since the end of a thought group is usually marked by a short pause. In addition, as mentioned in section 5.1, the last syllable of a thought group is usually longer and more prominent in Korean.

월요일 밤 에   극장에 갔 어

Although arrangement of words into thought groups can vary depending on the speed at which one is speaking, this sort of grouping is especially important in longer sentences, which might well be difficult to process if they were not broken into more manageable parts with the help of pauses.

Under some circumstances, the placement of a pause can dramatically change a sentence's meaning. In the following sentence, for example, a slight pause after 너 gives the meaning 'Aren't you going outside?', while a pause after 너밖에 (or no pause at all) results in the meaning 'Is no one but you going out?'. (In addition, because 밖에 is a word and is focused in the first sentence, it has a higher pitch on its first syllable, blocking the voicing of the ㅂ sound. This does not happen in the second sentence, where -밖에 is a suffix.)

너 밖에 안 나가? 'Aren't you going outside?'

너밖에 안 나가? 'Is no one but you going out?'

Section P-5 on the CD provides many examples of longer sentences that have been divided into thought groups. Practicing with them will help you become familiar with natural groupings of words in Korean utterances.

The interplay of pitch, length, and loudness is a vital part of every sentence that is uttered in any language. Poor prosody not only contributes to a foreign accent in a second language, it can create misunderstandings that lead to breakdowns in communication. Practicing with a clear understanding of how Korean prosody works and how it differs from English prosody will lead to fast and dramatic improvements in your speech and comprehension.

References

Celce-Murcia, Marianne, Donna Brinton, & Janet Goodwin. 1996. *Teaching pronunciation: A reference for teachers of English to speakers of other languages*. New York: Cambridge University Press.

Eimas, Peter. 1996. The perception and representation of speech by infants. In *Signal to syntax*, edited by J. Morgan & K. Demuth, 25–39. Mahwah, N.J.: Erlbaum.

Han, Mieko, & Raymond Weitzman. 1970. Acoustic features of Korean /P,T,K/, /p,t,k/ and /pʰ,tʰ,kʰ/. *Phonetica* 22:112–128.

Iverson, Gregory. 1983. Korean *s*. *Journal of Phonetics* 11:191–200.

Jun, Sun-Ah. 1993. The phonetics and phonology of Korean prosody. Ph.D. diss., University of California at Los Angeles.

Kagaya, Ryohei. 1974. A fiberscopic and acoustic study of the Korean stops, affricates and fricatives. *Journal of Phonetics* 2:161–180.

Kim, Chin-Wu. 1965. On the autonomy of the tensity feature in stop classification. *Word* 21:339–359.

Kim, Hyunsoon. 1999. The place of articulation of Korean affricates revisited. *Journal of East Asian Linguistics* 8:313–346.

Kim-Renaud, Young-Key. 1997. *The Korean alphabet: Its history and structure*. Honolulu: University of Hawai'i Press.

Ladefoged, Peter. 1999. Recording the phonetic structures of endangered languages. Talk given at the University of Hawai'i, April 27, 1999.

Ladefoged, Peter, & Ian Maddieson. 1996. *The sounds of the world's languages*. Oxford: Blackwell.

Lee, Iksop, & S. Robert Ramsey. 2000. *The Korean language*. Albany: State University of New York Press.

Lee, Jeong-Hoon. 1995. The /e/–/œ/ merger in Modern Seoul Korean is a 'near merger'. *Harvard Studies in Korean Linguistics* 6:108–120.

Lisker, Leigh, & Arthur Abramson. 1964. A cross language study of voicing in intial stops: Acoustical measurements. *Word* 20:384–422.

Lisker, Leigh, & Arthur Abramson. 1967. Some effects of context on voice onset time in English stops. *Language and Speech* 10:1–28.

Martin, Samuel. 1992. *A reference grammar of Korean*. Rutland, Vt.: Tuttle.

Sampson, Geoffrey. 1985. *Writing systems: A linguistic introduction*. Stanford: Stanford University Press.

Shin, Jiyoung, & Katrina Hayward. 1997. Some articulatory characteristics of Korean: Three types of alveolar stops and alveo-palatal fricatives. *SOAS Working Papers in Linguistics and Phonetics* 7:301-320.

Silva, David. 1998. The effects of prosodic structure and consonant phonation on vowel FØ in Korean: An examination of bilabial stops. In *Description and explanation in Korean linguistics*, edited by R. King, 11–34. Ithaca: Cornell University East Asian Program.

Sohn, Ho-min. 1994. *Korean*. New York: Routledge.

Suh, Chang-Kook. 1995. Palatalization, opacity and umlaut in Korean. *Harvard Studies in Korean Linguistics* 6:121–137.

Werker, Janet, Valerie Lloyd, Judith Pegg, & Linda Polka. 1996. Putting the baby in the bootstraps: Toward a more complete understanding of the role of the input in infant speech processing. In *Signal to syntax*, edited by J. Morgan & K. Demuth, 427–447. Mahwah, N.J.: Erlbaum.

Yang, Byunggon. 1996. A comparative study of American English and Korean vowels produced by male and female speakers. *Journal of Phonetics* 24:245–261.

Glossary

aspirated: pronounced with an accompanying puff of air. The sounds ㅍ, ㅌ, ㅋ, and ㅊ are aspirated.

blade: the part of the tongue immediately behind the tip.

bound roots: items that have wordlike meanings but cannot stand alone as independent words. The compound 전력 'electricity' consists of two such roots, 전 'electric' and 력 'power', neither of which can function as a word on its own.

compound: a multipart word made up of two or more smaller words (e.g., 책방 'bookstore').

consonant relinking: the adjustment process that results in a consonant that occurs at the end of one syllable being pronounced at the beginning of the next syllable. For instance, 언어 'language' is pronounced as if it were [어너].

dental ridge: the bony ridge immediately behind the upper front teeth.

diphthong: two-part sounds consisting of a glide and a vowel. ㅑ, ㅘ, and ㅢ are examples of diphthongs in Korean.

full closure: articulation of a consonant without releasing the closure in front of a consonant or at the end of a word. This results in the loss of the aspirated-lax-tense contrast.

glide: a 'y' or 'w' sound.

larynx (voice box): the part of the throat containing the vocal cords.

lax: produced with relatively little force and with little or no aspiration. The sounds ㅂ, ㄷ, ㄱ, ㅈ, and ㅅ are lax.

nasal: produced as vibrating air passes through the nose. ㅁ, ㄴ, and ㅇ are the nasal consonants of Korean.

nasalization: an adjustment process that gives consonants a nasal pronunciation. As a result of this process, for example, ㅂ is pronounced as if it were ㅁ in the word 십년 'ten years'.

prosody: the interaction of pitch, loudness, and length.

semi-compound: a multipart word made up of a smaller word and a bound root (e.g., 한약 'Chinese medicine', in which 한 is a bound root and 약 is a word).

stress: the loudness that makes one syllable more prominent and audible than another in English. The first syllable carries stress in the word *sofa*.

tense: pronounced with extra muscular effort. The sounds ㅃ, ㄸ, ㄲ, ㅉ, and ㅆ are tense.

voiced: pronounced with vocal cord vibrations. Vowels and the sounds ㅁ, ㄴ, ㅇ, and ㄹ are always voiced.

voiceless: pronounced without vocal cord vibrations. The sounds ㅍ, ㅌ, ㅋ, and ㅊ are always voiceless.

voicing: an adjustment process that makes a voiceless consonant voiced. The lax consonants ㅂ, ㄷ, ㄱ, and ㅈ become voiced when they occur between voiced sounds.

wh **question**: a question built around interrogative words such as *who*, *what*, *where*, *why*, and so on.

word: a noun root or a verb root together with any associated particles and suffixes (the subject marker, the direct object marker, the location particles -에 and -에서, tense markers, the copula verb 이다, and so on).

Part II

Practice Exercises

How to Use the Practice Exercises

The following sections of *The Sounds of Korean* contain practice exercises designed for use with the CD that accompanies this book. Because the exercises highlight and reinforce specific points in the text, you may wish to reread the relevant section(s) of the book before or after a practice session. Reading the text will help maximize the benefits of the CD, just as doing the practice exercises will enhance your understanding of the text. An index at the end of the book matches the practice exercises with the topics covered in the text.

The exercises were recorded by two native speakers of standard Korean, one male and one female, employing a natural colloquial style and speaking at slow to moderate speed. Some exercises involve listening and repetition, while others focus just on listening skills alone. Many of the latter exercises require you to respond by marking a choice, as illustrated below.

Circle the item in parentheses that you hear.

(불, 풀)이 안 붙어요.   The glue doesn't stick.

In the vast majority of exercises of this type, either word is compatible with the meaning and structure of the rest of the sentence, so choice of the correct item depends entirely on your ability to hear the relevant phonetic contrast. Because the translation may give away the correct answer (as happens in the example above if you know that 풀 means 'glue'), we advise you to cover up the English while listening to the CD.

In some cases, where spelling does not straightforwardly capture a word's pronunciation, we indicate it with the help of square brackets, as we often did in part I of the book. For example:

Circle the pronunciation of the italicized item.

십육년 됐습니다.   [심늉   십늉]   It's been sixteen years.

After completing an exercise, you can check your responses against the answer guide found at the end of the book. Because the exercises are intended for repeated use, you should indicate your answers on a separate sheet rather than in the book itself.

You may need to go through the exercises many times before feeling comfortable with some of the subtler contrasts of Korean. This is to be expected, however, and you should not feel discouraged.

The vocabulary used in the practice exercises was chosen with great care to ensure that it consists primarily of words that are both commonly used and relevant to second language learners. Only in a very few cases was it necessary to employ uncommon words to illustrate speech contrasts and adjustments.

In order to help make your listening practice a meaningful experience, we have provided translations for all the sentence-sized practice items. Because direct translation from Korean to English is often impractical, we have adopted the following general policies.

- In cases where the sentence's subject or direct object has been dropped (as happens routinely in Korean) and would normally be inferred from the context in normal conversation, we translate it by means of an English pronoun (*I, you, she, he, it*) that seems natural for the context in which the sentence is likely to be uttered. For example:

  수영할 수 있어요?   Can you swim?

- In cases where a Korean noun occurs without a definite or indefinite article (as frequently happens), we generally translate it with *the* or *a* in order to create a natural-sounding English sentence. For example:

  약 어때요?   How's the medicine?

- Korean has four major ways of ending sentences, each denoting a different level of formality. The following endings are used for statements.

  -니다   (formal)   -요 (semi-formal)
  -아/어 (intimate casual)   -다 (non-conversational/plain casual)

We have used a mixture of endings for our examples, even though it is not possible to translate the subtle distinctions that they convey.

Practice: Vowels

Section V-1: ㅡ & ㅜ

Exercise 1
Listen and repeat.

1. 그   구
2. 극   국
3. 글   굴
4. 든   둔
5. 은   운
6. 즉   죽
7. 쓴다 쏜다

Exercise 2
Circle the number corresponding to the word that sounds different.

1. [1   2   3]
2. [1   2   3]
3. [1   2   3]
4. [1   2   3]
5. [1   2   3]

Exercise 3
Circle the item in parentheses that you hear.

1. (극, 국)이 싱거워요.   The soup is not salty enough.
2. (글, 굴)을 씁니다.   I'm writing (a novel).
3. (글, 굴)이 길어요.   The tunnel is long.
4. 이 속에 (든, 둔) 거요?   The thing that is contained in here?
5. 이 속에 (든, 둔) 거요?   The thing that I put in here?
6. 학생(들, 둘)도 많아요.   There are also many students.
7. (은, 운)이 좋아요.   The silver is good.
8. (은, 운)이 나빠요.   I'm unlucky.

9. (음, 움)이 높아요.   The note is a high one.
10. 죽 (쓴다, 쑨다).   I'm making gruel./I'm messing it up.

Exercise 4
Fill in the blank with the syllable that you hear.

그/구

1. ___름이 한 점도 없어요.   There's not a speck of cloud.
2. ___림을 잘 그립니다.   She draws well.

을/울

3. 가___을 좋아합니다.   I like autumn.
4. 겨___도 따뜻해요.   Winter too is warm.

음/움

5. ___악을 좋아하세요?   Do you like music?
6. ___직이지 마세요.   Please don't budge.

극/국

7. 연___ 배우입니다.   He's a drama actor.
8. 영___ 사람이에요.   He's British.

Exercise 5
Listen and repeat. You will first hear just the part in italics and then the entire sentence.

1. *구름이* 한 점도 없다.   There's not a speck of cloud.
2. *그림을* 잘 그려요.   He draws well.
3. *가을을* 좋아해요.   I like autumn.
4. *겨울도* 따뜻합니다.   Winter too is warm.
5. *연극* 배우야.   She's a drama actor.
6. *영국* 사람입니다.   She's British.

Section V-2: ㅐ & ㅔ

Exercise 1
Listen and repeat.

1.   개   게
2.   때   떼
3.   배   베
4.   새   세

Exercise 2
Circle the number corresponding to the word that sounds different.

1.   [1   2   3   ]
2.   [1   2   3   ]
3.   [1   2   3   ]

Exercise 3
Circle the item in parentheses that you hear.

1.   (개, 게)장이 맛있어요.   The seasoned crab is delicious.
2.   (개, 게)가 귀여워요.   The dog is cute.
3.   (때, 떼)가 안 좋아요.   The timing isn't good.
4.   (때, 떼)를 써요.   He's pestering me for the impossible.
5.   (배짱, 베짱)이에요.   I'm going to be bold.
6.   (새, 세)가 비싸요.   The rent is expensive.
7.   (새, 세) 잔에 마셔요.   I'm drinking from a new glass.
8.   (새, 세) 잔 마셔요.   I drink three glasses.

Exercise 4
Fill in the blank with the syllable that you hear.

개 / 게

1.   ___을러요.   I'm lazy.
2.   ___성이 강해요.   She's very unique.

배 / 베

3. ___개를 베요.   Use the pillow for your head.
4. ___가 달아요.   The pear is sweet.

샘 / 셈

5. ___이 많아요.   She's a jealous person.
6. ___이 틀렸어요.   The calculation has come out wrong.

Exercise 5
Listen and repeat. Notice that when the vowels ㅐ and ㅔ are not at the beginning of the word, they sound the same.

1. 지내   지네
2. 모래   모레
3. 아내   안에

Section V-3: ㅓ & ㅗ

Exercise 1
Listen and repeat.

1. 덜   돌
2. 먹   목
3. 번   본
4. 섬   솜
5. 얼   올
6. 텅   통
7. 거기   고기
8. 저금   조금
9. 커피   코피
10. 주러   주로

Exercise 2
Circle the number corresponding to the word that sounds different.

1. [1   2   3]
2. [1   2   3]
3. [1   2   3]
4. [1   2   3]
5. [1   2   3]
6. [1   2   3]

Exercise 3
Circle the item in parentheses that you hear.

1.   (먹, 목)이 짧아요.   My neck is short.
2.   (벌, 볼)에 쏘였어요.   I got stung by a bee.
3.   (벌, 볼)이 빨개졌어요.   My cheeks became red.
4.   (섬, 솜)이 아름다워요.   The island is beautiful.
5.   언제 (언, 온) 거예요?   When is it that you came?
6.   (얼, 올)이 빠졌어요.   I'm out of it.
7.   (정, 종)이 들었어요.   We became attached to each other.
8.   (텅, 통) 비었어요.   The can is empty.
9.   (저금, 조금)밖에 없어요.   There's no more than a bit.
10. (저금, 조금)이 얼마예요?   How much is in your savings account?
11. (거기, 고기)가 어디예요?   Where's that place?
12. (거기, 고기)가 연해요.   The meat is tender.
13. (서리, 소리)가 안 들려요.   I can't hear the sound.
14. (커피, 코피)가 나요.   My nose is bleeding.
15. (커피, 코피) 마셔요.   I'm drinking coffee.

Exercise 4

Fill in the blank with the syllable that you hear.

러 / 로

1. 왼쪽으___ 가십시오.   Please go to the left.
2. 밥 먹으___ 갑니다.   I'm going in order to eat a meal.
3. 책 돌려주___ 가요.   I'm going in order to return the book.

터 / 토

4. 언제부___ 방학이니?   From when is your school vacation?
5. ___ 요일부터요.   It's from Saturday.

얼 / 올

6. ___ 마예요?   How much is it?
7. 값이 ___랐습니다.   The price has gone up.

번 / 본

8. 전화___호가 어떻게 돼요?   Can I have your phone number?
9. 일___ 사람이에요.   He's Japanese.

겁 / 곱

10. 여섯, 일___ , 여덟   six, seven, eight
11. ___ 이 많아요.   I'm timid.

청 / 총

12. ___소 좀 해야겠어요.   I'll have to clean (the place).

Exercise 5

Listen and repeat. You will first hear just the part in italics and then the entire sentence.

1. *여섯, 일곱, 여덟*   six, seven, eight
2. *얼마야?*   How much is it?
3. *고기가* 연하다.   The meat is tender.
4. *거기가* 어딘데?   Where's that place?
5. *밥 먹으러* 가요.   I'm going in order to eat a meal.
6. *왼쪽으로* 가세요.   Please go to the left.
7. *언제부터* 방학이야?   From when is your school vacation?

8. 일본 사람입니다.   She's Japanese.
9. 전화번호가 어떻게 돼요?   Can I have your phone number?
10. 커피 마시러 가요.   I'm going in order to drink coffee.

Section V-4: ㅡ & ㅓ

Exercise 1
Listen and repeat.

1. 금   검
2. 틀   털
3. 들어   덜어
4. 뜹니다   떱니다
5. 기증   기정

Exercise 2
Circle the number corresponding to the word that sounds different.

1. [1   2   3]
2. [1   2   3]
3. [1   2   3]
4. [1   2   3]

Exercise 3
Circle the item in parentheses that you hear.

1. (틀, 털)을 깎아요.   He's cutting (a dog's) hair.
2. (틀, 털)이 잡혔어요.   The framework is in place.
3. (금은, 검은) 색이에요.   It's black.
4. 시간 좀 (들어, 덜어)요.   It takes a little time.
5. 밥 좀 (들어, 덜어) 주세요.   Please scoop out some rice for me.
6. 물에 (뜹니다, 떱니다).   It floats on water.

Exercise   4
Fill in the blank with the syllable that you hear.

음 / 엄

1.   ___악을 좋아합니다.   I like music.
2.   부모님이 ___하세요.   My parents are strict.

증 / 정

3.   기___사실이에요.   It's an established fact.
4.   기___품이에요.   It's a donated thing/gift.

Exercise   5
Listen and repeat. You will first hear just the part in italics and then the entire sentence.

1.   *검은* 색이야.   It's black.
2.   좀 *들어* 주세요.   Please help me lift/hold this.
3.   물에 *떠요*.   It floats on water.
4.   *음악*을 좋아해요.   I like music.
5.   부모님이 *엄하셔*.   Her parents are strict.

Section   V-5:   ㅏ & ㅓ

Exercise   1
Listen and repeat.

1.   발   벌
2.   잠   점
3.   달아   덜어
4.   막아   먹어
5.   이상   이성

Exercise 2
Circle the number corresponding to the word that sounds different.

1. [1   2   3]
2. [1   2   3]
3. [1   2   3]
4. [1   2   3]

Exercise 3
Circle the item in parentheses that you hear.

1. 같은 (반, 번)이에요.   We're in the same class.
2. 여기서 (사, 서)요.   Please stand/stop here.
3. (발, 벌)이 커요.   My feet are big.
4. (상, 성)이 뭐예요?   What's your last name?
5. (잘, 절) 하셨어요?   Did you do it well?
6. (잠, 점)이 많아요.   There are a lot of spots on the skin.
7. 안 (남아, 넘어)요.   There won't be any leftovers.
8. 꼭 (막아, 먹어)요.   Be sure to eat, please.

Exercise 4
Fill in the blank with the syllable that you hear.

한/헌

1. ___ 집에 살아요.   They live in the same house.
2. ___ 책방에 가요.   I'm going to a used bookstore.

파/퍼

3. 영화가 슬___요.   The movie is sad.
4. 배가 고___요.   I'm hungry.

반/번

5. 전화___호 좀 주세요.   Please give me the phone number.
6. 정 ___대예요.   It's the exact opposite.

Exercise 5
Listen and repeat. You will first hear just the part in italics and then the entire sentence.

1. 영화가 *슬퍼요*.   The movie is sad.
2. 배가 *고파요*.   I'm hungry.
3. *같은* 반이에요.   We are in the same class.
4. 전화번호 좀 주세요.   Please give me the phone number.
5. *이상*해요   It's strange.
6. *이성*을 잃었어요.   He took leave of his senses.

Section V-6: ㅑ, ㅒ, ㅕ, ㅖ, ㅛ, & ㅠ

Section V-6.1: Simple vowel versus diphthong

Exercise 1
Listen and repeat.

1. 악   약
2. 애기   얘기
3. 거울   겨울
4. 에비   예비
5. 수포   수표
6. 후식   휴식

Exercise 2
Circle the number corresponding to the word that sounds different.

1. [1   2   3]
2. [1   2   3]
3. [1   2   3]
4. [1   2   3]

Exercise 3
Circle the item in parentheses that you hear.

1.   (악, 약)을 써요.   He's shouting.
2.   (애기, 얘기)해 주세요.   Please tell me the story.
3.   (애기, 얘기)가 재미있어요.   The baby is fun.
4.   (얼음, 여름)이 길어요.   Summer is long.
5.   (거울, 겨울)은 짧아요.   As for winter, it's short.
6.   (거울, 겨울) 좀 보세요.   Please look in the mirror.
7.   (수포, 수표)가 생겼어요.   I've received a cashier's check.
8.   (굴, 귤)이 싱싱해요.   The oyster is fresh.
9.   (여우, 여유)가 없어요.   I have no time/money/etc. to spare.
10. (후식, 휴식)이 필요해요.   You need to rest.

Exercise 4
Listen and repeat. You will first hear just the part in italics and then the entire sentence.

1.   *얘기*해 줘요.   Please tell me the story.
2.   *애기*가 울어요.   The baby's crying.
3.   *겨울*은 추워요.   As for winter, it's cold.
4.   *거울* 좀 봐요.   Please look in the mirror.
5.   *여유*가 없어요.   I have no time/money/etc. to spare.
6.   *여우같이* 생겼어.   She looks as cunning as a fox.

Exercise 5
Fill in the blank with the syllable that you hear.

에 / 예

1.   ___의가 없어.   He has no manners.
2.   친구___게 전화했습니다.   I phoned a friend.

후 / 휴

3.   정기___일입니다.   It's a regular holiday.
4.   ___식이 나옵니까?   Is dessert coming?

향 / 항
5. 고___이 어디세요?   Where's your hometown?
6. 공___으로 갑시다.   Let's go to the airport.

Section V-6.2: Diphthong versus diphthong

Exercise 1
Listen and repeat.

ㅐ / ㅖ
1. 애   예
2. 얘기   예기

ㅑ / ㅕ
3. 약   역
4. 향   형

ㅕ / ㅛ
5. 펴   표
6. 여행   요행

Exercise 2
Circle the number corresponding to the word that sounds different.

1. [1   2   3]
2. [1   2   3]
3. [1   2   3]
4. [1   2   3]
5. [1   2   3]

Exercise 3
Circle the item in parentheses that you hear.

1. (얘기, 예기) 들었습니다.   I heard the story.
2. (애, 예)를 들어 보세요.   Please try to give an example.

3. (약, 역) 어때요?　　　　　How's the medicine?

4. 정말 (고약, 고역)이에요.　It's real drudgery.

5. (향, 형)이 좋아요.　　　　The scent is nice.

6. (향수, 형수)가 둘이에요.　He has two sisters-in-law.

7. 물이 (얕아, 옅어)요.　　　The water is shallow.

8. 책 (퍼지, 표지)요?　　　　The book cover?

9. (수영, 수용)할 수 있어요?　Can you swim?

10. (여행, 요행)을 바라지 마.　Don't rely on luck.

Exercise 4

Listen and repeat. You will first hear just the part in italics and then the entire sentence.

1. *얘기* 들었어요.　　　　　I heard the story.

2. *예*를 들어 보세요.　　　　Please try to give an example.

3. *약* 드셨어요?　　　　　Did you take the medicine?

4. *기차역*으로 가죠?　　　　Why don't we go to the train station?

5. *여행*하고 싶다.　　　　　I want to travel.

6. *요행*을 바라지 마.　　　　Don't rely on luck.

Exercise 5

Fill in the blank with the syllable that you hear.

얘 / 예

1. ＿＿ 가 왜 안 오지?　　　Why is this kid not coming, I wonder.

2. 표를 ＿＿ 약 했어요.　　　I reserved a ticket.

양 / 영

3. ＿＿ 양실조예요.　　　　It's malnutrition.

4. ＿＿말 안 신어요?　　　　Aren't you going to wear socks?

여 / 요

5. ＿＿ 관에 묵었어요.　　　We stayed at an inn.

6. ＿＿ 리를 잘해요.　　　　He's a good cook.

Section V-7: ㅢ

Exercise 1
Listen and repeat.

At the beginning of a word, ㅣ and ㅢ have distinct pronunciations.
1.   이사   의사
2.   이자   의자

In a position other than the beginning of a word, ㅢ is pronounced as if it were ㅣ.
3.   희망   흰색
4.   무늬   유희
5.   예의   주의

When used to express the possessive particle, ㅢ is pronounced as if it were ㅔ.
6.   그림의 떡   pie in the sky
7.   대한민국의 수도   capital of the Republic of Korea

Exercise 2
Circle the number corresponding to the word that sounds different.

1.   [1   2   3   ]
2.   [1   2   3   ]
3.   [1   2   3   ]

Exercise 3
Circle the item in parentheses that you hear.

1.   (이자, 의자)가 편해요.   The chair is comfortable.
2.   (이자, 의자)가 비싸요.   The interest rate is high.
3.   (이사, 의사)를 만났어요. I met a doctor.
4.   (이미, 의미) 늦었어요.   It's already too late.
5.   (이리, 의리)가 없어.   He has no sense of duty toward friends.

Exercise 4
Circle the pronunciation of the vowel in the italicized syllable.

1. 정말 의심스러워요.   [ㅢ] ㅔ]   It's really doubtful.
2. 줄무늬 옷이 좋아요.   [ㅢ] ㅔ]   Clothes with a striped design
                                                are good.

3. 흰색을 좋아합니다.   [ㅢ] ㅔ]   I like white.

4. 저희집으로 오세요.   [ㅢ] ㅔ]   Please come to our house.

5. 그림의 떡이지요.   [ㅢ] ㅔ]   It's pie in the sky, of course.

6. 무소식이 희소식이다.   [ㅢ] ㅔ]   No news is good news.

7. 회의실이 어디예요?   [ㅢ] ㅔ]   Where's the conference room?

8. 의사가 되고 싶습니다.   [ㅢ] ㅔ]   I'd like to become a doctor.

9. 성공의 비결이 뭐예요?   [ㅢ] ㅔ]   What's the secret of success?

10. 거의 다 했습니다.   [ㅢ] ㅔ]   I'm almost finished.

Exercise 5
Listen and repeat. You will first hear just the part in italics and then the entire sentence.

1. 정말 의심스러워요.   It's really doubtful.
2. 줄무늬 옷이 좋아요.   Clothes with a striped design are good.
3. 흰색을 좋아합니다.   I like white.
4. 저희집으로 오세요.   Please come to our house.
5. 그림의 떡이지요.   It's pie in the sky, of course.
6. 무소식이 희소식이다.   No news is good news.
7. 의사가 되고 싶습니다.   I'd like to become a doctor.
8. 거의 다 했습니다.   I'm almost finished.

Section V-8: ㅟ, ㅚ, ㅙ, ㅞ, ㅘ, & ㅝ

Exercise 1
Listen and repeat.

ㅣ/ㅟ

1.   이   위
2.   시어   쉬어

ㅢ/ㅟ

3.   의기   위기
4.   의한   위한

ㅚ/ㅙ

5.   외   왜

ㅙ/ㅞ

6.   괘도   궤도

ㅘ/ㅝ

7.   관   권
8.   완만   원만

Exercise 2
Circle the number corresponding to the word that sounds different.

1.   [1   2   3   ]
2.   [1   2   3   ]
3.   [1   2   3   ]
4.   [1   2   3   ]
5.   [1   2   3   ]

Exercise 3
Circle the item in parentheses that you hear.

1. (이, 위)가 약해요.   My stomach is weak.
2. (이, 위)가 아파요.   My tooth is hurting.
3. (이쪽, 위쪽)으로 가세요.   Please go up.
4. 국민에 (의한, 위한) 정치   Government by the people
5. 국민을 (의한, 위한) 정치   Government for the people
6. (의기, 위기)왕성합니다.   They're in high spirits.
7. (외, 왜) 할머니가 오세요?   Why is your grandmother coming?
8. (외, 왜)아들입니까?   Are you an only son?
9. 경사가 (완만, 원만)해요.   The slope is gradual.
10. 성격이 (완만, 원만)해요.   Her personality is well-rounded.
11. 책 한 (관, 권) 샀어요.   I bought one book.
12. 한 (관, 권)은 3.75 kg입니다.   One *gwan* is 3.75 kg.

Exercise 4
Listen and repeat. You will first hear just the part in italics and then the entire sentence.

1. *위쪽*으로 가세요.   Please go up.
2. *의기*왕성합니다.   They're in high spirits.
3. *위기*는 모면했어요.   As for the crisis, we've pulled through it.
4. *외*할머니가 오세요?   Is your maternal grandmother coming?
5. 책 *한 권* 샀어요.   I bought one book.
6. 한 *관*은 3.75 kg입니다.   One *gwan* is 3.75 kg.
7. 날씨가 *더워*요.   The weather's hot.
8. 좀 *도와* 주세요.   Please help.

Exercise 5
Fill in the blank with the syllable that you hear.

이 / 위

1. ___ 험합니다.   It's dangerous.
2. ___ 해해요.   I understand.

좌 / 줘

3. ___ 회전하세요.   Make a left turn, please.
4. 좀 빌려 ___ 요.   Lend it to me, please.

와 / 워

5. 날씨가 더 ___ 요.   The weather's hot.
6. 좀 도 ___ 주세요.   Please help.

Practice: Consonants

Section C-1: ㅂ

Exercise 1
Listen and repeat. Notice that the ㅂ sound is fully voiced when it occurs between two voiced sounds (vowels or ㅁ, ㄴ, ㅇ, ㄹ), even when there is a word boundary.

1. 비   나비   갈비
2. 발   가발   신발
3. 십   십원   십이월
4. 바지   내 바지   청바지
5. 겁   겁 안 나   겁 없어
6. 잎*   잎 안

*ㅍ is pronounced here as if it were ㅂ; see section C-4.2.

Exercise 2
Each sentence contains two (italicized) ㅂ sounds. Circle the one that is fully voiced.

1. 형 *부*가 *부*자예요.   Her brother-in-law is rich.
2. *비*누가 안 *비*싸요.   The soap is inexpensive.
3. 국수를 *비*/*비*세요.   Please mix the noodle with sauce and stuff.
4. 갈*비*가 *비*싸요.   The rib is expensive.
5. 불고기는 9*불*이에요.   *Bulgogi* is nine dollars.
6. *방*금 다*방*에 갔어요.   He just went to a coffee shop.
7. 신*발*이 작아서 *발*이 아파요.   The shoes are so small that my feet hurt.
8. 청*바*지가 *바*랬어요.   The blue jeans have become faded.
9. *바*지 입어요.   I'm putting on pants.
10. *벌*은 겁 안 나요.   Bees, I'm not scared of them.
11. *백*오*십*원이에요.   It's 150 *won*.
12. 잎 안에 *벌*레가 있어요.   There's a worm inside the leaf.

Section C-2: ㅂ & ㅍ

Exercise 1
Listen and repeat.

1. 발   팔
2. 밭   팥
3. 봄   폼
4. 분   푼
5. 불   풀
6. 비   피
7. 보기   포기
8. 반사   판사
9. 벌벌   펄펄
10. 사발   사팔

Exercise 2
Circle the number corresponding to the word that sounds different.

1. [1   2   3]
2. [1   2   3]
3. [1   2   3]
4. [1   2   3]
5. [1   2   3]
6. [1   2   3]
7. [1   2   3]

Exercise 3
Circle the item in parentheses that you hear.

1. (비, 피)가 와요.   It's raining.
2. (비, 피)가 나요.   It's bleeding.
3. 한 (분, 푼)이세요?   Is there just one person?
4. 한 (분, 푼)도 없어요.   I'm penniless.
5. 밭에 (불, 풀)이 많아요.   There are lots of weeds in the patch.

6. 산에 (불, 풀)이 났어요.   Fire broke out on the mountain.

7. (팔, 발)꿈치가 까졌어요.   My elbow got scraped.

8. (발, 팔)이 저려요.   My foot is asleep.

9. (봄, 폼)이 좋아요.   Spring is good.

10. (보기, 포기)하지 마세요.   Please don't give up.

11. (보기, 포기)는 어려워요.   As for seeing it, it's difficult.

12. (벌벌, 펄펄) 떨어요.   She's trembling with nervousness.

13. (벌벌, 펄펄) 끓어요.   It's boiling hard.

14. 꽃이 (비었어, 피었어)요.   The flower has bloomed.

15. 완전히 (비었어, 피었어)요.   It's completely empty.

Exercise 4

Listen and repeat. You will first hear just the part in italics and then the entire sentence.

1. *비* 온다.   It's raining.

2. *피* 난다.   It's bleeding.

3. 돈이 *한 푼*도 없어.   I'm penniless.

4. *풀이* 많네요.   Oh, there are lots of weeds.

5. *불이* 났네요.   Wow, fire broke out.

6. 긴 *팔* 입을까?   Shall I wear a long-sleeved shirt?

7. 가발이에요.   It's a wig.

8. 봄에는 따뜻해요.   In the spring it's warm.

9. 꽃이 *피었어요*.   The flower has bloomed.

10. 텅 *비었어요*.   It's totally empty.

11. 빛을 *반사*해요.   It reflects light.

12. 판사가 꿈이에요.   A judgeship is my dream.

Exercise 5
Fill in the blank with the syllable that you hear.

바/파

1. 햇빛에 ___래요.   It fades in the sun.
2. 하늘이 ___래요.   The sky is blue.
3. 머리가 아___요.   My head hurts.

버/퍼

4. ___룻이 없어요.   He [the kid] has no courtesy.
5. 너무 슬___요.   It's so sad.
6. ___리지 마세요.   Please don't throw it away.

발/팔

7. 사___면 먹었어.   I ate a cup of instant noodles.
8. 반 ___ 입을까?   Shall I wear a short-sleeved shirt?
9. ___음이 좋아요.   Your pronunciation is good.

Section C-3: ㅂ & ㅃ

Exercise 1
Listen and repeat.

1. 배   빼
2. 벼   뼈
3. 방   빵
4. 분   뿐
5. 불   뿔
6. 비어   삐어
7. 부리   뿌리
8. 벌벌   뻘뻘
9. 이발   이빨

Exercise 2

Circle the number corresponding to the word that sounds different.

1. [1 2 3]
2. [1 2 3]
3. [1 2 3]
4. [1 2 3]
5. [1 2 3]
6. [1 2 3]
7. [1 2 3]

Exercise 3

Circle the item in parentheses that you hear.

1. (벼, 뼈)가 부러졌어요.   A bone's been broken.
2. (방, 빵)이 작아요.   The room is small.
3. (방, 빵)이 없어요.   There's no bread.
4. 저 (분, 뿐)이에요?   Is it that person?
5. 저 (분, 뿐)이에요.   I'm the only one.
6. 산에 (불, 뿔)이 났어요.   Fire broke out on the mountain.
7. 사슴은 (불, 뿔)이 있어요.   Deer have horns.
8. (벌벌, 뻘뻘) 떨려요.   I'm trembling with nervousness.
9. 땀을 (벌벌, 뻘뻘) 흘려요.   He's sweating profusely.
10. 얼룩을 (배, 빼)요.   Take the stain out.
11. 새끼를 (뱄어, 뺐어)요.   She [the animal] is pregnant.
12. 이를 (뱄어, 뺐어)요.   I had my tooth extracted.
13. 발목을 (비었어, 삐었어)요.   I sprained my ankle.
14. (빈, 삔) 손으로 왔습니다.   I came empty-handed.
15. (이발, 이빨)하러 갑니다.   He's going in order to get a haircut.

Exercise 4

Listen and repeat. You will first hear just the part in italics and then the entire sentence.

1. *방이* 좋아.   The room is small.
2. *빵이* 맛있다!   Wow, the bread is delicious.
3. 저 *분이*에요?   Is it that person?
4. 저 *뿐이*에요.   I'm the only one.
5. *불이* 났어요.   Fire broke out.
6. *뿔이* 있어요.   It has horns.
7. *벌벌* 떨려요.   I'm trembling with nervousness.
8. 땀을 *뻘뻘* 흘려요.   He's sweating profusely.
9. 새끼를 *뱄어요*.   She [the animal] is pregnant.
10. 이를 *뺐어요*.   I had my tooth extracted.
11. 발목을 *삐었어요*.   I sprained my ankle.
12. 텅 *비었어요*.   It's totally empty.

Exercise 5

Fill in the blank with the syllable that you hear.

바 / 빠

1. 요즘 바___요.   I'm busy these days.
2. 비___람이 쳐요.   It's stormy.
3. 눈이 나___졌어요.   My eyesight has gotten bad.

발 / 빨

4. ___리 오세요.   Please come quickly.
5. ___이 아파요.   My feet hurt.

번 / 뻔

6. 번___이 죄송해요.   I'm sorry to trouble you so often.
7. 정말 뻔___해요.   He's really shameless.
8. 죽을 ___했어요.   I almost died.

봉 / 뽕

9. 짬___이 매워요.   The *jjamppong* is spicy.
10. 비닐 ___지 있으세요?   Do you have a plastic bag?

Section C-4: ㅂ, ㅍ, & ㅃ
Section C-4.1: Basic pronunciation

Exercise 1
Listen and repeat.

1. 배   패   빼
2. 비   피   삐
3. 방   팡   빵
4. 빈   핀   삔
5. 분   푼   뿐
6. 불   풀   뿔
7. 비어   피어   삐어
8. 벌벌   펄펄   뻘뻘

Exercise 2
Circle the contrast that you hear.

1. [ㅍㅃ   ㅍㅂ   ㅃㅂ   ]
2. [ㅂㅃ   ㅃㅃ   ㅂㅍ   ]
3. [ㅍㅍ   ㅍㅂ   ㅃㅂ   ]
4. [ㅂㅍ   ㅍㅂ   ㅃㅍ   ]
5. [ㅂㅍ   ㅍㅃ   ㅃㅂ   ]
6. [ㅂㅃ   ㅃㅂ   ㅃㅍ   ]
7. [ㅂㅍ   ㅃㅂ   ㅃㅍ   ]

Exercise 3

Circle the item in parentheses that you hear.

1. (불, 풀)이 안 붙어요.   The glue doesn't stick.
2. (풀, 뿔)이 뾰족해요.   The horn is pointy.
3. (불, 뿔)이 났어요.   Fire broke out.
4. 두 (분, 푼)이세요?   Are there two of you?
5. 저 (분, 뿐)이에요.   I'm the only one.
6. 한 (분, 푼)도 안 남았어요.   Not a single penny is left.
7. (배, 패)가 안 좋아요.   The pear isn't good.
8. (패기, 빼기)가 있어요.   He has an ambitious spirit.
9. (패지, 빼지) 마세요.   Please join in.
10. (발레, 빨래)를 배웁니다.   I'm learning ballet.
11. 이 옷은 (팔래, 빨래).   This piece of clothing, I'm going to sell it.
12. (발레, 빨래)가 힘들어요.   Laundry is tough.
13. 꽃이 (비었어, 피었어)요.   The flower has bloomed.
14. 손이 (비었어, 삐었어)요.   My hands are free.
15. 다리를 (피었어, 삐었어)요.   I sprained my leg.

Exercise 4

Fill in the blank with the syllable that you hear.

북 / 푹 / 뿍

1. ___ 쉬세요.   Please have a good rest.
2. 듬___ 넣어요.   Put in lots.
3. 동, 서, 남, ___   east, west, south, north

빈 / 핀 / 삔

4. ___ 병을 모아요.   I collect empty bottles.
5. 활짝 ___ 꽃이 예뻐요.   The fully-bloomed flower is beautiful.
6. 어제 ___ 다리예요.   It's the leg I sprained yesterday.

방 / 팡 / 빵

7. 곰___이에요.   It's mold.

8. 찐___이 달아요.   The *jjinppang* (steamed bread) is sweet.

9. 주___이 넓어요.   The kitchen is spacious.

Exercise 5

Listen and repeat. You will first hear just the part in italics and then the entire sentence.

1. 풀로 *붙여요*.   Paste it with glue.

2. *뿔이* 났어요.   Horns have grown./He's vexed.

3. *불고기* 먹자.   Let's eat *bulgogi*.

4. 두 *분*이세요?   Are there two of you?

5. 저 *뿐*이에요.   I'm the only one.

6. 한 *푼*도 없어요.   I'm penniless.

7. *발레* 공연 보러 가요.   I'm going in order to see a ballet performance.

8. 차를 *팔래*.   I'm going to sell the car.

9. *빨래*가 많아요.   There's a lot of laundry.

10. *빈 병*을 모아요.   I collect empty bottles.

11. 꽃 *핀 것* 보세요.   Look at the flower that has bloomed.

12. 손을 *삔 것* 같아요.   It looks like I sprained my hand.

Section C-4.2: ㅂ & ㅍ in front of a consonant or at the end of a word

Exercise 1

Listen and repeat. Notice that ㅂ and ㅍ sound different at the beginning of a word, but that they are both pronounced as an unreleased ㅂ sound at the end of a word or in front of a consonant.

1.   비   피   beginning of a word   (ㅂ ≠ ㅍ)

      입   잎   end of a word   (ㅂ = ㅍ) —> ㅂ

2. 버   퍼   beginning of a word   (ㅂ ≠ ㅍ)
    덥지   덮지   in front of a consonant (ㅂ = ㅍ) —> ㅂ

Exercise 2

Listen and repeat. Notice that ㅂ and ㅍ are both pronounced as if they were ㅂ at the end of a word or in front of a consonant, but that their pronunciations differ from each other in front of a suffix that begins with a vowel.

end of a word (ㅂ = ㅍ) —> ㅂ

1.   입   잎

2.   입 안   잎 안

in front of a consonant (ㅂ = ㅍ) —> ㅂ

3.   입술   잎사귀

in front of a suffix that begins with a vowel (ㅂ ≠ ㅍ)

4.   입에   잎에

Exercise 3

Circle the italicized syllable that sounds different.

1.   a. 엽서를 써요.   I'm writing a postcard.
     b. 옆을 봐요.   Look to the side.
     c. 옆집에 살아요.   She lives next-door.

2.   a. 안 덮어요?   Aren't you going to cover it?
     b. 덮지 않아요?   Aren't you going to cover it?
     c. 덥지 않아요?   Aren't you hot?

3.   a. 앞집에 살아.   He lives in the house in front.
     b. 앞치마를 입어.   Wear the apron.
     c. 앞이 안 보여.   I can't see ahead.

4.   a. 잎이 떨어진다.   The leaves are falling.
     b. 입안이 헐었어.   Inside the mouth is sore.
     c. 잎 안에 벌레가 있어. There's a worm inside the leaf.

Exercise 4
Fill in the blank with the syllable that you hear.

압 / 앞

1. ___이 깜깜해요.   I see only darkness.
2. 수___이 세요.   The water pressure is high.

입 / 잎

3. ___이 떨어져요.   The leaves are falling.
4. 수___이 줄었어요.   The income has diminished.

Section C-5: ㄷ

Exercise 1
Listen and repeat. Notice that the ㄷ sound is fully voiced when it occurs between two voiced sounds (vowels or ㅁ, ㄴ, ㅇ, ㄹ), even when there is a word boundary.

1. 다   바다   멀다
2. 두   구두   만두
3. 맏   맏아들
4. 곧   곧 올게.   곧 언제?
5. 꽃*   꽃 어때?   꽃 안 사.
6. 맛*   맛 어때?   맛 없어.

*ㅊ and ㅅ are pronounced as if they were ㄷ; see sections C-16.2 and C-17.2.

Exercise 2
Each sentence contains two (italicized) ㄷ sounds. Circle the one that is fully voiced.

1. *다*음엔 바*다*로 가요.   Next time, let's go to the beach.
2. *다다*음주 어때요?   How is the week after next?
3. 오늘도 도서관에 가요?   Are you going to the library again today?

4. 만두국 두 개 주세요.   Give me two *mandugguk* (dumpling soup),
                                   please.
5. 구두가 두켤레예요.   I have two pairs of dress shoes.
6. 덜덜 떨려요.   I'm trembling with nervousness.
7. 동생은 자동차 없어?   Does your younger brother/sister not
                                   have a car?
8. 답이 안 들려요.   I can't hear the answer.
9. 대답하세요.   Please answer.
10. 다시 곧 올게요.   I'll come back soon.
11. 다 맛 없어.   Nothing has any taste.
12. 다시는 꽃 안 사.   I'm not buying flowers again.

Section C-6: ㄷ & ㅌ

Exercise 1
Listen and repeat.

1. 달   탈
2. 답   탑
3. 덕   턱
4. 덜   털
5. 돈   톤
6. 동   통
7. 도끼   토끼
8. 들려   틀려
9. 동지   통지
10. 배달   배탈

Exercise 2
Circle the number corresponding to the word that sounds different.

1. [1   2   3]
2. [1   2   3]

3.   [1   2   3   ]
4.   [1   2   3   ]
5.   [1   2   3   ]
6.   [1   2   3   ]
7.   [1   2   3   ]

Exercise 3
Circle the item in parentheses that you hear.

1.	누구 (덕, 턱)이야?	Thanks to whom is that?
2.	금이 두 (돈, 톤)이에요.	The gold is two *don*. (1 *don* = 3.76 grams)
3.	(달, 탈)이 멋있다!	The moon is spectacular!
4.	(달, 탈)도 많다.	You are full of trouble.
5.	(답, 탑)이 뭐예요?	What's the correct answer?
6.	공든 (답, 탑)이 무너지랴.	Is hard work ever wasted?
7.	(도끼, 토끼)가 귀여워요.	The rabbit's cute.
8.	(도끼, 토끼)가 무서워요.	The ax is scary.
9.	(동지, 통지)를 만났네요.	Hey, I've met a person in the same situation.
10.	(동지, 통지)가 언제 와요?	When will the notice come?
11.	답이 (들려, 틀려)요.	The answer is wrong.
12.	소리가 (들려, 틀려)요.	I hear a sound.
13.	가방 좀 (들어, 틀어) 줘.	Hold the bag for me.
14.	라디오 좀 (들어, 틀어) 봐.	Try to turn on the radio.
15.	(교동, 교통)이 복잡해요.	The traffic is heavy.

Exercise 4
Listen and repeat. You will first hear just the part in italics and then the entire sentence.

1.	*한달* 됐습니다.	It's been one month.
2.	*배탈*이 났어요.	My stomach is upset.
3.	*정답*이 뭐예요?	What's the correct answer?
4.	*시계탑*에서 만나.	Let's meet at the clock tower.
5.	좀 *덜* 추워요.	It's a bit less cold.

6.	털이 많아요.	He's hairy.
7.	동지를 만났네요.	Hey, I've met a person in the same situation.
8.	통지를 받았어요.	I've received a notice.
9.	답이 틀려요.	The answer is wrong.
10.	소리가 들려요.	I hear a sound.
11.	배탈이 났어요.	My stomach is upset.
12.	배달 됩니까?	Is delivery available?

Exercise 5

Fill in the blank with the syllable that you hear.

다/타

1.	고기가 ___ 탔어.	The meat is all burnt.
2.	차 ___고 가자.	Let's go, riding in the car.
3.	비___민 부족이야.	I'm short of vitamins.

동/통

4.	도___ 모르겠어요.	I don't think I know at all.
5.	___네 친구예요.	He's a neighborhood friend.
6.	쓰레기___ 있어요?	Is there a trashcan?
7.	___메달을 땄습니다.	I won a bronze medal.

당/탕

8.	설___ 넣으세요?	Do you put in sugar?
9.	___연하죠.	It goes without saying.

Section C-7: ㄷ & ㄸ

Exercise 1

Listen and repeat.

1.	도	또
2.	달	딸
3.	담	땀

4.   덕   떡
5.   대문   때문
6.   닳아   땋아
7.   덜어   떨어
8.   듣고   뜯고
9.   진담   진땀
10. 마당   마땅

Exercise 2
Circle the number corresponding to the word that sounds different.

1.   [1   2   3]
2.   [1   2   3]
3.   [1   2   3]
4.   [1   2   3]
5.   [1   2   3]
6.   [1   2   3]
7.   [1   2   3]

Exercise 3
Circle the item in parentheses that you hear.

1.   그 친구(도, 또) 왔어?   Did that friend also come?
2.   그 친구 (도, 또) 왔어?   Did that friend come again?
3.   (담, 땀) 좀 닦아요.   Wipe off your sweat.
4.   (달, 딸)이 안 보여요.   I can't see the moon.
5.   (달, 딸)이 예뻐요.   Your daughter is pretty.
6.   누구 (덕, 떡)이에요?   Whose rice cake is it?
7.   (덕, 떡)이 부족해요.   I'm short of virtue.
8.   남(대문, 때문)에 가요.   I'm going to Namdaemun (market).
9.   남(대문, 때문)에요?   Because of others?
10. (달기, 딸기)만 해.   Just get/use only the strawberry.
11. (달기, 딸기)는 달아.   As for sweetness, it's sweet (but . . .).
12. 머리 (닿아, 땋아)요.   The head is touching it.

13. 머리 (닿아, 땋아)요.   I'm braiding my hair.

14. 라디오 (듣고, 뜯고) 싶다.   I want to listen to the radio.

15. 선물 (듣고, 뜯고) 있어.   I'm opening my presents.

Exercise 4
Listen and repeat. You will first hear just the part in italics and then the entire sentence.

1. *땀* 좀 닦아라.   Wipe off your sweat.

2. *달이* 떴네요.   The moon is out.

3. *딸이* 시집가요.   My daughter's getting married.

4   *떡이* 맛있네요.   Wow, the rice cake is delicious.

5. *남대문에* 가요.   I'm going to Namdaemun (market).

6. *남때문에* 요?   Because of others?

7. *딸기가* 달죠?   The strawberry is sweet, isn't it?

8. 커피가 *달기*만 해.   The coffee is nothing but sweet.

9. 음악을 *듣고* 있어요.   I'm listening to music.

10. 선물을 *뜯고* 있어요.   I'm opening my presents.

11. *진담*이야.   I mean it.

12. *진땀*이 나요.   I'm sweating from anxiety.

Exercise 5
Fill in the blank with the syllable that you hear.

동 / 똥

1. 개___을 밟았어.   I stepped on dog dirt.

2. 차가 수___이에요?   Is your car a manual [transmission]?

3. ___차예요.   It's a lemon. (slang)

당 / 땅

4. ___콩이 고소해요.   The peanuts taste good.

5. 마___이 넓어요.   The yard is spacious.

6. 마___히 벌을 받아야죠.   I deserve to be punished.

득/뜩

7. 잔___ 먹었어요.   I ate to my heart's content.

8. 이___이 안 돼요.   It doesn't make a profit.

Exercise 6
Listen and repeat. Even if you can't follow along, notice the many instances of ㄷ and ㄸ in this children's song.

달 달 무슨달	Moon, moon, what kind of moon?
쟁반같이 둥근 달	A round moon like a tray.
어디 어디 떴나	Where, where has it risen?
남산 위에 떴지	It's risen over the *Namsan* (mountain).

Section C-8: ㄷ, ㅌ, & ㄸ
Section C-8.1: Basic pronunciation

Exercise 1
Listen and repeat.

1.	다	타	따
2.	더	터	떠
3.	덕	턱	떡
4.	단	탄	딴
5.	든	튼	뜬
6.	달	탈	딸
7.	들	틀	뜰
8.	담	탐	땀
9.	당	탕	땅
10.	동	통	똥

Exercise 2
Circle the contrast that you hear.

1. [ㄷㄸ   ㄸㄷ   ㄸㅌ   ]
2. [ㄷㄸ   ㄸㄷ   ㅌㄸ   ]
3. [ㅌㄸ   ㅌㄷ   ㄸㄷ   ]
4. [ㅌㄸ   ㄸㅌ   ㅌㄷ   ]
5. [ㄷㅌ   ㅌㅌ   ㄷㄸ   ]
6. [ㄷㅌ   ㅌㄷ   ㄷㄸ   ]
7. [ㅌㄸ   ㄸㅌ   ㄸㄷ   ]

Exercise 3
Circle the item in parentheses that you hear.

1. 물에 (터, 떠)요.   It floats on water.
2. 손이 (터, 떠)요.   My hands are getting chapped.
3. 좀 (더, 떠) 주세요.   Give me some more, please.
4. (단, 탄) 고기는 버려.   Throw away the burnt meat.
5. (탄, 딴) 종이에 쓰세요.   Write on a separate sheet, please.
6. (단, 탄) 과자를 좋아해요.   I like sweet cookies.
7. (탈, 딸)도 많다.   You are full of trouble.
8. (달, 딸)이 예쁘네요.   Wow, your daughter is pretty.
9. (달, 탈)이 동그래요.   The moon is round.
10. 다 부모님 (덕, 떡)이에요.   It's all thanks to my parents.
11. (턱, 떡)이 길어요.   His chin is long.
12. 생일(턱, 떡)이에요.   It's birthday rice cake.
13. (새통, 새똥)에 맞았어요.   I got hit by bird dirt.
14. (교동, 교통)이 복잡해요.   The traffic is heavy.
15. 정말 (동물, 똥물)이야.   He's really an animal.

Exercise 4

Listen and repeat. You will first hear just the part in italics and then the entire sentence.

1. *탄 고기*는 먹지 마.   Don't eat the burnt meat.
2. *딴소리* 하지 마.   Don't talk nonsense.
3. *단 걸* 좋아해요.   I love sweet things.
4. 차가 *탐이* 나요.   The car tempts me.
5. *땀이* 나요.   I'm sweating.
6. *담을* 쌓았어요.   They built a wall.
7. 부모님 *덕이에요*.   It's thanks to my parents.
8. 맛있는 *떡이에요*.   It's a delicious rice cake.
9. 한 *턱* 내세요.   Give us a treat, please.
10. 새*똥*에 맞았어요.   I got hit by bird dirt.
11. 쓰레기*통* 있어요?   Is there a trash can?
12. 동*쪽*에 있어요.   It's on the east side.
13. 눈을 *뜬* 것 같아요.   It seems like he opened his eyes.
14. 철이 *든* 것 같아요.   It seems like he's matured.
15. 싹이 *튼* 것 같아요.   It seems like the bud's come out.

Exercise 5

Fill in the blank with the syllable that you hear.

다/타/따

1. 왕__가 뭐예요?   What's a *wangdda* (social outcast)?
2. 고기 다 ___요.   The meat is all burning.
3. 기__ 잘 쳐요?   Do you play the guitar well?

두/투/뚜

4. ___ 껑이 안 보여요.   The lid is nowhere to be seen.
5. 항상 __덜거려요.   He always grumbles.
6. ___통이 심해요.   The headache is severe.

당 / 탕 / 땅

7. 설＿＿을 넣으세요.   Please put in sugar.

8. ＿＿콩 과자예요.   It's a peanut cookie.

9. ＿＿분이 많아요.   The sugar content is high.

덕 / 턱 / 떡

10. ＿＿분에 잘 지내요.   I'm doing well thanks to your concern.

11. 벌＿＿ 일어나.   Jump right up to your feet.

12. 주걱＿＿이에요.   He has a jutting jaw.

Section C-8.2: ㄷ & ㅌ in front of a consonant or at the end of a word

Exercise 1

Listen and repeat. Notice that ㄷ and ㅌ sound different at the beginning of a word, but that they are both pronounced as an unreleased ㄷ sound in front of a consonant.

1.   다   타   beginning of a word   (ㄷ ≠ ㅌ)

     받다   밭다   in front of a consonant (ㄷ = ㅌ) —> ㄷ

2.   디   티   beginning of a word   (ㄷ ≠ ㅌ)

     믿지는   밑지는   in front of a consonant (ㄷ = ㅌ) —> ㄷ

Exercise 2

Listen and repeat. Notice that ㄷ and ㅌ are both pronounced as if they were ㄷ at the end of a word or in front of a consonant, but that their pronunciations differ from each other in front of a suffix that begins with a vowel.

end of a word (ㄷ = ㅌ) —> ㄷ

1.   곧   솥

2.   곧 와   솥 없어

in front of a consonant (ㄷ = ㅌ) —> ㄷ

3.   곧장   솥뚜껑

in front of a suffix that begins with a vowel (ㄷ ≠ ㅌ)

4.   믿어   밑에

Exercise 3
Circle the italicized syllable that sounds different.

1.   a. 간격이 너무 *밭*아.   The space/time in between is too small.
     b. 전화 *받*아.   Answer the phone.
     c. 콩*밭* 아냐?   Isn't it a bean patch?

2.   a. *솥*에 끓여요.   Boil it in the kettle.
     b. *솥* 없어요.   There's no kettle.
     c. *솥* 안 닦아요?   Aren't you cleaning the kettle?

3.   a. 딸기 *밭*에 가자.   Let's go to a strawberry field.
     b. 딸기 *밭* 없어?   There's no strawberry field?
     c. 전화 *받*았어?   Did you receive the phone call?

4.   a. *믿*지는 장사예요.   It's a losing business.
     b. *믿*지는 마세요.   Please don't trust it.
     c. *밑*에 떨어졌어요.   It fell down.

Exercise 4
Fill in the blank with the syllable that you hear.

겉 / 겉

1.   ___으로 드러나요.   It shows on the surface.
2.   소매를 ___으세요.   Please roll up your sleeves.

맏 / 맡

3.   ___아들입니다.   I'm the eldest son.
4.   냄새를 ___아 보세요.   Please try to smell it.

Section C-9: ㄱ

Exercise 1
Listen and repeat. Notice that ㄱ is fully voiced when it occurs between two voiced sounds (vowels or ㅁ, ㄴ, ㅇ, ㄹ), even when there is a word boundary.

1.	구	누구	친구
2.	국	미국	한국
3.	백	백원	백일
4.	가방	내 가방	흰 가방
5.	꼭	꼭 와	꼭 안아

Exercise 2
Each sentence contains two (italicized) ㄱ sounds. Circle the one that is fully voiced.

1.	*가*방이 비싼*가*요?	Is the bag expensive, I wonder?
2.	내 *가*방은 *가*벼워요.	My bag is light.
3.	*개*미가 불*개*미야.	The ant is a fire ant.
4.	*거*의 본 *거*예요.	It's what I almost finished watching.
5.	과일은 사*과*를 좋아해요.	As for fruit, I like apples.
6.	9일날 야*구*하자.	Let's play baseball on the ninth.
7.	*김*하고 물*김*치 있어요.	There's *gim* (dried seaweed) and *mulgimchi*.
8.	목요일에 *교*실에서 보자.	Let's meet in the classroom on Thursday.
9.	*구*백원입니다.	It's 900 *won*.
10.	같이 꼭 오세요.	Please be sure to come together.

Section C-10: ㄱ & ㅋ

Exercise 1
Listen and repeat.

1.	개	캐
2.	기	키

3. 간   칸
4. 근   큰
5. 금   큼
6. 겁   컵
7. 공   콩
8. 그게   크게
9. 그림   크림
10. 골라   콜라

Exercise 2
Circle the number corresponding to the word that sounds different.

1. [1   2   3]
2. [1   2   3]
3. [1   2   3]
4. [1   2   3]
5. [1   2   3]
6. [1   2   3]
7. [1   2   3]

Exercise 3
Circle the item in parentheses that you hear.

1. 감자를 (개, 캐)요.   They are digging potatoes.
2. 옷을 (개, 캐)요.   I'm folding up clothes.
3. (기, 키)가 부족해요.   I'm short of vitality.
4. (간, 칸)이 콩알만해 졌어요.   My heart leaped into my throat.
5. (겁, 컵)이 많아요.   I'm timid.
6. 무슨 (공, 콩)이에요?   What kind of bean is it?
7. 주인(공, 콩)이에요.   She's the protagonist.
8. (공, 콩)들인 보람이 있네요.   Wow, the hard work was worth it.
9. (공, 콩)떡이 맛있어요.   Rice cake with beans in it is delicious.
10. (골라, 콜라) 가지세요.   Please pick one and take it.
11. (골라, 콜라) 드세요.   Help yourself to the cola.

12. (근시, 큰 시)예요.   I'm near-sighted.
13. 이 (근방, 큰 방)에 사세요?   Do you live in this vicinity?
14. (그림, 크림)이 맛있어요.   The cream is delicious.
15. (그림, 크림)이 멋있어요.   The picture is beautiful.

Exercise 4

Listen and repeat. You will first hear just the part in italics and then the
entire sentence.

1.   *키가* 작아요.   He's short.
2.   *기가* 막혀요.   I'm dumbfounded.
3.   무슨 *콩이*에요?   What kind of bean is it?
4.   *야구공이*에요.   It's a baseball.
5.   *간이* 콩알만해 졌어요.   My heart leaped into my throat.
6.   *골라* 가지세요.   Please pick one and take it.
7.   *크게* 써 주세요.   Please write it big for me.
8.   *그게* 뭐예요?   What's that?
9.   *크림*이 맛있어요.   The cream is delicious.
10. *그림*이 멋있어요.   The picture is beautiful.
11. *칼국수* 끓여요.   I'm making *kalguksoo* (noodle soup).
12. *갈비* 먹읍시다.   Let's eat *galbi.*

Exercise 5

Fill in the blank with the syllable that you hear.

고 / 코

1.   들창___예요.   He has a turned-up nose.
2.   ___집이 세요.   She's stubborn.

갈 / 칼

3.   ___국수 끓여요.   I'm making *kalguksoo* (noodle soup).
4.   ___비 먹읍시다.   Let's eat *galbi.*

근 / 큰

5. 당___ 쥬스예요.   It's carrot juice.

6. ___ 5만명이에요.   There are approximately 50,000 people.

7. 찌게가 얼___해요.   The stew is mildly spicy.

금 / 큼

8. 옷이 ___직해요.   The clothes are loose-fitting.

9. ___연입니다.   It's "no smoking".

Section C-11: ㄱ & ㄲ

Exercise 1
Listen and repeat.

1. 가   까
2. 개   깨
3. 굴   꿀
4. 강   깡
5. 가지   까지
6. 고리   꼬리
7. 기어   끼어
8. 갈아   깔아
9. 토기   토끼
10. 곰곰이   꼼꼼히

Exercise 2
Circle the number corresponding to the word that sounds different.

1. [1   2   3]
2. [1   2   3]
3. [1   2   3]
4. [1   2   3]
5. [1   2   3]

6. [1   2   3   ]
7. [1   2   3   ]

Exercise 3
Circle the item in parentheses that you hear.

1. 언제 (가, 까)요?   When are you going?
2. (가지, 까지) 마세요.   Please don't peel it.
3. 언제 (가지, 까지) 먹어?   When are we eating eggplant?
4. 세(가지, 까지) 받았어.   I received three kinds.
5. (개, 깨)소금 맛이다!   Serves him right!
6. (굴, 꿀)이 시원해요.   The oyster is refreshing.
7. (굴, 꿀)맛이 변했어요.   The taste of the honey has changed.
8. (고리, 꼬리)가 길면 잡혀요.   Wrongdoing gets caught eventually.
9. 열쇠 (고리, 꼬리)예요.   It's a keychain.
10. 천천히 (기어, 끼어) 왔어.   I got here, crawling slowly.
11. 간신히 (기어, 끼어) 왔어.   I got here, barely squeezed in.
12. 방석을 (갈아, 깔아)요.   Use the seat cushion.
13. 전구를 (갈아, 깔아)요.   Change the light bulb.
14. (토기, 토끼)가 귀여워요.   The rabbit is cute.
15. (곰곰이, 꼼꼼히) 생각 중이야. I'm mulling it over.

Exercise 4
Listen and repeat. You will first hear just the part in italics and then the
entire sentence.

1. *가지* 마세요.   Please don't go.
2. *언제까지* 해요?   By when do I do it?
3. *깨소금* 맛이다!   Serves you right!
4. *개가* 짖어요.   The dog is barking.
5. *강이* 깊어요.   The river is deep.
6. *깡이* 세요.   She has a lot of guts.
7. 설설 *기어요.*   He's groveling with fear.
8. 팔짱을 *끼어요.*   Put your arm in my arm.

9. 방석을 *깔아요*.   Use the seat cushion.
10. 칼을 *갈아요*.   Sharpen the knife.
11. *가끔* 전화해요.   Call me from time to time.
12. *방금* 왔어요.   I just got here.

Exercise 5
Fill in the blank with the syllable that you hear.

가/까

1. 집이 가___워요.   My house is nearby.

개/깨

2. 어___에 메.   Put it on your shoulder.
3. 지우___ 있어요?   Do you have an eraser?
4. 주근___가 많아.   I have a lot of freckles.

간/깐

5. 잠___ 기다리세요.   Just a moment, please.
6. 시___ 없어요.   I don't have time.

곱/꼽

7. 피부가 참 ___다!   Wow, your skin is so smooth.
8. 배보다 배 ___이 커요.   The belly button is bigger than the belly.
                              (The expense that should be smaller is actually
                                  bigger.)

금/끔

9. 가___ 전화하세요.   Please call from time to time.
10. 방___ 도착했어요.   I've just arrived.

Section C-12: ㄱ, ㅋ, & ㄲ
Section C-12.1: Basic pronunciation

Exercise 1
Listen and repeat.

1. 개   캐   깨
2. 겨   켜   껴
3. 기   키   끼
4. 간   칸   깐
5. 근   큰   끈
6. 글   클   끌
7. 감감   캄캄   깜깜
8. 굴굴   쿨쿨   꿀꿀

Exercise 2
Circle the contrast that you hear.

1. [ㄱㄲ   ㅋㄲ   ㄱㅋ   ]
2. [ㄱㄲ   ㅋㄲ   ㅋㄱ   ]
3. [ㅋㄲ   ㅋㄱ   ㄱㅋ   ]
4. [ㄱㄲ   ㅋㅋ   ㄱㅋ   ]
5. [ㄱㄲ   ㅋㄱ   ㄱㅋ   ]
6. [ㅋㄲ   ㅋㄱ   ㄱㅋ   ]
7. [ㄱㅋ   ㅋㄱ   ㄲㅋ   ]

Exercise 3
Circle the item in parentheses that you hear.

1. (기, 키)가 모자라요.   He is short of vitality.
2. (키, 끼)가 있어요.   She has a wild/risqué spirit.
3. (기, 키)가 커요.   He's tall.
4. (기, 끼)가 멋있다!   Wow, the flag is beautiful.
5. 진흙을 (개, 깨)요.   I'm kneading clay.
6. 인삼을 (캐, 깨)요.   I dig ginseng roots.

7. 얼음을 (캐, 깨)요.　　Break the ice.

8. 좀 (클, 끌) 거예요.　　It'll be a little big.

9. 성냥을 (글, 끌)게요.　　I will put out the match.

10. 옷을 (겨, 껴) 입었어요.　　I'm bundled up in layers of clothes.

11. 불 좀 (켜, 껴) 주세요.　　Please turn on the light for me.

12. (겨자, 껴 자)요?　　Mustard?

13. 방이 (감감, 깜깜)해요.　　The room is pitch-dark.

14. (감감, 캄캄) 무소식이야.　　There's been no news for a long time.

15. 하늘이 (캄캄, 깜깜)해요.　　The sky is completely dark.

Exercise 4

Listen and repeat. You will first hear just the part in italics and then the entire sentence.

1. 좀 *큰 것* 같아요.　　It seems like it's a little big.

2. *근* 이틀을 잤어요.　　I slept for almost two days.

3. *끈이* 끊어졌어요.　　The string is broken.

4. *글씨*를 잘 써요.　　She has good handwriting.

5. 좀 *클 거야*.　　It'll be a little big.

6. 불 *끌게*.　　I'll turn off the light.

7. 옷이 *큼직*해요.　　The clothes are loose-fitting.

8. 정말 *끔찍*해요.　　It's really horrible.

9 주차*금지*예요.　　It's "no parking".

10. 방이 *깜깜*해요.　　The room is pitch dark.

11. *감감* 무소식이에요.　　There's been no news for a long time.

12. 앞이 *캄캄*해요.　　Things look grim.

Exercise 5

Fill in the blank with the syllable that you hear.

게 / 케 / 께

1. 그저___ 뭐 했어?　　What did you do the day before yesterday?

2. ___으름 피우지 마.　　Don't be lazy.

거 / 커 / 꺼

3. 얼굴이 두___워.   He's thick-skinned.

4. 손이 ___요.   She has big hands/does things on a big scale.

5. ___실에 있어요.   It's in the living room.

굼 / 쿰 / 꿈

6. ___벵이 같애.   He's as slow as a snail.

7. ___이 커요.   I have big dreams.

금 / 큼 / 끔

8. 가___ 봐요.   I see it once in a while.

9. 옷이 ___직해요.   The clothes are loose-fitting.

10. 정말 ___찍해요.   It's really horrible.

Exercise 6
Listen and repeat. Even if you can't follow along, notice the many instances of ㄱ and ㄲ in this children's song.

산토끼 토끼야	Hey, mountain rabbit, rabbit
어디를 가느냐	Where are you going?
깡총깡총 뛰면서	Hopping like that
어디를 가느냐	Where are you going?

Exercise 7
Listen and repeat. Even if you can't follow along, notice the many instances of ㅋ and ㄲ in this traditional tongue twister.

저기 저 콩깍지는	Over there, that bean pod
깐 콩깍지냐	Is it a shelled one?
안 깐 콩깍지냐	Or an unshelled one?

Section C-12.2: ㄱ, ㅋ, & ㄲ in front of a consonant or at the end of a word

Exercise 1

Listen and repeat. Notice that ㄱ, ㅋ, and ㄲ sound different at the beginning of a word, but that they are all pronounced as an unreleased ㄱ sound at the end of a word.

1. 가 　 까 　 카 　　 beginning of a word 　(ㄱ ≠ ㄲ ≠ ㅋ)
　　박 　 밖 　 부엌 　 end of a word 　　　(ㄱ = ㄲ = ㅋ) —> ㄱ

Exercise 2

Listen and repeat. Notice that ㄱ, ㅋ, and ㄲ are all pronounced as if they were ㄱ at the end of a word or in front of a consonant, but that their pronunciations differ from each other in front of a suffix that begins with a vowel.

　 end of a word (ㄱ = ㄲ = ㅋ) —> ㄱ
1. 　수박 　　　　　밖 　　　　　부엌
2. 　수박 안 사 　　밖 안 보여 　부엌 안

　 in front of a consonant (ㄱ = ㄲ = ㅋ) —> ㄱ
3. 　수박까지 　　　밖까지 　　　부엌까지

　 in front of a suffix that begins with a vowel (ㄱ ≠ ㄲ ≠ ㅋ)
4. 　수박에 　　　　밖에 　　　　부엌에*

* ㅋ can be pronounced ㄱ here; see section A-15.

Exercise 3

Circle the italicized syllable that sounds different.

1. a. *박*씨가 없어요. 　　　　There's no one whose last name is Bak.
　 b. *밖*에 나가요. 　　　　　Let's go outside.
　 c. *밖*까지 나갈게요. 　　　I'll go just to the outside.

2. a. *낚*시를 좋아해. 　　　　I like fishing.
　 b. *낚*싯줄이 끊어졌어. 　　The fishing line broke.
　 c. 한 마리도 못 *낚*아. 　　I cannot catch a single fish.

3.   a. 고기 좀 볶지.   I wish you had stir-fried some meat.
      b. 볶음밥 시킬까?   Shall we order fried rice?
      c. 복지 사업 해.   I do welfare work.

4.   a. 사과 깎아?   Are you peeling the apple?
      b. 깎지 마.   Don't peel it.
      c. 연필깎이 있어?   Do you have a pencil sharpener?

Exercise 4
Fill in the blank with the syllable that you hear.

박 / 밖
1.   ___이 어두워요.   Outside is dark.
2.   수___이 시원해요.   The watermelon is refreshing.

석 / 섞
3.   물을 ___어요.   Mix it with water.
4.   좌___이 없습니다.   There's no seat.

Section C-13: ㅈ

Exercise 1
Listen and repeat. Notice that ㅈ is fully voiced when it occurs between two voiced sounds (vowels or ㅁ, ㄴ, ㅇ, ㄹ), even when there is a word boundary.

1.   자   모자   상자
2.   절   계절   품절
3.   낮   낮에   낮은
4.   자리   내 자리   다른 자리

Exercise 2

Each sentence contains two (italicized) ㅈ sounds. Circle the one that is fully voiced.

1.	*자*기 모*자*야.	It's your hat.
2.	*주*로 양*주* 마셔요.	I mainly drink Western liquor.
3.	*지*갑에 휴*지* 있어요.	There's tissue in the purse.
4.	*전* 오*전*에 왔어요.	As for me, I got here in the morning.
5.	정말 인*정*이 없어.	He's really coldhearted.
6.	*자*리에 앉아요.	Please have a seat.
7.	*자*꾸 내 *자*리로 와요.	He keeps coming to my seat.
8.	*제*가 낮에 갈게요.	I'll go during the daytime.

Section C-14: ㅈ & ㅊ

Exercise 1

Listen and repeat.

1. 자 차
2. 절 철
3. 질 칠
4. 짐 침
5. 종 총
6. 주워 추워
7. 중고 충고
8. 진해 친해
9. 기자 기차
10. 가지 가치

Exercise 2

Circle the number corresponding to the word that sounds different.

1. [1 2 3]
2. [1 2 3]

3. [1   2   3]
4. [1   2   3]
5. [1   2   3]
6. [1   2   3]
7. [1   2   3]

Exercise 3

Circle the item in parentheses that you hear.

1.	밤에는 (자, 차)요.	At night it's cold.
2.	아기가 (자, 차)요.	The baby is sleeping.
3.	(자고, 차고) 할까요?	Shall we do it after sleeping?
4.	(질, 칠)이 나빠요.	The quality is bad.
5.	테니스를 (졌어, 쳤어).	I played tennis.
6.	내가 (졌어, 쳤어).	I lost.
7.	(종, 총) 소리가 나요.	There's a gunshot sound.
8.	(종, 총) 울렸어요?	Did the bell ring?
9.	커피가 (진해, 친해)요.	The coffee is strong.
10.	걔하고 (진해, 친해)?	Are you close to that kid?
11.	(짐, 침)이 바뀌었어요.	The luggage got switched.
12.	(짐, 침) 넘어 가요.	My mouth is watering.
13.	(기자, 기차)예요.	She's a journalist.
14.	(기자, 기차)가 빨라요.	The train is fast.
15.	(가지, 가치)가 떨어져요.	The value is diminishing.

Exercise 4

Listen and repeat. You will first hear just the part in italics and then the entire sentence.

1.	공을 *차요.*	He's kicking a ball.
2.	잘 *자요.*	Sleep tight.
3.	*총에* 맞았어요.	He got shot by a gun.
4.	*종* 쳤어요?	Did the bell ring?
5.	*짐이* 무거워요.	The luggage is heavy.

6.   *침*을 맞았어요.   I was treated with acupuncture.
7.   테니스 *쳤어*.   I played tennis.
8.   게임에 *졌어*.   I lost the game.
9.   *충*고 좀 주세요.   Please give me some advice.
10. *중*고차 샀어요.   I bought a used car.
11. *가지*나물이에요.   It's seasoned eggplant.
12. *가치*가 없어요.   It's worthless.

Exercise 5
Fill in the blank with the syllable that you hear.

주 / 추

1.   ___말 잘 보내세요.   Have a good weekend.
2.   ___석 잘 보내세요.   Happy *Choosuk*.

잠 / 참

3.   ___이 안 와.   I can't sleep.
4.   밤___ 먹을까?   Shall we eat a night-time snack?

정 / 청

5.   ___이 들었어요.   We became attached to each other.
6.   ___색을 좋아해요.   I like blue.

즘 / 츰

7.   요___ 어떠세요?   How are you these days?
8.   차___ 나아질 거예요.   It will get better gradually.

Section C-15: ㅈ & ㅉ

Exercise 1
Listen and repeat.

1.   자   짜
2.   족   쪽

3.   짐   찜
4.   자리   짜리
5.   졸면   쫄면
6.   쟁쟁   쨍쨍
7.   짖어   찢어
8.   가자   가짜
9.   팔지   팔찌
10. 공자   공짜

Exercise 2
Circle the number corresponding to the word that sounds different.

1.   [1   2   3   ]
2.   [1   2   3   ]
3.   [1   2   3   ]
4.   [1   2   3   ]
5.   [1   2   3   ]
6.   [1   2   3   ]
7.   [1   2   3   ]

Exercise 3
Circle the item in parentheses that you hear.

1.   그 친구 (자, 짜)요.   That friend is stingy.
2.   실컷 (자, 짜)요.   Sleep to your heart's content.
3.   (잠, 짬)이 안 와요.   I can't sleep.
4.   (잠, 짬)이 안 나요.   I have no time to spare.
5.   (짐, 찜)은 다 쌌어요?   Have you finished packing?
6.   이 (족, 쪽)을 보세요.   Look this way, please.
7.   옥수수 (지고, 찌고) 있어.   I'm steaming corn.
8.   걔한테 (질렸어, 찔렸어).   I've had it with that kid.
9.   좀 (질리네, 찔리네)요.   Well, I feel a little pang of conscience.
10. (졸면, 쫄면) 안 돼요.   You'd better not doze off.
11. (졸면, 쫄면) 먹어야지.   I'd better eat *jjolmyeon* (noodles).

12. 개가 (짖어, 찢어)요.   The dog is barking.
13. 왜 (짖어, 찢어)?   Why are you tearing it up?
14. 귀에 (쟁쟁, 쩽쩽)해요.   They [the words] are ringing in my ears.
15. 해가 (쟁쟁, 쩽쩽) 나요.   The sun is blazing.

Exercise 4
Listen and repeat. You will first hear just the part in italics and then the
entire sentence.

1. *얼마짜리*예요?   How much are they each?
2. *자리*에 앉으세요.   Please have a seat.
3. *이 쪽*으로 오세요.   Come this way, please.
4. *짐 쌌*어요.   I packed the luggage.
5. *갈비찜* 먹자.   Let's eat steamed ribs.
6. *졸면* 안돼요.   You'd better not doze off.
7. *쫄면* 먹자.   Let's eat *jjolmyeon* (noodles).
8. 같이 *가자*.   Let's go together.
9. 이건 *가짜*야.   This is fake.
10. *공짜*로 얻었어요.   I got it for free.
11. 차를 *팔지* 그래?   Why don't you sell the car?
12. *팔찌*가 예뻐요.   The bracelet is pretty.

Exercise 5
Fill in the blank with the syllable that you hear.

작 / 짝

1. 단___이에요.   Those two are an inseparable pair.
2. ___심삼일이에요.   My resolution is good for three days.

점 / 쩜

3. 어___ 그렇게 잘 해?   Wow, how do you do it so well?
4. 아___ 먹었어.   I had brunch.

졸/쫄

5. ___바지 입어.   Put on the leggings.
6. 언제 ___업해요?   When do you graduate?

즘/쯤

7. 요___ 바쁘세요?   Are you busy these days?
8. 언제___ 오세요?   About when are you coming?

Section C-16: ㅈ, ㅊ, & ㅉ
Section C-16.1: Basic pronunciation

Exercise 1
Listen and repeat.

1. 자   차   짜
2. 져   쳐   쪄
3. 족   촉   쪽
4. 잔   찬   짠
5. 짐   침   찜
6. 절절   철철   쩔쩔
7. 가자   가차   가짜
8. 지르지   치르지   찌르지

Exercise 2
Circle the contrast that you hear.

1. [ㅈㅊ   ㅊㅉ   ㅊㅊ   ]
2. [ㅈㅊ   ㅉㅊ   ㅉㅈ   ]
3. [ㅈㅊ   ㅊㅉ   ㅊㅈ   ]
4. [ㅈㅊ   ㅊㅉ   ㅊㅈ   ]
5. [ㅈㅊ   ㅉㅊ   ㅊㅈ   ]
6. [ㅈㅉ   ㅊㅉ   ㅉㅉ   ]
7. [ㅈㅊ   ㅊㅉ   ㅊㅈ   ]

Exercise 3
Circle the item in parentheses that you hear.

1. (자, 차, 짜) 드세요.   Please have some tea.
2. (자, 차) 있으세요?   Do you have a ruler?
3. 바닷물이 (차, 짜)요.   The seawater is salty.
4. (잔, 짠)돈 있으세요?   Do you have change?
5. (찬, 짠)물 한 잔 주세요.   Give me a glass of cold water, please.
6. (짐, 찜)이 오래 걸려요.   It takes a long time to steam food.
7. (짐, 침) 넘어 가요.   My mouth is watering.
8. (짐, 침) 싸야지요.   I'd better pack the luggage.
9. 피아노를 (져, 쳐)요.   I play the piano.
10. 옥수수를 (져, 쪄)요.   I'm steaming corn.
11. (질, 칠)이 안 좋아요.   The quality is not good.
12. (질, 칠)을 조심하세요.   Watch out for the wet paint.
13. 몇 (촉, 쪽)이에요?   How many watts is it [the bulb]?
14. (밤잠, 밤참)이 꿀맛이야.   The night-time snack is scrumptious.
15. (잠, 짬)이 안 나요.   There's no time to spare.

Exercise 4
Listen and repeat. You will first hear just the part in italics and then the entire sentence.

1. *차* 드세요.   Please have some tea.
2. *자*, 드세요.   Please, go ahead and eat.
3. 계획을 *짜요*.   I'm making a plan.
4. *잔*돈 있으세요?   Do you have change?
5. *찬*물 한 잔 주세요.   Give me a glass of cold water, please.
6. *짠* 건 못 먹어요.   I can't eat salty things.
7   군*침*이 도는데요.   Wow, my mouth is watering.
8. *짐*을 부치세요.   Please check in the luggage/send the package by mail.
9. 소금 좀 *쳐요*.   Sprinkle some salt.
10. 살 *쪄요*.   You're going to gain weight.

11. 왜 소리 질러요?   Why are you screaming?
12. 양심에 찔려요?   Do you have a guilty conscience?

Exercise 5
Fill in the blank with the syllable that you hear.

재 / 채 / 째

1. 재___기가 나요.   I am sneezing.
2. 눈치 ___요.   They are going to sense it.
3. 세___딸이에요.   She's the third daughter.

저 / 처 / 쩌

4. 어___면 못 와요.   I may not be able to come.
5. 어___구니가 없어.   It's preposterous.

장 / 창 / 짱

6. 동___이에요.   He's my fellow alumnus.
7. 배___이 두둑해요.   He has a lot of guts.
8. 정___을 하세요.   Please dress formally.

족 / 촉 / 쪽

9. 어느___이에요?   Which side is it?
10. ___감이 좋은데요.   Wow, the texture is good.

Section C-16.2: ㅈ & ㅊ in front of a consonant
or at the end of a word

Exercise 1
Listen and repeat. Notice that ㅈ and ㅊ sound different at the beginning of a word, but that they are both pronounced as an unreleased ㄷ sound at the end of a word.

1. 자   차   beginning of a word   (ㅈ ≠ ㅊ)
    낮   낯   end of a word   (ㅈ = ㅊ) —> ㄷ

2.　지　　치　　beginning of a word　(ス ≠ ㅊ)

　　빚　　빛　　end of a word　　　(ス = ㅊ) —> ㄷ

Exercise 2

Listen and repeat. Notice that ㅈ and ㅊ are both pronounced as if they were ㄷ at the end of a word or in front of a consonant, but that their pronunciations differ from each other in front of a suffix that begins with a vowel.

end of a word　(ス = ㅊ) —> ㄷ

1.　빚　　　빛

2.　빚 안 져　빛 안 나

in front of a consonant　(ス = ㅊ) —> ㄷ

3.　빚장이　　빛깔

in front of a suffix that begins with a vowel　(ス ≠ ㅊ)

4.　빚이　　　빛이

Exercise 3

Circle the italicized syllable that sounds different.

1.　a. *꽃*가루가 날려요.　　　Pollen is flying around.

　　b. *꽃*이 예뻐요.　　　　　The flower is pretty.

　　c. 꽃*꽃*이 배워요.　　　　I'm learning flower arrangement.

2.　a. *빛*이 안 나요.　　　　　It doesn't shine.

　　b. *빛*깔이 고와요.　　　　The color is pretty.

　　c. *빚*까지 졌어요.　　　　I even got into debt.

3.　a. 사람이 *몇* 안 돼.　　　There aren't many people.

　　b. 친구 *몇*이 와?　　　　How many friends are coming?

　　c. *몇*월 며칠이야?　　　　What month and what day is it?

4.　a. *낯*이 설어요.　　　　　It looks unfamiliar.

　　b. *낮*잠 자요.　　　　　　I'm taking a nap.

　　c. *낯* 뜨거워요.　　　　　My face is burning with shame.

Exercise 4
Fill in the blank with the syllable that you hear.

빗 / 빛

1.   송편을 ___어요.   We are making *songpyeon* (rice cake).
2.   달___이 밝아요.   The moonlight is bright.

낮 / 낯

3.   ___을 붉혀요.   His face is red with anger/shame.
4.   밤___이 없어요.   It's day in and day out.

Section C-17: ㅅ & ㅆ

Section C-17.1: Basic and 'sh'-like pronunciation

Exercise 1
Listen and repeat. Notice that ㅅ and ㅆ have a 'sh'-like pronunciation when they come before ㅣ or a 'y' diphthong.

1.   소   시
2.   싸   씨
3.   술   실
4.   서   셔

Exercise 2
Circle the italicized syllable in which the consonant ㅅ or ㅆ sounds different.

1.   삼   심   솜
2.   사와   샤워   쉬워
3.   맛은   맛있어   마셔
4.   도시   가수   교실
5.   씨름   싸움   씨앗

Exercise 3
Listen and repeat.

1.   사   싸
2.   서   써
3.   시   씨
4.   속   쏙
5.   살   쌀
6.   상   쌍
7.   시름   씨름
8.   수다   쑤다
9.   설어   썰어
10. 가서   갔어

Exercise 4
Circle the number corresponding to the word that sounds different.

1.   [1   2   3   ]
2.   [1   2   3   ]
3.   [1   2   3   ]
4.   [1   2   3   ]
5.   [1   2   3   ]
6.   [1   2   3   ]
7.   [1   2   3   ]

Exercise 5
Circle the item in parentheses that you hear.

1.   책을 (사, 싸)요.   Buy a book.
2.   컴퓨터를 (사, 싸)요.   Wrap the computer.
3.   (시, 씨)를 빼요.   Take out the seeds.
4.   (시, 씨)를 써요.   I write poems.
5.   (살, 쌀)이 탔어요.   My skin got tanned.
6.   (살, 쌀)이 떨어졌어요.   The rice ran out.
7.   (살, 쌀)이 좀 빠졌어요.   I've lost some weight.

8. 차가 (서, 써)요.   The tea is bitter.
9. 들러리 (섰어, 썼어)요.   I played second fiddle. (slang)
10. (삼, 쌈) 먹어요.   I'm eating the lettuce wrap.
11. 떡 (설어, 썰어)요.   I'm slicing the rice cake.
12. 비 (와서, 왔어)요.   It rained.
13. 피곤(해서, 했어)요.   Because I am/was tired.
14. (아파서, 아팠어)요.   Because I am/was sick.
15. 재미(있어서, 있었어)요.   It was fun.

Exercise 6
Listen and repeat. You will first hear just the part in italics and then the entire sentence.

1. 옷이 *싸*요.   Clothes are cheap.
2. 옷을 *사*요.   Buy clothes.
3. *씨가* 없네요.   Wow, there are no seeds.
4. *도시가* 커요.   The city is big.
5. 너무 *속이* 상해요.   I'm so upset.
6. 마음에 *쏙* 들어요.   It's to my complete satisfaction.
7. 새로 *샀어*요.   I bought a new one [to replace the old one].
8. 포장지에 *쌌어*요.   I wrapped it in wrapping paper.
9. 날씨가 *쌀쌀해*요.   The weather is chilly.
10. *살살* 만져요.   Touch it gently.
11. 왜 안 *왔어*요?   Why didn't you come?
12. 비가 *와서*요.   Because it is raining/rained.

Exercise 7
Fill in the blank with the syllable that you hear.

서 / 써

1. 벌___ 구월이에요.   It's already September.
2. 줄 ___야죠.   We'd better stand in line.

시 / 씨

3.   영화가 시___해요.   The movie is dull.

4.   솜___가 좋으시네요.   Wow, you're skillful.

수 / 쑤

5.   죽을 ___었어요.   I made gruel./I messed it up.

6.   ___다쟁이예요.   She's a blabbermouth.

7.   온몸이 ___셔요.   I'm aching all over.

신 / 씬

8.   날___해졌어요.   You've become slender.

9.   정___ 없어요.   I'm out of my mind.

10. 이게 훨___ 커요.   This is far bigger.

Section C-17.2: ㅅ & ㅆ in front of a consonant
or at the end of a word

Exercise 1
Listen and repeat. Notice that ㅅ and ㅆ sound different at the beginning of
a word, but that they are both pronounced as an unreleased ㄷ sound in
front of a consonant.

1.   사   싸   beginning of a word   (ㅅ ≠ ㅆ)

      잇다   있다   in front of a consonant (ㅅ = ㅆ) —> ㄷ

Exercise 2
Listen and repeat. Notice that ㅅ and ㅆ are pronounced as ㄷ at the end of
a word or in front of a consonant but retain their usual pronunciation in
front of a suffix that begins with a vowel.

   end of a word   (ㅅ = ㅆ) —> ㄷ

1.   옷   (ㅆ does not occur in this position)

2.   옷 없어   (ㅆ does not occur in this position)

in front of a consonant   (ㅅ = ㅆ) —> ㄷ

3.   옷감   있고

in front of a suffix that begins with a vowel   (ㅅ ≠ ㅆ)

4.   옷에   있어

Exercise 3
Circle the italicized syllable that sounds different.

1.   a. 맛있어?   Is it tasty?
      b. 맛없어.   It's tasteless.
      c. 맛이 없어.   It's tasteless.

2.   a. 멋있어요?   Is it nice?
      b. 멋없어요.   It's not nice.
      c. 멋 안 나요.   It doesn't look nice.

3.   a. 옷 있어요?   Do you have clothes?
      b. 옷 없어요.   I don't have clothes.
      c. 옷을 사요.   Buy clothes.

4.   a. 줄을 잇지요.   Let's connect the strings.
      b. 줄 있지요?   There's a string, isn't there?
      c. 줄 있어요.   There's a string.

5.   a. 집에 있다 왔어.   I came here from home.
      b. 줄 잇다 왔어.   I was connecting the strings before I got here.
      c. 재미 있어?   Is it fun?

Exercise 4
Fill in the blank with the syllable that you hear.

갓 / 갔

1.   ___을 썼어요.   He's wearing a traditional bamboo hat.
2.   ___을 거예요.   I bet he went.

Section C-18: ㅎ

Section C-18.1: Basic pronunciation

Exercise 1
Listen and repeat. Notice the difference between syllables that begin with a vowel and those that begin with ㅎ.

1. 와   화
2. 영   형
3. 악기   학기
4. 유지   휴지

Exercise 2
Circle the item in parentheses that you hear.

1. (악기, 학기)가 끝났어요.   The semester is over.
2. 손이 (얼었어, 헐었어)요.   My hands are frozen.
3. (양수, 향수) 냄새가 나요.   You smell of perfume.
4. (유지, 휴지) 있으세요?   Do you have tissue?
5. (영, 형)이 몇이에요?   How many brothers do you have?

Section C-18.2: ㄷ, ㅌ, ㅈ, ㅊ, ㅅ, & ㅆ in front of a consonant or at the end of a word

These consonants are all pronounced as unreleased ㄷ in front of a consonant or at the end of a word. But their pronunciations differ from each other in front of a suffix that begins with a vowel.

Exercise 1
Circle the one that sounds different.

1. 낫   낮   날   낯
2. 갖다   간다   갔다   같다
3. 이고   잇고   있고   잊고
4. 낫지   낮지   났지   남지

Exercise 2
Circle the italicized syllable that sounds different.

1. a. 똑같지 않아?   Aren't they the same?
   b. 똑같다.   They're the same.
   c. 똑같애.   They're the same.

2. a. 시간 있어요?   Do you have time?
   b. 시간 있지요?   You have time, don't you?
   c. 잊지 마세요.   Please don't forget.

3. a. 이게 낫지?   This is better, isn't it?
   b. 화 났지?   You're angry, aren't you?
   c. 화 났어?   Are you angry?

4. a. 빚 없어요.   I have no debt.
   b. 빛 안 나요.   It doesn't shine.
   c. 빛이 안 나요.   It doesn't shine.

Exercise 3
Indicate whether the italicized items sound the same (S) or different (D).

1. 똑같지?   [S   D]   They're the same, aren't they?
   못 갔지?   You couldn't go, could you?

2. 낯 안 가려요.   [S   D]   He [the baby] takes to strangers.
   낯이 뜨거워요.   My face is burning with shame.

3. 시간 있지?   [S   D]   You have time, don't you?
   시간 잊지 마.   Don't forget the time.

4. 빚 없어요.   [S   D]   I have no debt.
   빗 없어요.   I don't have a comb.

Exercise 4
Listen and repeat. You will first hear just the part in italics and then the entire sentence.

1. *빗* 있어요?   Do you have a comb?
2. *빗이* 없어요?   You don't have a comb?
3. *빛* 안 나요.   It doesn't shine.
4. *빛이* 안 나요.   It doesn't shine.
5. *잊지* 마세요.   Please don't forget.
6. *잊어버렸어요.*   I forgot.
7. *똑같죠?*   They're the same, aren't they?
8. *못 갔죠?*   You couldn't go, could you?

Exercise 5
Fill in the blank with the syllable that you hear.

났 / 낮 / 낯

1. ___이 짧아요.   Daytime is short.
2. ___이 뜨거워요.   My face is burning with shame.
3. 떠 ___어요.   They left.

빗 / 빚 / 빛

4. ___이 안 나요.   It doesn't shine.
5. 머리 ___어요.   I'm combing my hair.
6. ___을 졌어요.   I fell into debt.

Section C-19: ㅁ, ㄴ, & ㅇ

Exercise 1
Listen and repeat.

1. 그물   금물
2. 몸에   몸매
3. 시는   신는

4.   많아   만나
5.   부어   붕어

Exercise 2
Circle the number corresponding to the word that sounds different.

1.   [1   2   3   ]
2.   [1   2   3   ]
3.   [1   2   3   ]
4.   [1   2   3   ]
5.   [1   2   3   ]

Exercise 3
Circle the item in parentheses that you hear.

1. (잠 안, 잠만) 자요.	I'm doing nothing but sleeping.
2. (잠 안, 잠만) 자요?	Are you not going to sleep?
3. (자만, 잠만)이 뭐예요?	What's *jaman* (conceit)?
4. (그물, 금물)이에요.	It's a fish net.
5. (그물, 금물)이 뭐예요?	What's *geummul* (forbidden thing)?
6. (몸에, 몸매) 딱 맞아요.	It fits perfectly on my body.
7. (몸에, 몸매)는 좋아요.	As far as her figure goes, it's nice.
8. 신발 (신은, 신는) 사람?	The person who is putting shoes on?
9. 신발 (신은, 신는) 사람?	The person who is wearing shoes?
10. (신은, 신는) 운동화가 편해.	As for shoes, sneakers are comfortable.
11. 친구 (많아, 만나)요.	I have many friends.
12. 친구 (많아, 만나)요.	I'm meeting a friend.
13. 고기 (타네, 탄 내).	Oh, the meat is burning.
14. (저 나무, 전나무)요?	That tree?
15. 물에 (부어, 붕어) 보세요.	Look at the fish in the water.

Exercise 4

Listen and repeat. You will first hear just the part in italics and then the entire sentence.

1.	*잠만* 자요.	I'm doing nothing but sleeping.
2.	잠 *안* 자요?	Are you not going to sleep?
3.	*자만하지* 마세요.	Please don't be conceited.
4.	몸에 *딱* 맞아요.	It fits perfectly on my body.
5.	*몸매가* 좋아요.	Your figure is nice.
6.	친구를 *만나요.*	I'm meeting a friend.
7.	친구가 *많아요.*	I have many friends.
8.	*탄* 내가 나요.	There's a burning smell.
9.	고기가 *타네요.*	Oh, the meat is burning.
10.	*금붕어* 보세요.	Look at the goldfish.

Exercise 5

Fill in the blank with the syllable that you hear.

아 / 나

1.	친구가 많___요.	I have many friends.
2.	친구를 만___요.	I'm meeting a friend.

이 / 미

3.	인공 감___료예요.	It's an artificial sweetener.
4.	감___ 익었어요.	The persimmon has ripened.

Section C-20: ㄹ

Exercise 1

Listen and repeat.

	end of a word	between vowels	double ㄹ
1.	달	다리	달리
2.	불	불어	불러
3.	길	길어	길러

Exercise 2
Listen and repeat. Notice how English loan words that begin with 'l' or 'r' are pronounced in Korean.

1. 레스토랑   restaurant   렌즈   lens
2. 리본   ribbon   립스틱   lipstick

Exercise 3
Listen and repeat.

1. 벌레를 버렸어요.   I threw out the bug.
2. 이름은 비밀이에요.   As for the name, it's a secret.
3. 로숀을 발라요.   Apply the lotion.

Exercise 4
Circle the number corresponding to the word that sounds different.

1. [1   2   3]
2. [1   2   3]
3. [1   2   3]
4. [1   2   3]
5. [1   2   3]

Exercise 5
Circle the item in parentheses that you hear.

1. 잠깐 (들어, 들러)요.   Stop by for a moment.
2. 노래 (들어, 들려)요.   I'm listening to songs.
3. 잘 (들어, 들려)요.   I can hear it well.
4. 시계가 (느려, 늘려)요.   The clock is slow.
5. 얼음 (어려, 얼려)요.   I'm making ice.
6. 배 (불어, 불러)요.   I'm full.
7. 바람 (불어, 불러)요.   It's windy.
8. 네 말이 (옳았, 올랐)어.   What you said was correct.
9. 값이 (옳았, 올랐)어.   The price has gone up.
10. 오래 (걸었어, 걸렸어)요.   I walked for a long time.

11. 오래 (걸었어, 걸렸어)요. It took a long time.

12. 몹시 (놀았어, 놀랐어)요. I was terribly surprised.

13. 너무 (놀았어, 놀랐어)요. I played too much (instead of working).

14. 머리 (자랐어, 잘랐어)요. I got a haircut.

15. 머리 (자랐어, 잘랐어)요. My hair has grown.

Exercise 6
Listen and repeat. You will first hear just the part in italics and then the entire sentence.

1. 노래 *들어요*.   I'm listening to songs.

2. 잘 *들려요*.   I can hear it well.

3. 바람이 *불어요*.   It's windy.

4. 배가 *불러요*.   I'm full.

5. 생선이 *비려요*.   The fish has a fishy taste.

6. 책을 *빌려요*.   I'm borrowing books.

7. 오래 *걸었어요*.   I walked for a long time.

8. 오래 *걸렸어요*.   It took a long time.

9. 신나게 *놀았어요*.   I played excitedly.

10. 깜짝 *놀랐어요*.   I was startled.

Exercise 7
Fill in the blank with the syllable that you hear.

이 / 리

1. 빨___ 오세요.   Get here quickly, please.

2. 발___ 아파요.   My feet hurt.

을 / 를

3. 음악 들___거야?   Are you going to listen to music?

4. 집에 들___거야?   Are you going to stop by your house?

5. 벌레___ 잡았어.   I caught a bug.

6. 월요일___ 싫어해.   He hates Mondays.

버 / 벌

7. 그냥 ___려요.   Just throw it away.
8. 크게 ___려요.   Open it up wide.

Exercise 8

Listen and repeat. Even if you can't follow along, notice the many instances of ㄹ in this traditional folk song.

아리랑 아리랑 아라리요   Arirang, Arirang, Arariyo
아리랑 고개를 넘어간다   You're going over the Arirang hill.
나를 버리고 가시는 님은   My beloved, who is going, abandoning me,
십리도 못 가서 발병 난다   You will get sore feet before going even ten *li*.

Practice: Adjustments

Section A-1: Consonant relinking

Exercise 1
Listen and repeat. Notice how the final consonant of the italicized syllable is pronounced at the beginning of the next syllable because it is followed by a vowel sound.

1. 음   음악
2. 일   일요일
3. 집   집에
4. 맛   맛이
5. 있-   있어
6. 먹-   먹어
7. 밖   밖에

Exercise 2
Listen and repeat. Notice that only one consonant at the end of the first syllable is pronounced when the next syllable begins with a consonant. When the next syllable begins with a vowel, though, both consonants are pronounced—the second one as part of the following syllable.

1. 앉고   앉아
2. 젊지   젊은
3. 읽고   읽어
4. 값진   값이

Exercise 3
Listen and repeat. Notice that consonant relinking occurs across a word boundary when the two words are pronounced as part of the same group.

1. 안 왔어요.   He didn't come.
2. 곧 올 거예요.   She'll be here soon.
3. 꼭 오세요.   Please be sure to come.

4.   꽃 안 사요.*   I'm not buying flowers.

5.   학교앞 어디?*   Where in front of the school?

*ㅊ is pronounced as if it were ㄷ, and ㅍ is pronounced as if it were ㅂ; see sections C-16.2 and C-4.2, respectively.

Exercise 4
Circle the item in parentheses that you hear.

1.   (백권, 백원)입니다.   It's 100 *won*.

2.   전화 (받다, 받아) 왔어.   I was answering the phone before getting here.

3.   (국기, 국이) 달아요.   The soup is sweet.

4.   (국기, 국이) 달아요.   Put up the national flag.

5.   애기 (안은, 안는) 사람?   The person who is holding a baby in his arms?

6.   바지 (입은, 입는) 사람?   The person who is wearing pants?

7.   책 값을 (물어, 물러)요.   Get a refund for the book.

8.   5분 (걸었어, 걸렸어)요.   I walked five minutes.

Exercise 5
Indicate whether the italicized items sound the same (S) or different (D).

1.   일이 많아요.   [S   D]   There's a lot of work.
     이리 오세요.   Come this way, please.

2.   국이 싱거워요.   [S   D]   The soup is not salty enough.
     국기 달아요.   Put up the national flag.

3.   목이 말라요.   [S   D]   I'm thirsty.
     모기 물어요.   The mosquitos are biting.

4.   전화 받아요.   [S   D]   Answer the phone.
     바다에 가요.   Let's go to the beach.

5.   아기를 안아요.   [S   D]   Hold the baby in your arms.
     소리가 안 나요.   The sound isn't coming out.

6.   인연이 많아요.   [S   D]   There's a predestined link between us.
     이년이 됐어요.   It's been two years.

Exercise 6
Draw a line to indicate consonant relinking in the following sentences.
For example, 월 요일 이에요.

1.	월요일이에요.	It's Monday.
2.	일이 힘들어요.	The work is tough.
3.	밥은 없어요?	Is there no cooked rice?
4.	책을 읽어요.	Read a book.
5.	낮이 짧아요.	Daytime is short.
6.	한국어 녹음을 해요.	We are recording Korean.
7.	곧 올게요.	I'll come back soon.
8.	화장실 어디예요?	Where's the restroom?
9.	빗 어디 있어요?	Where's the comb?

Exercise 7
Listen and repeat. You will first hear the item in italics and then the entire sentence.

1.	*월요일*이에요.	It's Monday.
2.	*책을 읽어*요.	Read a book.
3.	*천오백원*이에요.	It's 1,500 *won*.
4.	*낮이 짧아*요.	Daytime is short.
5.	*병원에 입원*해요.	I'm being hospitalized.
6.	*곧 올게*요.	I'll come back soon.
7.	*빗 있어*요?	Do you have a comb?

Exercise 8
Fill in the blank with the syllable that you hear.

리 / 이

1.	물___ 안 나와요.	No water comes out [of the tap].
2.	무___하지 마세요.	Don't overdo it, please.

버 / 벗

3.	코트 ___어요.	Take off the coat.
4.	___섯이에요.	It's a mushroom.

늘 / 을

5. 오___ 월요일이에요.   Today is Monday.

6. 등산___ 했어요.   I did hiking.

막 / 악

7. 음___ 들어요?   Are you listening to music?

8. 자___ 있어요?   Does it have a subtitle?

Section A-2: Voicing

Exercise 1
Listen and repeat. Notice that ㅂ, ㄷ, ㄱ, and ㅈ are fully voiced in the second and third columns, where they occur between two voiced sounds (vowels and ㅁ, ㄴ, ㅇ, or ㄹ).

1. 발   이발   금발
2. 다   크다   간다
3. 구   야구   농구
4. 정   다정   인정

Exercise 2
Listen and repeat. Notice the joint effects of consonant relinking and voicing.

1. 입   입원   입양
2. 받-   받아   받은
3. 국   국어   국에

Exercise 3
Listen and repeat. Notice that voicing occurs across a word boundary when two words are pronounced as a group.

1. 꼭 오세요.   Please be sure to come.

2. 좋은 자리예요.   It's a good seat/position.

3. 곧 올 거예요.   He'll be here soon.

4. 맛 없어요.*   It's not tasty.

*The ㅅ in 맛 is pronounced as if it were ㄷ; see section C-17.2.

Exercise 4
Circle the italicized item in which the indicated consonant sounds different.

1. ㅂ
    a. 갈*비*요.   It's *galbi*.
    b. *비*싸요?   Is it expensive?
    c. 안 *비*싸요.   It's not expensive.

2. ㅂ
    a. 금*발*이에요?   Is she blonde?
    b. 가*발*이에요.   It's a wig.
    c. *발*소리에요.   It's the sound of a footstep.

3. ㄱ
    a. 농*구*해요?   Do you play basketball?
    b. 야*구*해요.   We play baseball.
    c. *구*월이에요.   It's September.

4. ㄱ
    a. 안 *가*요?   Aren't you going?
    b. *가*수예요.   He's a singer.
    c. 약*아*요.   She's clever.

5. ㄷ
    a. 옻 올라요.*   You may get a poison oak rash.
    b. 돌떡이에요.   It's rice cake for her [the baby's] birthday.
    c. 두돌이에요.   He [the baby] is two years old.

6. ㄷ
    a. *더* 추워요.   It's colder.
    b. 옷 없어요.*   I don't have clothes.
    c. 얻었어요.   I got it for free.

7. ㅈ
    a. 지갑이요?   Wallet?
    b. 휴지요.   Tissue.
    c. 편지 써요.   I'm writing a letter.

*The ㅊ in 옻 and the ㅅ in 옷 are pronounced as if they were ㄷ; see sections C-16.2 and C-17.2.

Section A-3: Diphthong reduction

Exercise 1

Listen and repeat. Notice how the diphthong undergoes glide reduction in non-initial positions in casually pronounced sentences.

ㅘ —> ㅏ
1. 과   사과 먹어요.   Eat the apple.
2. 봐   여기 봐요.   Look here.

ㅖ —> ㅔ
3. 계   안녕히 계세요.   Goodbye.
4. 예   얼마예요?   How much is it?

ㅝ —> ㅓ
5. 뭐   뭐 하세요?   What are you doing?
6. 워   고마워요.   Thank you.

ㅚ —> ㅔ
7. 쇠   열쇠 있어요?   Do you have the key?
8. 죄   죄송합니다.   I'm sorry.

ㅟ —> ㅣ
9. 뒤   뒤에 있어.   It's in the back.
10. 쉬   좀 쉬어.   Get some rest.

ㅙ —> ㅔ
11. 괜   괜찮아.   It's okay.
12. 돼   안 돼.   No way./It doesn't work.

Exercise 2

Listen carefully, paying special attention to the italicized items. Notice that the italicized words in each pair sound almost the same due to glide reduction.

1. 사과 먹어.　　　　　Eat the apple.
   케익을 사가.　　　　Buy and take the cake.

2. 영하 5도예요.　　　It's five degrees below zero.
   영화 봐요.　　　　　I'm watching a movie.

3. 계란 과자　　　　　Egg cookie
   이제 가자.　　　　　Let's go now.

4. 멉니까?　　　　　　Is it far?
   뭡니까?　　　　　　What's that?

5. 우리집 열쇠예요.　　It's our house key.
   우리가 열세예요.　　We are inferior in strength/numbers.

6. 포도가 시어요.　　　The grapes are sour.
   잠깐 쉬어요.　　　　Get some rest.

Exercise 3

Indicate whether the vowel in the italicized syllable is fully pronounced (FP) or reduced (R).

1. 예술적이에요.　　　[FP　R] It's artistic.
2. 어디예요?　　　　　[FP　R] Where is it?
3. 빨리 와요.　　　　　[FP　R] Get here quickly.
4. 도와 주세요.　　　　[FP　R] Please help.
5. 전화왔어요.　　　　[FP　R] There is/was a phone call.
6. 분위기가 좋아요.　　[FP　R] The ambience is good.
7. 위치가 좋아요.　　　[FP　R] The location is good.
8. 사귄지 오래 됐어.　[FP　R] It's been a while since we started going out.
9. 워낙 잘해요.　　　　[FP　R] He does it so well.
10. 뭘 샀어요?　　　　[FP　R] What did you buy?/Did you buy something? *
11. 고마워요.　　　　　[FP　R] Thank you.

12. 외국에 살아요.   [FP   R] I live abroad.
13. 기회가 없어요.   [FP   R] There's no opportunity.
14. 회사 다녀요.   [FP   R] I work for a company.
15. 괜찮습니다.   [FP   R] It's okay.

*The female speaker gives the sentence the first interpretation, and the male speaker gives it the second interpretation; see section P-2.

Section A-4: Contraction

Exercise 1
Listen and repeat.

1.	나의	내	저의	제
2.	나는	난	이것은	이건
3.	저를	절	이것을	이걸
4.	그것이	그게	이것이	이게
5.	무엇	뭐	-것이에요	-거예요
6.	마음	맘	다음주	담주
7.	이 아이	애	이야기	얘기
8.	그런데	근데	그러면	그럼
9.	보아요	봐요	지어요	져요
10.	주어요	줘요	되어요	돼요
11.	가지오	가죠	아니오	아뇨
12.	재미있다	재밌다	의사입니다	의삽니다

Exercise 2
Underline the contracted items in the following sentences. (Some items have a contracted pronunciation only, while others have both a contracted pronunciation and a contracted spelling.)

1. 사과를 좋아하세요?   Do you like apples?
2. 과자는 안 먹어요.   I don't eat cookies.
3. 이게 뭡니까?   What's this?

4.	우리는 못 가요.	We can't go.
5.	그럼, 다음주에 오세요.	Then, please come next week.
6.	걔 이름이 뭐야?	What's the kid's name?
7.	그런데, 왜 안 간 거야?	By the way, why was it that you didn't go?
8.	얘기 좀 합시다.	Let's have a talk.
9.	매운 건 못 먹어요.	I can't eat spicy things.
10.	영화를 참 재미있게 봤어.	I watched the movie with great enjoyment.
11.	뭘 그렇게 봐요?	What are you looking at like that?
12.	어쩌면 못 가요.	I may not be able to go.
13.	그 사람 가수입니다.	That person is a singer.
14.	그게 어디 있어요?	Where's that?
15.	날씨가 추워졌어요.	The weather has gotten cold.

Section A-5: Pronunciation of ㅗ as if it were ㅜ

Exercise 1

Listen and repeat. Notice that 고, 도, and 로 can be pronounced [구], [두], and [루], respectively, in colloquial speech.

고/구

1.	친구하고 갔어요.	I went with a friend.
2.	그리고 뭐 했어?	And what did you do?
3.	보고 싶어요.	I want to see it.
4.	뭐라고요?	What did you say?

도/두

5.	빵도 사.	Buy bread too.
6.	나도 갈게.	I'll go too.

로/루

7.	어디로 가요?	Where are you going?
8.	비행기로 가?	Are you going by plane?
9.	바로 갈게.	I'll go right away.

Exercise 2
Circle the italicized syllable in which the pronunciation of the vowel cannot change (from ㅗ to ㅜ).

1.   a. 뭐 먹고 싶다.   I want to eat something.
     b. 자고 나서 할게.   I'll do it after sleeping.
     c. 냉장고에 있어.   It's in the refrigerator.

2.   a. 고장났어.   It's out of order.
     b. 간다고?   Did you say you are going?
     c. 나하고 가.   Go with me.

3.   a. 지도 있어요?   Is there a map?
     b. 배도 샀어요?   Did you buy pears too?
     c. 하도 졸라서요.   Because he begged me for it so much.

4.   a. 과로하지 마세요.   Please don't overexert yourself.
     b. 따로 왔어요.   We came separately.
     c. 연필로 쓰세요.   Please write in pencil.

5.   a. 바로 갈게.   I'll go right away.
     b. 위로 올라 와.   Come on up.
     c. 위로해 주자.   Let's console him.

Section A-6: ㅎ reduction

Exercise 1
Listen and repeat. Notice that ㅎ is reduced between voiced sounds (vowels and ㅁ, ㄴ, ㅇ, or ㄹ) and can even be deleted. The degree of reduction is in proportion to the speed of one's speech—the faster one speaks, the more weakly ㅎ is pronounced.

1.   화   소화   영화
2.   해   새해   올해
3.   학   대학   방학

4. 혼   이혼   결혼
5. 합니다   감사합니다 죄송합니다

Exercise 2
Listen and repeat. Notice that deletion of ㅎ is obligatory in the following items, where it occurs at the end of a verb root.

1. 좋아   놓아
2. 많아   괜찮아
3. 싫어   끓어

Exercise 3
Listen and repeat. Notice that the items in each pair have about the same pronunciation due to the effects of ㅎ reduction and of processes such as consonant relinking (examples 2–4) and diphthong reduction (example 4).

1. 고향이요?   Hometown?
    고양이요?   Cat?

2. 올해 가요.   I'm going this year.
    오래 가요.   It lasts long.

3. 환해요.   It's bright.
    화내요.   He's getting angry.

4. 만화요?   Cartoon?
    많아요?   Is it a lot?

Exercise 4
Indicate whether the ㅎ in the italicized syllable is fully pronounced (FP) or reduced (R).

1. 오후에 봐요.   [FP   R] See you in the afternoon.
2. 후추 좀 주세요.   [FP   R] Please give me the black pepper.
3. 방학이에요.   [FP   R] It's school vacation.
4. 지하에 있어요.   [FP   R] It's in the basement.
5. 통화중이에요.   [FP   R] The line's busy./I'm on the phone.
6. 화가 나요.   [FP   R] I'm getting angry.

7. 영화 봤어요?/.   [FP   R] Did you see a movie?/I saw a movie.*
8. 인형을 샀어요.   [FP   R] I bought a doll.
9. 형이에요.   [FP   R] He's my older brother.
10. 공항에 가요.   [FP   R] I'm going to the airport.

*The female speaker gives the sentence the first interpretation, and the male speaker gives it the second interpretation.

Exercise 5
Listen and repeat. You will first hear the item in italics and then the entire sentence.

1. *죄송합니다.*   I'm sorry.
2. *오후에* 봐요.   See you in the afternoon.
3. *은행에* 가요.   I'm going to the bank.
4. *여행* 가요.   I'm going on a trip.
5. *비행기로* 가요?   Are you going by plane?
6. *전화가* 안 돼요.   The phone doesn't work.
7. *통화중*이에요.   The line's busy./I'm on the phone.
8. *기숙사* 생활이 어때?   How is dorm life?

Section A-7: Aspiration

Exercise 1
Listen and repeat. Notice that ㅎ combines with a preceding consonant to produce an aspirated consonant in the second and third columns.

1. 해   착해   답답해
2. 화   국화   삽화
3. 회   학회   집회
4. 학   약학   입학

5. 합   백합   집합
6. -하고   옷하고*   꽃하고*

*Because of full closure, ㅅ and ㅊ correspond to the ㄷ sound before undergoing aspiration; see sections C-17.2 and C-16.2, respectively.

Exercise 2

Listen and repeat. Notice that ㅎ combines with a following consonant to produce aspiration in the second and third columns.

1. 좋아   좋다   좋게
2. 많아   많다   많지
3. 괜찮아   괜찮다   괜찮지

Exercise 3

Listen and repeat. Notice that aspiration takes place even across a word boundary when the two words are pronounced in the same group. (The chances of this happening increase in proportion to the speed of one's speech.)

1. 꼭 할게요.   I'll do it for sure.
2. 딱 하루면 돼요.   Just one day will do.
3. 잘 못 합니다.   I don't do it well.
4. 백합 향기가 좋아요.   The lily smell is nice.

Exercise 4

Indicate whether the ㅎ in the italicized syllable is reduced (R) or causes aspiration (A).

1. 그렇지 않아요. [R   A] It's not that way.
2. 날씨가 좋지요? [R   A] The weather is nice, isn't it?
3. 올해 입학해요. [R   A] I enter school this year.
4. 어떡 해요?   [R   A] What should I do?
5. 국화가 예뻐요. [R   A] The mums are beautiful.
6. 만화 봐요.   [R   A] I'm reading/watching a cartoon.
7. 백화점에 가요. [R   A] I'm going to the department store.
8. 급히 나갔어요. [R   A] He went out hurriedly.

9.   특히 어려워요.   [R   A] It's especially difficult.
10. 천천히 가요.   [R   A] Let's go slowly.
11. 잘 해요?   [R   A] Do you do it well?
12. 잘 못 해요.   [R   A] I don't do it well.

Exercise 5

Indicate the sound that results from aspiration in the italicized portion of the following sentences.

1.   깨끗해요.*   [ㅌ]   It's clean.
2.   축하합니다.   [   ]   Congratulations.
3.   날씨 좋지요?   [   ]   The weather is nice, isn't it?
4.   별로 안 좋다.   [   ]   It's not really good.
5.   백화점에 가요.   [   ]   I'm going to the department store.
6.   늦지 않도록 해.   [   ]   Try not to be late.
7.   잘 부탁합니다.   [   ]   I'd appreciate your favorable consideration.
8.   딱 하루면 돼.   [   ]   Just one day will do.
9.   옷 한 벌 사요.*   [   ]   Buy a suit of clothes.
10. 답답해요.   [   ]   It's stifling./I feel suffocated.

*ㅅ in 끗 and 옷 is pronounced as if it were ㄷ; see section C-17.2.

Exercise 6

Listen and repeat. You will first hear the item in italics and then the entire sentence.

1.   집이 깨끗해요.   The house is clean.
2.   축하합니다.   Congratulations.
3.   날씨가 좋죠?   The weather is nice, isn't it?
4.   백화점에 갑니다.   I'm going to the department store.
5.   늦지 않도록 해.   Try not to be late.
6.   잘 부탁합니다.   I'd appreciate your favorable consideration.
7.   백합 향기가 좋아요.   The lily smell is nice.
8.   꽃하고 케익 하나 사.   Buy flowers and a cake.
9.   대답해요.   Answer, please.
10. 그렇지 않아요?   Isn't it that way?

Exercise 7
Fill in the blank with the syllable that you hear.

과 / 화

1. 국___를 좋아해요.   I like mums.
2. 사___가 맛있어요.   The apple is delicious.
3. 벽___가 멋있어요.   The mural is beautiful.

이 / 히

4. 특___ 잘 해요.   She does it especially well.
5. 참 특___해요.   It's really unique.
6. 극___ 드물어요.   It's extremely rare.

Section A-8: Pronunciation of ㄴ as if it were ㄹ

Exercise 1
Listen and repeat.

ㄴ —> ㄹ after ㄹ

1.   나   찰나
2.   내   실내
3.   남   월남
4.   날   칼날
5.   넷   열넷

ㄴ —> ㄹ before ㄹ

6.   신   신라
7.   연   연락
8.   원   원래
9.   진   진로
10. 편   편리

Exercise 2

Listen and repeat. Notice that ㄴ is pronounced as if it were ㄹ because of the ㄹ at the end of the preceding word.

1.	잘 나와요.	It comes out well.
2.	매일 늦어요.	I'm late every day.
3.	큰일 났어요.	There's been a disaster.
4.	설탕을 넣으세요.	Please put in sugar.

Exercise 3

Listen carefully, paying special attention to the italicized items. These items have the same pronunciation, because ㄴ is pronounced as if it were ㄹ.

1.	일년 지났어요.	One year has passed.
	일련 번호예요.	It's the serial number.
2.	논리는 분명해요.	As for the logic, it's clear.
	놀리는 거예요?	Are you making fun of me, or what?
3.	둘로 분리해요.	Divide it in two.
	우리가 불리해요.	We're at a disadvantage.
4.	불변의 진리죠.	It's definitely an eternal truth.
	좀 질리죠?	It's a bit tiring to take, isn't it?

Exercise 4

Circle the italicized syllable that sounds different.

1.	a. 일요일날 만나.	Let's meet on Sunday.
	b. 무슨 날이야?	What kind of day is it?
	c. 설날이야.	It's New Year's Day.
2.	a. 일년 됐어요.	It's been one year.
	b. 십년 됐어요.	It's been ten years.
	c. 훈련 받아요.	We are getting training.
3.	a. 불 났어요.	Fire broke out.
	b. 큰일 났어요.	There's been a disaster.
	c. 언제 났어요?	When did it happen?

4. a. 항상 늦어.   I'm always late.

    b. 매일 늦어.   I'm late everyday.

    c. 한발 늦었어.   We've fallen a step behind.

5. a. 연극을 봤어요.   I saw a play.

    b. 연락 하세요.   Please get in touch.

    c. 연령제한이 있습니까?   Is there an age limit?

6. a. 원래 그래요.   It was originally like that.

    b. 월례 행사예요.   It's a monthly event.

    c. 원칙대로 해요.   Let's do it according to the rules.

Exercise 5
Listen and repeat. You will first hear the item in italics and then the entire sentence.

1. 일요일날 만나요.   Let's meet on Sunday.

2. 제 생일날 오세요.   Please come by on my birthday.

3. 일년 됐습니다.   It's been one year.

4. 팔팔년생이에요.   I was born in 1988.

5. 열네명이에요.   There are fourteen people.

6. 잘났어, 정말.   You're great, really! (sarcastic)

7. 곤란해요.   There's a problem with doing that.

8. 연락 주세요.   Please get in touch.

9. 정말 편리해요.   It's really convenient.

10. 물난리가 났어요.   There's been a disastrous flood.

Section A-9: Nasalization
Section A-9.1: Before ㅁ or ㄴ

Exercise 1
Listen and repeat. Notice that a consonant is nasalized when there is an immediately following nasal ㅁ or ㄴ.

1. 십   십만
2. 합   합니다
3. 앞   앞머리
4. 몇   몇 명
5. 여섯   여섯명
6. 꽃   꽃무늬
7. 겉   겉모습
8. 백   백만
9. 한국   한국말
10. 창밖   창밖만

Exercise 2
Listen and repeat. Notice that nasalization occurs across a word boundary when the two words are pronounced together in the same group.

1. 답 맞아요?   Is the answer correct?
2. 밥 먹어요.   I'm eating rice/a meal.
3. 못 나가요.   I can't go out.
4. 못 마셔요.   I can't drink.
5. 목 말라요.   I'm thirsty.
6. 깜짝 놀랐어요.   I got startled.

Exercise 3
Circle the item in parentheses that you hear.

1. (닭, 답) 맞아요?   Is the answer correct?
2. (닭, 답) 맞아요?   Chicken, right?
3. (방, 밥) 많죠?   There's plenty of rice, isn't there?

4. (꽃, 꼭) 남아요.   There are flowers left over.

5. (꽃, 꼭) 나와요.   Be sure to come out.

6. (목, 못) 나와요.   I can't come out.

7. (자나, 잤나) 봐요.   It looks like I slept.

8. (우나, 웃나) 봐요.   It looks like she's crying.

9. (천운, 첫눈)이에요.   It's the first snow.

Exercise 4
Circle the italicized syllable that sounds different.

1.   신년   십년   심장

2.   감이다   갑시다   갑니다

3.   많네   맞네   막내

4.   콩장   콘칩   콧노래

5.   작년   장난   잔디

6.   박수   방수   박물관

7.   궁전   국어   한국말

Exercise 5
Circle the pronunciation of the italicized item.

1.   겁나요.   [건   검] I'm scared.

2.   지금 없는데요.   [언   엄] Oh, he's not here right now.

3.   도서관에 갑니다.   [간   감] I'm going to the library.

4.   몇 명이에요?   [면   명] How many people are there?

5.   화났나 봐요.   [난   낭] It looks like he's gotten angry.

6.   어디 갔는데요./?   [간   감] Oh, he's gone somewhere./Where
                                         did he go?*

7.   못 만났어요.   [몬   몽] I couldn't meet her.

8.   국물 좀 주세요.   [굼   궁] Please give me some broth.

9.   저녁 먹어요.   [넌   녕] I'm eating dinner.

10. 백만원 벌었어요.   [뱀   뱅] I made one million *won*.

11. 딱 맞아요.   [땀   땅] It fits perfectly.

12. 창밖만 바라 봐요. [밤   방] He's just looking out the window.

*The female speaker gives the sentence the first interpretation and the male speaker gives it the second interpretation.

Exercise 6

Listen and repeat. You will first hear the item in italics and then the entire sentence.

1. *밥 먹어요.*   I'm eating rice/a meal.

2. 집에 *없는데요.*   Oh, he's not home.

3. 비 *왔네요.*   Oh, it rained.

4. *끝났나 봐요.*   It looks like it's finished.

5. 어디 *갔는데요.*   Oh, he's gone somewhere.

6. *꽃무늬로 해요.*   Let's do it in a floral design.

7. *못 말려요.*   We can't stop him.

8. *저녁 먹어요.*   I'm eating dinner.

9. *한국말이* 재미있어요.   The Korean language is fun.

10. *생각 났어요.*   It has come to mind.

Exercise 7

Fill in the blank with the syllable that you hear.

명 / 몇

1. ___ 명이에요?   How many people are there?

2. ___ 마리예요?   How many animals are there?

목 / 못

3. 술 ___ 마셔요.   I can't drink alcohol.

4. ___ 말라요.   I'm thirsty.

5. 정말 ___ 말려요.   We really can't stop him.

나 / 났

6.   다 끝___는 데요.   Oh, it's all finished.

7.   겁___나 봐요.   It looks like he's getting scared.

8.   화___나 봐요.   It looks like she's gotten angry.

한 / 합

9.   공부___니다.   I'm studying.

10. 언제 ___니까?   When are you doing it?

Section A-9.2: Nasalization of ㄹ after a consonant other than ㄴ or ㄹ

Exercise 1
Listen and repeat.

ㄹ is pronounced as if it were ㄴ after ㅁ.

1.   여려   염려

2.   그리   금리

ㄹ is pronounced as if it were ㄴ after ㅇ.

3.   조류   종류

4.   저력   정력

ㄹ is pronounced as if it were ㄴ after ㄱ, which is then nasalized.

5.   서류   석류

6.   라면   떡라면

ㄹ is pronounced as if it were ㄴ after ㅂ, which is then nasalized.

7.   서리   섭리

8.   다래   답례

Exercise 2
Listen and repeat. Notice that nasalization can take place across a word boundary.

1. 꼭 *라*면만 먹어요.   He makes sure to eat only ramen.
2. 지금 *라*디오 들어요.   I'm listening to the radio right now.
3. 고급 *레*스토랑이에요.   It's an upscale restaurant.

Exercise 3
Circle the item in parentheses that you hear.

1. (금리, 금이) 비싸죠?   Gold is expensive, isn't it?
2. (실리, 심리)학을 공부합니다.   I study psychology.
3. (공룡, 공용)이에요.   It's a dinosaur.
4. (정류장, 정유장)이에요.   It's a (bus) stop.
5. 자연 (섭이, 섭리)예요.   It's the law of nature.
6. (석류, 석유)가 비싸요.   Petroleum is expensive.

Exercise 4
Circle the italicized syllable that sounds different.

1. a. 악*랄*해요.   He's cruel.
    b. 발*랄*해요.   She's lively.
    c. 신*랄*해요.   It's incisive.

2. a. 방*랑*자예요.   He's a wanderer.
    b. 신*랑*이에요.   He's the bridegroom.
    c. 명*랑*해요.   She's cheerful.

3. a. 실*력*이 좋아요.   He has great ability.
    b. 경*력*이 많아요.   She has a lot of (work) experience.
    c. 박*력*있어요.   You have energy/forcefulness.

4. a. 입장*료*가 얼마예요?   How much is the admission fee?
    b. 진*료*중이십니다.   She's in the middle of treating a patient.
    c. 음*료*수 마셔요.   Please drink the beverage.

5.   a. 합*리*적이에요.   It's reasonable.
     b. 궁*리*중이에요.   I'm mulling it over.
     c. 불변의 진*리*예요.   It's an eternal truth.

6.   a. 군중 심*리*예요.   It's mass psychology.
     b. 4킬로가 십*리*예요.   Four kilometers is ten *li*.
     c. 실*리*적이에요.   It's practical.

Exercise 5
Circle the pronunciation of the italicized item.

1.   *금리*가 내렸어요.   [그미   금니] The interest rate has gone down.
2.   *염려* 마세요.   [여며   염녀] Please don't worry.
3.   *공립*학교예요.   [공닙   공입] It's a public school.
4.   *공룡*을 봤어요.   [고농   공농] I saw a dinosaur.
5.   *석류*가 시어요.   [성뉴   성유] The pomegranate is sour.
6.   *식량*이 부족해요.   [싱냥   싱양] They are short of provisions.
7.   *확률*이 적어요.   [환뉼   황뉼] There's little probability.
8.   주식이 *폭락*했어요.   [퐁낙   퐁악] The stock price plummeted.
9.   *압력*이 세요.   [아멱   암녁] The pressure is high.
10. 자연 *섭리*예요.   [섭니   섭리] It's the law of nature.

Exercise 6
Listen and repeat. You will first hear the item in italics and then the entire sentence.

1.   *염려* 마세요.   Please don't worry.
2.   *음료수* 한 잔 주세요.   Please give me a glass of beverage.
3.   성격이 *명랑*해요.   Her personality is cheerful.
4.   *등록금*이 비싸요.   The tuition is expensive.
5.   방 *정리* 좀 해라.   Get the room organized, please.
6.   *확률*이 높아요.   There's a high probability.
7.   *국립*대학이에요.   It's a national university.
8.   *박력*이 부족해요.   He lacks energy/forcefulness.

9.	합리적이에요.	It's reasonable.
10.	독립기념일이에요.	It's Independence Day.

Exercise 7
Fill in the blank with the syllable that you hear.

리 / 이

1.	무슨 심___예요?	What kind of psychology is that?
2.	연필 심___에요?	Is it a pencil lead?

략 / 약

3.	이하 생___이에요.	The rest is omitted.
4.	이거 생___이에요?	Is this herbal medicine?

률 / 율

5.	확___이 높아요.	There's a high probability.
6.	환___이 높아요.	The exchange rate is high.

력 / 역

7.	협___해 주세요.	Please cooperate for me.
8.	비밀번호를 입___하십시오.	Please put in the secret number/password.

Section A-10: Pronunciation of ㄴ as if it were ㅁ or ㅇ

Exercise 1
Listen and repeat. Each item is pronounced twice—first with no change in the pronunciation of the ㄴ and then with a change.

ㄴ —> ㅁ before ㅁ, ㅂ, ㅍ, or ㅃ

1. 신문
2. 몇 명*
3. 한번
4. 건포도
5. 찐빵

*The ㅊ in 몇 is nasalized to ㄴ before being modified to ㅁ; see section A-9.1.

ㄴ —> ㅇ before ㄱ, ㅋ, or ㄲ

6.   한국
7.   빈칸
8.   단꿈

Exercise 2

Listen and repeat. Notice that the change in the pronunciation of ㄴ is triggered by the consonant from the next word.

1.	못 마셔요.*	I can't drink it.
2.	좋은 물건이에요.	It's a good product.
3.	안 가요.	I'm not going.

*The ㅅ in 못 is nasalized to ㄴ before being modified to ㅁ; see section A-9.1.

Exercise 3

Circle the two italicized syllables that can sound the same.

1.	a.	방 말이에요?	Are you talking about the room?
	b.	반말로 하세요.	Please speak to me, using the informal style.
	c.	밤말은 쥐가 들어요.	Walls have ears.
2.	a.	신문 봐요.	I'm looking at the newspaper.
	b.	심문하는 거예요?	Are you interrogating me, or what?
	c.	신 식문이에요.	It's a new-style door.
3.	a.	겁이 많아.	I'm timid.
	b.	겁만 많아.	I'm nothing but timid.
	c.	겉만 번지르르해.	It's showy just on the outside.
4.	a.	꽃무늬야.	It's a floral design.
	b.	꼼짝 못 하겠어.	I can't budge.
	c.	꽁무니 빼지 마.	Don't turn tail.
5.	a.	한국에 가요.	I'm going to Korea.
	b.	함구하세요.	Please keep it to yourself.
	c.	항구예요.	It's a port.

Exercise 4
Fill in the blank with the syllable that you hear.

간/감

1. ___격이 넓어요.   The space in between is wide.
2. ___격이 커요.   I am deeply moved.

단/담

3. ___배 끊었어요.   I've quit smoking.
4. ___골이에요.   I'm a regular customer./It's my regular place.

인/임

5. ___기가 좋아요.   It's popular.
6. ___기가 끝났어요.   My term is over.

명/몇

7. 학생이 ___명이에요?   How many students are there?
8. 개가 ___마리예요?   How many dogs are there?

Section A-11: Addition of ㄴ

Exercise 1
Listen and repeat. Notice the presence of an added ㄴ sound in the italicized syllable.

1. 요   담요
2. 일   웬일
3. 육   만육천
4. 여름   한여름

Addition of ㄴ, which triggers nasalization of the preceding consonant

5. 육   십육
6. 일   막일
7. 잎   꽃잎
8. 약   염색약
9. 연필   색연필

Addition of ㄴ, which is pronounced as if it were ㄹ; see section A-8.

10. 약   물약
11. 역   전철역
12. 육   칠육
13. 잎   풀잎

Exercise 2
Listen and repeat. Notice the added ㄴ sound at the beginning of the second word and its effect on neighboring sounds. In example 5, the ㄴ is pronounced as if it were ㄹ.

1.	문 열어 주세요.	Please open the door for me.
2.	무슨 요일이에요?	What day of the week is it?
3.	집 열쇠예요.	It's the house key.
4.	옷 입어요.	I'm putting on clothes.
5.	볼 일이 있어요.	I have something to see to.

Exercise 3
Listen and repeat. Notice how the addition of a ㄴ sound can affect the pronunciation of the number six in these examples.

1.   16
2.   160
3.   1,600
4.   16,000
5.   362-2636
6.   916-0666

Exercise 4
Circle the italicized syllable that sounds different.

1.	a. 무슨 약이야?	What kind of medicine is that?
	b. 염색 약이야?	Is it hair dye?
	c. 감기 약이야.	It's cold medicine.

2. a. 십육   16
    b. 육십   60
    c. 백육   106

3. a. 막일 해요?   Do you do manual labor?
    b. 부엌일 해요.   I do kitchen work.
    c. 하루종일 해요?   Do you do it all day long?

4. a. 꽃잎이에요?   Is it a petal?
    b. 풀잎이에요?   Is it a grass leaf?
    c. 깻잎이에요.   It's a sesame leaf.

5. a. 한 일이 없어요.   There's not a thing that I've done.
    b. 무슨 일이에요?   What's up?/What's the matter?
    c. 별일 아니에요.   It's nothing in particular.

6. a. 절약하자.   Let's be frugal.
    b. 물약이야?   Is it liquid medicine?
    c. 알약이야.   It's tablet medicine.

Exercise 5
Circle the pronunciation of the italicized item.

1. *웬* 일이에요?   [웨닐   웬닐]   What's up?
2. *십육*년 됐습니다.   [심늉   십늉]   It's been 16 years.
3. *꽃잎이* 시들어요.   [꼬디피   꼰니피]   The petals are
                                                        withering.
4. *나뭇잎이* 떨어져요.   [나문니피   나묻디피]   The tree's leaves are
                                                        falling.
5. *색연필* 있어요?   [새견필   생년필]   Do you have a color
                                                        pencil?
6. *앞일이* 걱정돼요.   [아빌   암닐]   I am worried about
                                                        future matters.
7. *뒷일도* 걱정돼요.   [뒤딜   뒨닐]   I'm also worried about
                                                        the aftermath.
8. *옛일이* 생각나네요.   [예딜   옌닐]   Oh, that brings back
                                                        old memories.

9. 전철역이 어딨어요? [전처력   전철력] Where's the subway
                                                station?
10. 362-36*76*이에요.   [치륙   칠륙]   It's 362-3676.

Exercise 6
Listen and repeat. You will first hear the item in italics and then the entire
sentence.

1. *웬* 일이에요?   What's up?
2. *십육*년 됐어요.   It's been sixteen years.
3. *앞일*이 걱정돼요.   I'm worried about future matters.
4. *깻잎*이 맛있어요.   The sesame leaves are tasty.
5. *낯익은* 얼굴이에요.   It's a familiar face.
6. *색연*필로 쓰세요.   Please write with a color pencil.
7. 옷 *입어*요.   I'm putting on clothes.
8. *외국여*행하고 싶다.   I want to travel abroad.
9. 별 일 *없으*시죠?   Everything's okay with you, isn't it?
10. 전철역으로 가죠.   Let's go to the subway station.

Section A-12: Tensing
Section A-12.1: Predictable tensing

Exercise 1
Listen and repeat. Notice that the first consonant in the italicized syllable is
tensed due to the preceding consonant.

1. 가부   갑*부*
2. 가다   갇*다*
3. 마시다   맛있*다*
4. 백원   백*권*
5. 수속   숲*속*
6. 찾아   찾*자*

Exercise 2
Listen and repeat. Notice that tensing takes place across a word boundary
when the two words are pronounced in the same group.

1.	못 봤어요.	I couldn't see it.
2.	옷 다려요.	I'm ironing clothes.
3.	책 갖고 오세요.	Please come with the book.
4.	약 사러 가요.	I'm going in order to buy medicine.
5.	계속 자요.	He's continuing to sleep.

Exercise 3
Circle the italicized syllable that contains a tensed consonant.

1.	가보	겁보	울보
2.	맛있다	마시다	마신다
3.	한권	두권	다섯권
4.	수속	금속	약속
5.	큰집	꽃집	새집

Exercise 4
Circle the one that sounds different.

1.	자비	잡비	잡이
2.	악기	악이	아기
3.	차자	찾자	찾아
4.	마시다	맛이다	맛있다

Exercise 5
Circle the item in parentheses that you hear.

1.	(자비, 잡비)가 들어요.	It requires miscellaneous expenses.
2.	(가다, 갔다) 왔어요.	I went and have come back.
3.	커피 (맛이다, 맛있다).	Oh, it's a coffee taste.
4.	(백권, 백원) 있어요.	I have 100 won.
5.	(악기, 아기)를 좋아해요.	I like musical instruments.
6.	(이 속, 잇속)에 있어요.	It's inside this.
7.	공 좀 (차자, 찾자).	Let's look for the ball, please.

Exercise 6
Listen and repeat. You will first hear the item in italics and then the entire sentence.

1. *대단한* 갑부예요.   He's a big millionaire.
2. *못* 봤어요.   I couldn't see it.
3. 커피 *맛있다!*   The coffee tastes good!
4. *학기가* 끝났어요.   The semester's over.
5. *옷 값이* 비싸요.   Clothing prices are high.
6. *약속* 있어요.   I have an appointment/engagement.
7. *잊지* 마세요.   Please don't forget.

Section A-12.2: Non-predictable tensing

Exercise 1
Listen and repeat. Notice that the consonant in the italicized syllable is tensed after a vowel or after ㅁ, ㄴ, ㅇ, ㄹ. Tensing in these contexts is irregular and cannot be predicted by a general rule; it must be learned on a case-by-case basis in accordance with the intended meaning.

1.	큰 *방*	big room	안*방*	main room
2.	콩*밥*	rice with beans in it	김*밥*	Korean-style sushi
3.	정*돈*	proper arrangement	용*돈*	spending money
4.	상*대*	opponent; match	절*대*	absolute(ly)
5.	사*과*	apple	치*과*	dentist's office
6.	공*격*	attack; offense	성*격*	personality
7.	중*성*	neutrality	가능*성*	possibility
8.	상*점*	store	장*점*	good points; advantage

Exercise 2
Indicate whether the consonant in the italicized syllable is tensed (T) or not (N).

1.   a. 열 *병*을 앓아요.   [T   N] He's sick with fever/a feverish
                                              desire.
      b. 열 *병*을 마셨어요. [T   N] I drank ten bottles.

2.   a. 책 판 돈이에요.   [T   N] It's money from selling books.
     b. 노름 판돈이에요.   [T   N] It's gambling money.

3.   a. 장기가 많아요.   [T   N] You have many special talents.
     b. 장기가 취미예요.   [T   N] Chess is my hobby.

4.   a. 정말 신기해요.   [T   N] It's really amazing.
     b. 구두 신기 싫어요. [T   N] I hate to wear dress shoes.

5.   a. 개가 물기때문에요. [T   N] Because the dog bites.
     b. 물기 닦으세요.   [T   N] Wipe off the moisture.

6.   a. 한자도 배웁니다.   [T   N] We learn Chinese characters too.
     b. 한 자도 몰라요.   [T   N] I don't know a word of it.

7.   a. 이점이 많아요.   [T   N] There are a lot of advantages.
     b. 이 점이 좋아요.   [T   N] This point is good.

Exercise 3
Circle the italicized syllable whose initial consonant is *not* tensed.

1.   a. 한번 해 보세요.   Please give it a try.
     b. 다섯번 했어요.   I did it five times.
     c. 열번 했어요.   I did it ten times.

2.   a. 수법이 다양해요.   You have various tricks.
     b. 그런 법이 어디 있어요?   Where is such a rule written?
     c. 비법이 있어요.   There's a secret method.

3.   a. 정돈 좀 해라.   Get organized, please.
     b. 용돈 좀 주세요.   Please give me some spending money.
     c. 푼돈을 아껴야지.   You'd better be penny wise.

4.   a. 절대 안 됩니다.   It's absolutely impossible.
     b. 상대가 안 됩니다.   He's no match for me.
     c. 장대비가 와요.   It's raining cats and dogs.

5. a. 누구거예요?   Whose is it?

    b. 이거요?   This thing?

    c. 제거예요.   It's mine.

6. a. 조건이 있어요.   There's a proviso.

    b. 용건이 뭐예요?   What's your point?

    c. 물건이 비싸요.   Things are expensive.

7. a. 중성이에요.   He's sexless./It's chemically neutral.

    b. 가능성이 커요.   There's a big possibility.

    c. 참을성이 없어요.   I have no patience.

8. a. 서점에서 샀어요.   I bought it at a bookstore.

    b. 문제점이 많아요.   There are a lot of problems.

    c. 장점도 많아요.   There are a lot of good points too.

Exercise 4

Listen and repeat. You will first hear the item in italics and then the entire sentence.

1.   문법이 어려워요.   Grammar is difficult.

2.   맥주 열 병 마셔요.   I drink ten bottles of beer.

3.   용돈 좀 주세요.   Please give me some spending money.

4.   절대 안 돼.   It's absolutely impossible.

5.   물가가 올랐어요.   The price of things has gone up.

6.   창가에 앉읍시다.   Let's sit by the window.

7.   치과에 가요.   I'm going to the dentist's.

8.   인기가 많아요.   He's popular.

9.   성격이 좋아요.   Her personality is good.

10. 단점도 있어요.   There are shortcomings too.

Exercise 5
Listen and repeat. Notice that the first consonant in the italicized syllable
(always word-initial except for -밖에) can be tensed.

1.	버스 *탈*까요?	Shall we take the bus?
2.	하루*밖*에 없어요.	There's no more than one day.
3.	이 *닦*아요.	I'm brushing my teeth.
4.	*달*러가 비싸요.	A dollar is expensive.
5.	*가*시에 찔렸어요.	I got pricked by a thorn.
6.	*거*꾸로 입었어요.	You've put it [clothes] on backwards.
7.	힘이 *세*요.	He has a lot of strength.
8.	너무 *작*아요.	It's too small.
9.	머리 *잘*랐어요.	I got a haircut.
10.	방이 *좁*아요.	The room is small.

Exercise 6
Indicate whether the first consonant in the italicized syllable can be tensed
(T) or not (N).

1.	차 *닦*아요.	[T N]	I'm washing the car.
2.	고집이 *세*요.	[T N]	He's stubborn.
3.	돈을 *세*요.	[T N]	I'm counting the money.
4.	숫자가 *줄*었어요.	[T N]	The number got reduced.
5.	고기에 *질*렸어요.	[T N]	I'm sick of meat.
6.	머리 *잘*랐어요?	[T N]	Did you get a haircut?
7.	*밖*에 안 나가요?	[T N]	Aren't you going outside?
8.	하나*밖*에 없어요.	[T N]	There's no more than one.

Section A-13:   ㅅ insertion

Exercise 1
Listen and repeat.

Inserted ㅅ causes tensing of the following consonant.

1.	해	sun	빛	light	햇빛	sunlight
2.	비	rain	길	road	빗길	rainy road
3.	코	nose	수염	facial hair	콧수염	beard
4.	차	tea	집	house	찻집	teahouse

Inserted ㅅ becomes nasalized due to the following consonant.

5.	예	past	날	day	옛날	old days
6.	코	nose	물	water	콧물	runny nose
7.	코	nose	노래	song	콧노래	hummed tune

Inserted ㅅ becomes nasalized due to the added ㄴ sound.

8.	예	past	일	matter	옛일	thing of the past
9.	깨	sesame	잎	leaf	깻잎	sesame leaf
10.	나무	tree	잎	leaf	나뭇잎	tree leaf

Exercise 2
Circle the italicized syllable that sounds different.

1. a. 바*닷*가에 가요.   We are going to the beach.
    b. 바*닷*물은 짜죠.   Sea water is salty, of course.
    c. 바*닷*바람이 세요.   The ocean wind is strong.

2. a. *콧*대가 높아요.   She's stuck-up.
    b. *콧*노래를 흥얼거려요.   She's humming a tune.
    c. *콧*물이 나요.   My nose is running.

3. a. 옛*날* 생각이 나요.   It brings back memories of the old days.
    b. 옛*일*이 생각나요.   It brings back old memories.
    c. 옛*친*구가 그리워요.   I miss old friends.

Exercise 3
Fill in the blank with the syllable that you hear.

다 / 닷

1. 바___가 보여요.   I can see the ocean.

2. 바___가에 가요.   Go to the beach.

비 / 빗

3. ___물이에요.   It's rainwater.

4. 준___물 잊지 마세요.   Please don't forget things to take.

Section A-14: Modifications to the pronunciation of ㄷ and ㅌ

Exercise 1
Listen and repeat. Notice that the ㄷ or ㅌ in the italicized syllable is pronounced as if it were ㅈ or ㅊ, respectively, because it occurs before an 이 suffix.

1. 마디   맏이
2. 굳어   굳이
3. 걷어   걷혀*
4. 닫아   닫혀*
5. 같은   같이
6. 붙어   붙여

*Examples 3 and 4 also show the effects of aspiration; see section A-7.

Exercise 2
Indicate whether the italicized items sound the same (S) or different (D).

1. 한 *마디* 하세요.   [S   D] Please say a word.
    제가 *맏이*예요.   I'm the eldest.

2. 빵이 *굳어*요.   [S   D] The bread is getting hard.
    날씨가 *궂어*요.   The weather is lousy.

3. 우표 *붙여요*.   [S   D] I'm putting the stamp on.
    편지 *부쳐요*.   I'm mailing a letter.

4. 안 *붙어요*.   [S   D] It doesn't stick.
    돌*부처*예요.   It's a stone Buddha.

5. *같이* 가요.   [S   D] Let's go together.
    *가치*가 없어요.   It's of no value.

6. 문이 안 *닫혀요*.   [S   D] The door doesn't close.
    조심해요. *다쳐요*.   Watch out. You'll get hurt.

7. 구름이 *걷혔어*.   [S   D] The cloud lifted.
    하와이를 *거쳤어*.   I passed through Hawaii.

Exercise 3
Circle the pronunciation of the final consonant in the italicized syllable.

1. 결심이 *굳었어요*.   [ㄷ   ㅈ] My mind has been made up.
2. 결심을 *굳혔어요*.   [ㅌ   ㅊ] I strengthened my resolve.
3. *굳이* 올 필요 없어요. [ㄷ   ㅈ] There's no need to make any special
                                        effort to come.
4. 마음이 *곧아요*.   [ㄷ   ㅈ] He has an upright character.
5. *곧이* 안 들려요.   [ㄷ   ㅈ] It doesn't ring true.
6. *곧이* 곧대로예요.   [ㄷ   ㅈ] He's rigid and unbending.
7. *같이* 해요.   [ㅌ   ㅊ] Let's do it together.
8. 거의 *같아요*.   [ㅌ   ㅊ] They are almost the same.
9. 잘 안 *붙어요*.   [ㅌ   ㅊ] It doesn't stick well.
10 다시 *붙여* 봐요.   [ㅌ   ㅊ] Try sticking it on again.

Exercise 4
Listen and repeat. You will first hear the item in italics and then the entire
sentence.

1. 제가 *맏이*예요.   I'm the eldest.
2. *굳이* 사양하지 마세요.   Please don't decline so firmly.
3. *해돋이* 보러 가요.   We are going in order to see the sunrise.

4. *미닫이예요.*   It's a sliding door.
5. *같이 가요.*   Let's go together.
6. *우표 붙여야지요.*   You'd better put a stamp on.
7. *문이 안 닫혀요.*   The door doesn't close.
8. *답을 맞혔어요.*   I guessed the answer correctly.
9. *결심을 굳혔어요.*   I strengthened my resolve.
10. *구름이 걷혔어요.*   The cloud lifted.

Exercise 5
Fill in the blanks with the syllable that you hear.

부 / 붙

1. 우표를 ___여요.   Put a stamp on.
2. 편지를 ___쳐요.   Mail the letter.

였 / 혔

3. 답을 다 맞___어요.   You guessed all the answers correctly.
4. 문이 안 닫___어요.   The door didn't close.
5. 돈이 많이 안 걷___어요.   Not much money was collected.

Section A-15: Consonant weakening

Exercise 1
Listen and repeat.

ㅊ can be pronounced as if it were ㅅ.

1. 꽃이
2. 빛을

ㅌ, normally pronounced as if it were ㅊ in this context (section A-14), can be pronounced as if it were ㅅ.

3. 끝이
4. 숱이

ㅌ can be pronounced as if it were ㅊ or ㅅ.

5. 곁을

6. 끝을

ㅍ can be pronounced as if it were ㅂ.

7. 숲이

8. 무릎이

ㅋ can be pronounced as if it were ㄱ.

9. 부엌에

Exercise 2
Indicate whether the final consonant in the italicized syllable can be weakened (W) or not (N).

1. *앞*을 보세요.   [W   N]   Look ahead.
2. *무릎*이 아파요.   [W   N]   My knee hurts.
3. *옆*에 앉아요.   [W   N]   Sit beside me.
4. *빛*이 나요.   [W   N]   It shines.
5. 나이가 *몇*이에요?   [W   N]   What's his age?
6. *꽃*을 샀어요.   [W   N]   I bought flowers.
7. *숱*이 많아요.   [W   N]   I have thick hair.
8. *부엌*에 있어요.   [W   N]   It's in the kitchen.

Exercise 3
Circle the two italicized items that can sound the same.

1. a. 꽃*꽂이* 배워요.   I'm learning flower arrangement.
    b. *꽃이* 예뻐요.   The flowers are beautiful.
    c. *꼬시*지 마세요.   Don't tempt me, please.

2. a. *낮이* 뜨거워요.   The daytime is hot.
    b. *낯이* 뜨거워요.   My face is burning with shame.
    c. *낫이* 잘 들어요.   The scythe cuts well.

3. a. *숱이* 없어요.   I have thin hair.
    b. *숯이* 필요해요.   We need charcoal.
    c. *수지* 맞았어요.   I made a big profit.

Practice: Prosody

Section P-1: Pitch, loudness, and length

Exercise 1
Listen and repeat. Notice how all the syllables are pronounced with roughly equal loudness. You may hear a slightly higher pitch on the first syllable.

1. -국   country   2. -원   institute
    한국   Korea   병원   hospital
    선진국   advanced nation   미장원   hair salon
    대한민국   Republic of Korea   종합병원   general hospital
    개발도상국   developing country   외국어학원   foreign language
                                                            institute

Exercise 2
Listen and repeat. Notice that all the syllables are pronounced with roughly equal loudness and that the final syllable of each sentence is longer and more prominent than the others.

1. 합니다.   I'm doing it.
    감사합니다.   Thank you.
    대단히 감사합니다.   Thank you very much.

2. 왔어요.   I'm here.
    어젯밤에 왔어요.   I got here last night.
    지난 일요일에 왔어요.   I got here last Sunday.

3. 했어요.   I did it.
    공부했어요.   I studied.
    친구하고 공부했어요.   I studied with a friend.

Section P-2: Focus

Exercise 1
Underline the word in speaker B's response that is emphasized.

1. A: 다음주에 한국에 가요?   Are you going to Korea next week?
   B: 아뇨, 한국에서 누가 와요.   No, someone is coming from Korea.

2. A: 도서관에 책 빌리러 가요?   Are you going to the library to borrow
                                      books?
   B: 아뇨, 도서관에 일하러 가요.   No, I'm going to the library to work.

3. A: 보통 새벽에 공부하세요?   Do you usually study in the early
                                      morning?
   B: 아뇨, 저녁에 공부해요.   No, I study in the evening.

Exercise 2
Circle the syllable with the highest pitch in speaker B's response.

1. A: 학생 아니죠?   You aren't a student, are you?
   B: 학생이에요.   I am a student.
      [학   이   요]

2. A: 오늘 월요일인가?   Is today Monday, I wonder?
   B: 네, 월요일이에요.   Yes, it is Monday.
      [네   월   이]

3. A: 차가 노란색이었어요?   Was the car yellow?
   B: 네, 노란색이었어요.   Yes, it was yellow.
      [네   노   이]

4. A: 숙제했어?   Did you do the homework?
   B: 응, 숙제했어.   Yes, I did the homework.
      [응   숙   했]

Exercise 3

Based on the element that is emphasized by speaker A, pick the right response for speaker B (before hearing the answer on the CD).

1. A: 콜라 두 잔 시켰는데...   I ordered two glasses of cola...

   B₁: 사이다 아니었어요?   Wasn't it cider?

   B₂: 세 잔 아니었어요?   Wasn't it three glasses?

2. A: 콜라 두 잔 시켰는데...   I ordered two glasses of cola...

   B₁: 사이다 아니었어요?   Wasn't it cider?

   B₂: 세 잔 아니었어요?   Wasn't it three glasses?

3. A: 그거 은 시계예요?   Is that a silver watch?

   B₁: 팔찌예요.   It's a bracelet.

   B₂: 백금이에요.   It's white gold.

4. A: 그거 은 시계예요?   Is that a silver watch?

   B₁: 팔찌예요.   It's a bracelet.

   B₂: 백금이에요.   It's white gold.

5. A: 책상 위에 있어?   Is it on the desk?

   B₁: 아니, 책상 밑에.   No, under the desk.

   B₂: 아니, 식탁 위에.   No, on the dining table.

Exercise 4

Based on the element that is emphasized by speaker A, pick the right response for speaker B (before hearing the answer on the CD). Remember that the verb is focused in *yes-no* questions and that the question word is focused in *wh* questions.

1. A: 어디 가요?

   B₁: 학교요.   School.

   B₂: 네, 어디 좀 가요.   Yes, I'm going somewhere.

A: 어디 가요?

B₁: 학교요.   School.

B₂: 네, 어디 좀 가요.   Yes, I'm going somewhere.

2. A: 누가 와요?

B₁: 친구요.   A friend.

B₂: 네.   Yes.

A: 누가 와요?

B₁: 친구요.   A friend.

B₂: 네.   Yes.

3. A: 언제 봤어요?

B₁: 조금 아까요.   A little while ago.

B₂: 네, 봤어요.   Yes, I saw it.

A: 언제 봤어요?

B₁: 조금 아까요.   A little while ago.

B₂: 네, 봤어요.   Yes, I saw it.

4. A: 몇 번 봤어요?

B₁: 두 번이요.   Twice.

B₂: 네, 봤어요.   Yes, I saw it.

5. A: 뭐 해요?

B₁: 아무 것도 안 해요.   I'm not doing anything.

B₂: 네.   Yes.

(Because the translations for A's utterances give away the right answers, they have been placed in the answer guide.)

Section P-3: Intonation

Exercise 1

Listen and repeat. Pay special attention to the intonation that is associated with each sentence type.

Neutral statements—falling or flat intonation

1.	한국에 갑니다.	I'm going to Korea.
2.	한국말 잘 해요.	He speaks Korean fluently.

Yes-no questions—rising intonation

3.	한국에 갑니까?	Are you going to Korea?
4.	한국말 잘해요?	Do you speak Korean well?
5.	누가 와요?	Is someone coming?
6.	어디 가요?	Are you going somewhere?

Wh questions—rising or falling intonation

7.	얼마예요?	How much is it?
8.	몇 시예요?	What time is it?
9.	누가 와요?	Who's coming?
10.	어디 가요?	Where are you going?

Soft-sounding, nondemanding *wh* questions—rising intonation

11.	얼마죠?	How much is it?
12.	몇 시죠?	What time is it?

Commands—falling or prolonged rising intonation

13.	숙제 좀 해라.	Do some homework.
14.	꼭 와.	Be sure to come.
15.	전화하세요.	Please call.

Exercise 2

Draw a pitch arrow at the end of each sentence (to indicate the intonation for each speaker).

1.	비 와요?	Is it raining?
2.	비 안 와요.	It's not raining.
3.	조용히 좀 해라.	Be quiet, please.
4.	내일 오세요?	Are you coming tomorrow?

5.	내일 오세요.	Please come tomorrow.
6.	전화해요?	Are you making a phone call?
7.	전화해요.	Please call.
8.	지금 몇 시죠?	What time is it now?
9.	누가 와요.	Someone's coming.

Exercise 3
Using the intonation, fill in the missing punctuation.

1. 파티에 오세요
2. 파티에 오세요

3. 전화하세요
4. 전화하세요

5. 한국에 가 봤어요
6. 한국에 가 봤어요

7. 언제 오세요
8. 언제 오세요

(Because the translations for the practice sentences give away the right answers, they have been placed in the answer guide.)

Exercise 4
Based on the intonation (and which element is focused), circle the appropriate sentence type. (Y/N = *yes-no* question; Wh = *wh* question; S = statement; P = proposal)

1.	저 영화 몇 번 봤어	[Y/N	Wh	S]
2.	저 영화 몇 번 봤어	[Y/N	Wh	S]
3.	저 영화 몇 번 봤어	[Y/N	Wh	S]
4.	오늘 어디 가요	[Y/N	Wh	S/P]
5.	오늘 어디 가요	[Y/N	Wh	S/P]
6.	오늘 어디 가요	[Y/N	Wh	S/P]

7.	내일 누가 와요	[Y/N	Wh	S]
8.	내일 누가 와요	[Y/N	Wh	S]
9.	내일 누가 와요	[Y/N	Wh	S]

(Punctuation marks have been deliberately omitted here. Because the translations give away the right answers, they have been placed in the answer guide.)

Exercise 5

Draw a pitch arrow at the end of each sentence in the following dialogue.

A:	안녕하세요?	Hi, how are you?
	어디 가세요?	Are you going somewhere?
B:	네, 볼 일이 좀 있어서요.	Yes, because I have something to see to.
A:	어디 가시는데요?	Where are you going?
B:	학교에를 좀 가려구요.	I'm going to go to school.
A:	오늘 일요일인데...	Today is Sunday, though.
	누구 만나세요?	Are you meeting someone?
B:	네, 누구 좀 만나려고요.	Yes, I'm going to meet someone.
A:	누굴요?	Who?
B:	친구 좀 만나려고요.	I'm going to meet a friend.
	그럼, 저 먼저 가 볼게요.	Then, I'll get going first.
A:	네, 그럼 안녕히 가세요.	Yes, then, goodbye.
B:	네, 안녕히 가세요.	Okay, goodbye.
	또 뵈요.	See you again.

Section P-4: Intonation and the expression of emotion

Exercise 1

Listen and repeat. Pay special attention to how intonation is used to express emotion.

Exclamation/surprise—dramatic tone

1.	정말 맛있다!	It's really delicious!
2.	와, 멋있네요!	Wow, it looks fantastic!
3.	정말 잘 하는데요!	She does it really well!

Speaking boastfully among close friends—rising intonation

4.	나 여자/남자 친구 생겼다.	I've got a girl/boyfriend.
5.	나 다음주에 하와이 간다.	I'm going to Hawai'i next week.

Gentle suggestion—gently rising intonation

6.	저쪽으로 가시죠?	Why don't you go over to that side?
7.	좀 앉지?	Why don't you have a seat?

Regret—falling intonation

8.	좀 앉지.	I wish he'd sit down.
9.	파티에 갈걸.	I wish I'd gone to the party.

Strong conjecture—rising intonation

10.	파티에 갈걸.	I bet she's going to the party.
11.	아닐걸, 안 갈걸.	I bet she isn't; I don't think she's going.
12.	틀림없이 갈텐데.	I bet she is going for sure.

Exercise 2

Listen carefully to the intonation used by speaker A, and pick the right response for speaker B (before hearing the answer on the CD).

1. A: 그 사람도 같이 갈걸.

	B₁: 정말이요?	Really?
	B₂: 그러게요.	(I wish s/he had), right.

2. A: 그 사람도 같이 갈걸.

    B₁: 정말이요?   Really?

    B₂: 그러게요.   (I wish s/he had), right.

3. A: 좀 앉지

    B₁: 정말, 저 사람 때문에   Right; oh, I can't see because
        안 보이네.   of that person.

    B₂: 네, 잠깐 앉을게요.   Yes, I'll sit for a moment.

4. A: 좀 앉지

    B₁: 정말, 저 사람 때문에   Right; oh I can't see because
        안 보이네.   of that person.

    B₂: 네. 잠깐 앉을게요.   Yes, I'll sit for a moment.

(Punctuation marks in examples 3 and 4 have been deliberately omitted here. Because the translations for A's utterances give away the right answers, they have been placed in the answer guide.)

Exercise 3
Draw a pitch arrow at the end of each sentence in the following dialogue.

A: 안녕하세요?   Hi, how are you?
    날씨가 꽤 추운데요.   Oh, the weather's quite cold.

B: 네, 정말 추워요.   Yes, it's really cold.
    어, 눈온다! 밖에 눈 와요!   Wow, it's snowing! It's snowing outside!

A: 와, 정말 첫눈이네요!   Wow, it's really the first snow!
    그런데, 우리 뭐 시킬까요?   By the way, what shall we order?

B: 전 냉커피로 할게요.   I'll have an iced coffee.

A: 여기 냉커피 하나하고   Here, please give us one iced coffee
    인삼차 하나 주세요.   and one ginseng tea.

B: 아, 춥다!   Oh, it's cold!

    찬 걸 마시니까 더 춥네요.   Oh, I feel colder, drinking something cold.

A: 그렇죠?   That's right, isn't it?

    뜨거운 걸 시키시지.   You should have ordered something hot.

Exercise 4

Draw a pitch arrow at the end of each sentence in the following dialogue.

(Between two close friends)

A: 나 여자친구 생겼다!   I've got a girlfriend now!

B: 정말? 예뻐?   Really? Is she pretty?

A: 끝내 줘.   She's a knockout.

    얼마나 예쁜데.   You can't imagine how pretty she is.

B: 와, 부럽다! 나도 네   Wow, I envy you! Please introduce

    친구 하나 소개시켜 주라.   one of your friends to me too.

A: 말만 해.   Just let me know.

    어떤 타입을 좋아하는데?   What type of guy do you like?

B: 난 이해심 많은 남자가   For me, I find that an understanding

    좋더라.   guy is my type.

A: 그래? 내 여자친구는   Is that so? You know what, my

    이해심도 많다.   girlfriend is very understanding too.

B: 야, 자랑 좀 그만해. 근데,   Hey, stop the bragging. By the way,

    나 언제 소개시켜 줄 거야?   when are you going to introduce the
                                     guy to me?

A: 이리 오기로 돼 있어, 이미.   It's already been arranged for him to come

    한 한 시간이면 될걸.   here. I bet it'll be in about an hour.

B: 그래? 어, 옷 좀 예쁘게   Really? Oh, I should've come dressed a bit

    입고 나올 걸.   nicely. I wish you had told me that

    미리 얘기 좀 해 주지.   in advance.

Section P-5: Thought groups

Exercise 1
Listen and repeat. Pay special attention to the location of the pauses (and high pitch) and to their role in determining the meaning of the sentence.

1. 여기 서요.   Stop/stand here.
   여기서요.   Here.

2. 아, 까먹었어요.   Oh, I forgot.
   아까 먹었어요.   I ate a little while ago.

3. 너 도사니?   Are you an expert?
   너도 사니?   Are you also buying it?

4. 너밖에 안 가?   Is no one but you going?
   너 밖에 안 가?   Aren't you going outside?

5. 이따가 보자.   Let's see it in a little while.
   이따 가보자.   Let's go see it in a little while.

Exercise 2
Based on the location of the pause (and high pitch), pick the right meaning for each sentence.

1. 여기서요.   a. Stop/stand here.
                           b. Here.

2. 아까먹었어요.   a. Oh, I forgot.
                           b. I ate a little while ago.

3. 너도사니?   a. Are you an expert?
                           b. Are you also buying it?

4. 너밖에안가?   a. Is no one but you going?
                           b. Aren't you going outside?

5. 이따가보자.   a. Let's see it in a little while.
                           b. Let's go see it in a little while.

(The spaces between words have been deliberately omitted here.)

Exercise 3
Place a slash (/) at each pause in the following sentences.

1. 매운 음식은 못 먹어요.

    I can't eat spicy food.

2. 내일부터는 저녁 먹기 전에 30분씩 운동하려고 해요.

    Starting from tomorrow, I plan to exercise for thirty minutes every day
    before eating dinner.

3. 어제는 너무 피곤해서 저녁도 안 먹은 채 그냥 잠이
    들었어요.

    Yesterday, I was so tired that I just fell asleep without even eating dinner.

4. 지금은 전화받기가 어려우니 메시지를 남겨 주시면
    감사하겠습니다.

    I am not able to take your call right now, so I'd appreciate it if you would
    leave a message for me.

5. 처음에 미국에 왔을때는 영어가 많이 서툴었는데 이제
    꽤 능숙해졌어요.

    My English was very clumsy when I first came to the United States, but I've
    become quite proficient now.

6. 이번 일요일에 친구들하고 등산을 가기로 했는데 갑자기
    일이 생겨서 못 갈 것 같아요.

    I was supposed to go hiking with friends this Sunday, but something came up
    all of a sudden, so I don't think I can go.

Exercise 4
Place a slash (/) at each pause in the following story.

작년 8월 말에 시작된 나의 대학 생활은 정말 값지고도
소중합니다. 비록 1년이 안된 짧은 기간이지만 그동안
나는 너무나 많은 것을 배우고 체험하고 또 느꼈습니다.
부모님으로부터 떨어져 자립이 무엇인가도 알게 되었습니다.

My college life, which began at the end of August last year, is really valuable and
precious. Although it's been a short time, not even a year, I've learned,

experienced, and felt so much during that period. I've also come to know what independence is all about, being away from my parents.

개성있고 멋진 나의 사랑하는 친구들과의 시간들은 대학 1년 생활 중 얻은 가장 큰 선물이었습니다. 그리고 이제는 제법 졸지 않고 꾸준히 공부하는 법도 터득하게 되었습니다.

The times I've had with my dear friends, who are unique and wonderful, were the greatest gift I've had during my first year in college. And I've now learned how to study quite steadily without dozing off.

부모님 품밖에* 나와 빨래와 요리도 스스로 할 수 있게 되었으며 학교 단체에서 여는 여러 행사에도 참여했고 대학생활의 첫 목적이라고도 할 수 있는 지식을 넓히게 되었습니다.

*The speaker on the CD inadvertently read this item as 품밖에서.

Having gotten away from my parents' protection, I now can also do laundry and cooking on my own. I've also participated in various events that are sponsored by school organizations, and I've expanded my knowledge, which may be considered to be the primary purpose of college.

그러나 대학생활 중 반성하고 고쳐야 할 점도 많았습니다. 갑자기 얻어진 자유 탓인지 정신적으로 많이 느슨해져 있었던 것 같습니다. 이제 3년 이상 남은 대학 생활, 나는 이 길고도 짧은 시간동안 최선을 다해 내 생애 최고의 가장 값진 시간을 보내려고 합니다.

However, there have been a lot of things that I had to reflect on and correct. I think that I might have been too undisciplined psychologically, perhaps because of the freedom that I had all of a sudden. Now that my college life has a little more than three years left, I am planning to do my best and to spend the seemingly long, but really short, time to make it the best and the most precious time of my life.

Answer Guide for the Practice Exercises

Practice: Vowels

Section V-1
Exercise 2
1. [2]   2. [3]   3. [2]   4. [3]   5. [2]

Exercise 3
1. 국   2. 글   3. 굴   4. 든   5. 둔   6. 들   7. 은   8. 운
9. 음   10. 쑨다

Exercise 4
1. 구   2. 그   3. 을   4. 울   5. 음   6. 움   7. 극   8. 국

Section V-2
Exercise 2
1. [1]   2. [2]   3. [1]

Exercise 3
1. 게   2. 개   3. 때   4. 떼   5. 배짱   6. 세   7. 새   8. 세

Exercise 4
1. 게   2. 개   3. 베   4. 배   5. 샘   6. 셈

Section V-3
Exercise 2
1. [1]   2. [3]   3. [2]   4. [2]   5. [3]   6. [2]

Exercise 3
1. 목   2. 벌   3. 볼   4. 섬   5. 온   6. 얼   7. 정   8. 통   9. 조금
10. 저금   11. 거기   12. 고기   13. 소리   14. 코피   15. 커피

Exercise 4
1. 로   2. 러   3. 러   4. 터   5. 토   6. 얼   7. 올   8. 번   9. 본
10. 곱   11. 겁   12. 청

Section V-4
Exercise 2
1. [2]   2. [2]   3. [2]   4. [3]

Exercise 3
1. 털   2. 틀   3. 검은   4. 들어   5. 덜어   6. 뜹니다

Exercise 4
1. 음   2. 엄   3. 정   4. 증

Section V-5
Exercise 2
1. [3]   2. [3]   3. [1]   4. [2]

Exercise 3
1. 반   2. 서   3. 발   4. 성   5. 잘   6. 점   7. 남아   8. 먹어

Exercise 4
1. 한   2. 헌   3. 퍼   4. 파   5. 번   6. 반

Section V-6
Section V-6.1
Exercise 2
1. [1]   2. [3]   3. [2]   4. [2]

Exercise 3
1. 악   2. 얘기   3. 애기   4. 여름   5. 겨울   6. 거울   7. 수표   8. 굴
9. 여유   10. 휴식

Exercise 5
1. 예   2. 에   3. 휴   4. 후   5. 향   6. 항

Section V-6.2
Exercise 2
1. [2]   2. [2]   3. [2]   4. [2]   5. [3]

Exercise 3
1. 얘기   2. 예   3. 약   4. 고역   5. 향   6. 형수   7. 앓아   8. 표지
9. 수영   10. 요행

Exercise 5
1. 애   2. 예   3. 영   4. 양   5. 여   6. 요

Section V-7
Exercise 2
1. [3]   2. [2]   3. [2]

Exercise 3
1. 의자   2. 이자   3. 의사   4. 이미   5. 의리

Exercise 4
1. [ㅢ]   2. [ㅣ]   3. [ㅣ]   4. [ㅣ]   5. [ㅔ]   6. [ㅣ]   7. [ㅣ]   8. [ㅢ]
9. [ㅔ]   10. [ㅣ]

Section V-8
Exercise 2
1. [1]   2. [2]   3. [1]   4. [2]   5. [1]

Exercise 3
1. 위   2. 이   3. 위쪽   4. 의한   5. 위한   6. 의기   7. 왜   8. 외   9. 완만
10. 원만   11. 권   12. 관

Exercise 5
1. 위   2. 이   3. 좌   4. 줘   5. 워   6. 와

Practice: Consonants

Section C-1
Exercise 2
1. 1st one   2. 2nd one   3. 2nd one   4. 1st one   5. 2nd one   6. 2nd one
7. 1st one   8. 1st one   9. 2nd one   10. 2nd one   11. 2nd one   12. 1st one

Section C-2
Exercise 2
1. [2]   2. [3]   3. [2]   4. [3]   5. [1]   6. [2]   7. [1]

Exercise 3
1. 비   2. 피   3. 분   4. 푼   5. 풀   6. 불   7. 팔   8. 발   9. 봄   10. 포기
11. 보기   12. 벌벌   13. 펄펄   14. 피었어   15. 비었어

Exercise 5
1. 바   2. 파   3. 파   4. 버   5. 퍼   6. 버   7. 발   8. 팔   9. 발

Section C-3
Exercise 2
1. [3]   2. [1]   3. [2]   4. [1]   5. [1]   6. [2]   7. [2]

Exercise 3
1. 뻐   2. 방   3. 빵   4. 분   5. 뿐   6. 불   7. 뿔   8. 벌벌   9. 뻘뻘
10. 빼   11. 뱄어   12. 뺐어   13. 삐었어   14. 빈   15. 이빨

Exercise 5
1. 빠   2. 바   3. 빠   4. 빨   5. 발   6. 번   7. 뻔   8. 뻔   9. 뽕   10. 봉

Section C-4
Section C-4.1
Exercise 2
1. [ㅍ ㅂ]   2. [ㅂ ㅃ]   3. [ㅍ ㅂ]   4. [ㅂ ㅍ]   5. [ㅍ ㅃ]   6. [ㅃ ㅂ]   7. [ㅃ ㅍ]

Exercise 3
1. 풀   2. 뿔   3. 불   4. 분   5. 뿐   6. 푼   7. 배   8. 패기   9. 빼지
10. 발레   11. 팔래   12. 빨래   13. 피었어   14. 비었어   15. 삐었어

Exercise 4
1. 푹   2. 뿍   3. 북   4. 빈   5. 핀   6. 삔   7. 팡   8. 빵   9. 방

Section C-4.2
Exercise 3
1. b   2. a   3. c   4. a

Exercise 4
1. 앞   2. 압   3. 잎   4. 입

Section C-5
Exercise 2
1. 2nd one   2. 2nd one   3. 1st one   4. 1st one   5. 1st one   6. 2nd one
7. 2nd one   8. 2nd one   9. 2nd one   10. 2nd one   11. 2nd one   12. 2nd one

Section C-6
Exercise 2
1. [2]　2. [1]　3. [2]　4. [2]　5. [3]　6. [2]　7. [3]

Exercise 3
1. 덕　2. 돈　3. 달　4. 탈　5. 답　6. 탑　7. 토끼　8. 도끼　9. 동지
10. 통지　11. 틀려　12. 들려　13. 들어　14. 틀어　15. 교통

Exercise 5
1. 다　2. 타　3. 타　4. 통　5. 동　6. 통　7. 동　8. 탕　9. 당

Section C-7
Exercise 2
1. [2]　2. [3]　3. [2]　4. [2]　5. [2]　6. [3]　7. [2]

Exercise 3
1. 도　2. 또　3. 땀　4. 달　5. 딸　6. 떡　7. 덕　8. 대문　9. 때문
10. 딸기　11. 달기　12. 닿아　13. 땋아　14. 듣고　15. 뜯고

Exercise 5
1. 똥　2. 동　3. 똥　4. 땅　5. 당　6. 땅　7. 뜩　8. 득

Section C-8
Section C-8.1
Exercise 2
1. [ㄸㄷ]　2. [ㄷㄸ]　3. [ㅌㄷ]　4. [ㅌㄸ]　5. [ㄷㅌ]　6. [ㄷㅌ]　7. [ㄸㅌ]

Exercise 3
1. 떠　2. 터　3. 더　4. 탄　5. 딴　6. 단　7. 탈　8. 딸　9. 달　10. 덕
11. 턱　12. 떡　13. 새똥　14. 교통　15. 동물

Exercise 5
1. 따　2. 타　3. 타　4. 뚜　5. 투　6. 두　7. 탕　8. 땅　9. 당　10. 덕
11. 떡　12. 턱

Section C-8.2
Exercise 3
1. a　2. a　3. a　4. c

Exercise 4
1. 겉　2. 걷　3. 맏　4. 맡

Section C-9
Exercise 2
1. 2nd one　2. 1st one　3. 2nd one　4. 2nd one　5. 2nd one　6. 2nd one
7. 2nd one　8. 1st one　9. 2nd one　10. 2nd one

Section C-10
Exercise 2
1. [2]　2. [2]　3. [3]　4. [2]　5. [2]　6. [3]　7. [1]

Exercise 3
1. 캐   2. 개   3. 기   4. 간   5. 겁   6. 콩   7. 공   8. 공   9. 콩
10. 골라   11. 콜라   12. 근시   13. 근방   14. 크림   15. 그림

Exercise 5
1. 코   2. 고   3. 칼   4. 갈   5. 근   6. 근   7. 큰   8. 큼   9. 금

Section C-11
Exercise 2
1. [3]   2. [3]   3. [2]   4. [2]   5. [2]   6. [1]   7. [2]

Exercise 3
1. 가   2. 까지   3. 가지   4. 가지   5. 깨   6. 굴   7. 꿀   8. 꼬리   9. 고리
10. 기어   11. 끼어   12. 깔아   13. 갈아   14. 토끼   15. 곰곰이

Exercise 5
1. 까   2. 깨   3. 개   4. 깨   5. 깐   6. 간   7. 곱   8. 꼽   9. 꿈   10. 금

Section C-12
Section C-12.1
Exercise 2
1. [ㄱ ㄲ]   2. [ㅋ ㄲ]   3. [ㅋ ㄱ]   4. [ㄱ ㅋ]   5. [ㄱ ㄲ]   6. [ㅋ ㄱ]   7. [ㄲ ㅋ]

Exercise 3
1. 기   2. 끼   3. 키   4. 기   5. 개   6. 캐   7. 깨   8. 클   9. 끌   10. 껴
11. 켜   12. 겨자   13. 깜깜   14. 감감   15. 캄캄

Exercise 5
1. 께   2. 게   3. 꺼   4. 커   5. 거   6. 굼   7. 꿈   8. 끔   9. 큼   10. 끔

Section C-12.2
Exercise 3
1. b   2. c   3. b   4. b

Exercise 4
1. 밖   2. 박   3. 섞   4. 석

Section C-13
Exercise 2
1. 2nd one   2. 2nd one   3. 2nd one   4. 2nd one   5. 2nd one   6. 2nd one
7. 2nd one   8. 2nd one

Section C-14
Exercise 2
1. [2]   2. [3]   3. [2]   4. [2]   5. [3]   6. [3]   7. [1]

Exercise 3
1. 차   2. 자   3. 자고   4. 질   5. 쳤어   6. 졌어   7. 총   8. 종   9. 진해
10. 친해   11. 짐   12. 침   13. 기자   14. 기차   15. 가치

Exercise 5
1. 주   2. 추   3. 잠   4. 참   5. 정   6. 청   7. 즘   8. 츰

Section C-15
Exercise 2
1. [1] 2. [3] 3. [1] 4. [3] 5. [3] 6. [2] 7. [2]

Exercise 3
1. 짜 2. 자 3. 잠 4. 짬 5. 집 6. 쪽 7. 찌고 8. 질렀어 9. 찔리네
10. 졸면 11. 쫄면 12. 짖어 13. 찢어 14. 쟁쟁 15. 쨍쨍

Exercise 5
1. 짜 2. 작 3. 쩜 4. 점 5. 쫄 6. 졸 7. 즘 8. 쯤

Section C-16
Section C-16.1
Exercise 2
1. [ㅈㅊ] 2. [ㅉㅈ] 3. [ㅊㅈ] 4. [ㅈㅊ] 5. [ㅉㅊ] 6. [ㅈㅉ] 7. [ㅈㅊ]

Exercise 3
1. 차 2. 자 3. 짜 4. 잔 5. 찬 6. 찜 7. 침 8. 짐 9. 쳐 10. 쩌
11. 질 12. 칠 13. 촉 14. 밤참 15. 짬

Exercise 5
1. 채 2. 채 3. 째 4. 쩌 5. 처 6. 창 7. 짱 8. 장 9. 쪽 10. 촉

Section C-16.2
Exercise 3
1. b 2. a 3. b 4. a

Exercise 4
1. 빛 2. 빛 3. 낮 4. 낫

Section C-17
Section C-17.1
Exercise 2
1. 심 2. 사와 3. 맛은 4. 가수 5. 싸움

Exercise 4
1. [1] 2. [2] 3. [1] 4. [2] 5. [3] 6. [2] 7. [2]

Exercise 5
1. 사 2. 싸 3. 씨 4. 시 5. 살 6. 쌀 7. 살 8. 써 9. 섰어 10. 쌈
11. 썰어 12. 왔어 13. 해서 14. 아파서 15. 있었어

Exercise 7
1. 써 2. 서 3. 시 4. 씨 5. 쑤 6. 수 7. 쑤 8. 씬 9. 신 10. 씬

Section C-17.2
Exercise 3
1. b 2. a 3. c 4. c 5. c

Exercise 4
1. 갓 2. 갔

Section C-18
Section C-18.1
Exercise 2
1. 학기 2. 얼었어 3. 향수 4. 휴지 5. 형

Section C-18.2
Exercise 1
1. 날 2. 간다 3. 이고 4. 남지

Exercise 2
1. c 2. a 3. c 4. c

Exercise 3
1. [S] 2. [D] 3. [S] 4. [S]

Exercise 5
1. 낮 2. 낯 3. 났 4. 빛 5. 빗 6. 빚

Section C-19
Exercise 2
1. [2] 2. [2] 3. [3] 4. [1] 5. [2]

Exercise 3
1. 잠만 2. 잠 안 3. 자만 4. 그물 5. 금물 6. 몸에 7. 몸매
8. 신는 9. 신은 10. 신은 11. 많아 12. 만나 13. 타네 14. 저 나무
15. 붕어

Exercise 5
1. 아 2. 나 3. 미 4. 이

Section C-20
Exercise 4
1. [2] 2. [1] 3. [3] 4. [3] 5. [2]

Exercise 5
1. 들러 2. 들어 3. 들려 4. 느려 5. 얼려 6. 불러 7. 불어 8. 옳았
9. 올랐 10. 걸었어 11. 걸렸어 12. 놀랐어 13. 놀았어 14. 잘랐어
15. 자랐어

Exercise 7
1. 리 2. 이 3. 을 4. 를 5. 를 6. 을 7. 버 8. 벌

Practice: Adjustments

Section A-1
Exercise 4
1. 백원 2. 받다 3. 국이 4. 국기 5. 안은 6. 입은 7. 물러
8. 걸었어

Exercise 5
1. [S] 2. [D] 3. [S] 4. [S] 5. [D] 6. [S]

Exercise 6

1. 월/요일/이에요.

2. 일/이 힘 들/어요.

3. 밥/은 없/어요?

4. 책/을 읽/어요.

5. 낮/이 짧/아요.

6. 한국/어 녹/음/을 해요.

7. 곧/올게요.

8. 화장실/어디예요?

9. 빗/어디 있/어요?

Exercise 8
1. 이   2. 리   3. 벗   4. 버   5. 늘   6. 을   7. 악   8. 막

Section A-2
Exercise 4
1. b   2. c   3. c   4. b   5. b   6. a   7. a

Section A-3
Exercise 3
1. [FP]   2. [R]   3. [FP]   4. [R]   5. [R]   6. [R]   7. [FP]   8. [R]   9. [FP]   10. [R]
11. [R]   12. [FP]   13. [R]   14. [FP]   15. [R]

Section A-4
Exercise 2
1. 사과를 is contracted to 사꽐 in speech.
2. 과자는 is contracted to 과잔 in speech.
3. 이게 and 뭡니까 are the contractions of 이것이 and 무엇입니까, respectively.
4. 우리는 is contracted to 우린 in speech.
5. 그럼 is the contraction of 그러면, and 다음주 is contracted to 담주 in speech.
6. 걔 and 뭐야 are contractions of 그 아이, and 무엇이야, respectively.
7. 그런데 is contracted to 근데 in speech, and 거야 is the contraction of 것이야.
8. 얘기 is the contraction of 이야기.
9. 건 is the contraction of 것은.
10. 영화를 and 재미있게 are contracted to 영활 and 재밌게, respectively, in speech and 봤어 is the contraction of 보았어.
11. 뭘 and 봐요 are the contractions of 무엇을 and 보아요, respectively.
12. 어쩌면 is contracted to 어쩜 in speech.
13. 가수입니다 is contracted to 가숩니다 in speech.
14. 그게 is the contraction of 그것이 and 어디 있어요 is contracted to 어딨어요 in speech.
15. -졌어요 is the contraction of -지었어요. (Nowadays it is always written and pronounced as the contracted 졌어요.)

Section A-5
Exercise 2
1. c 2. a 3. a 4. a 5. c

Section A-6
Exercise 4
1. [R] 2. [FP] 3. [R] 4. [R] 5. [R] 6. [FP] 7. [R] 8. [R] 9. [FP]
10. [R]

Section A-7
Exercise 4
1. [A] 2. [A] 3. [A] 4. [A] 5. [A] 6.[R] 7. [A] 8. [A] 9. [A] 10. [R]
11. [R] 12. [A]

Exercise 5
1. [ㅌ] 2. [ㅋ] 3. [ㅊ] 4. [ㅌ] 5. [ㅋ] 6. [ㅌ] 7. [ㅋ] 8. [ㅋ] 9. [ㅌ]
10. [ㅍ]

Exercise 7
1. 화 2. 과 3. 화 4. 히 5. 이 6. 히

Section A-8
Exercise 4
1. b 2. b 3. c 4. a 5. a 6. c

Section A-9
Section A-9.1
Exercise 3
1. 답 2. 닭 3. 밥 4. 꽃 5. 꼭 6. 못 7. 잤나 8. 우나 9. 첫눈

Exercise 4
1. 신년 2. 갑시다 3. 막내 4. 콩장 5. 잔디 6. 박수 7. 국어

Exercise 5
1. [겸] 2. [엄] 3. [감] 4. [면] 5. [난] 6. [간] 7. [몬] 8. [궁] 9. [녕]
10. [뱅] 11. [땅] 12. [방]

Exercise 7
1. 몇 2. 몇 3. 못 4. 목 5. 못 6. 났 7. 나 8. 났 9. 합 10. 합

Section A-9.2
Exercise 3
1. 금이 2. 심리 3. 공룡 4. 정류장 5. 섭리 6. 석유

Exercise 4
1. a 2. b 3. a 4. b 5. c 6. c

Exercise 5
1. [금니] 2. [염녀] 3. [공닙] 4. [공농] 5. [성뉴] 6. [싱냥] 7. [황뉼]
8. [퐁낙] 9. [암녁] 10. [섬니]

Exercise 7
1. 리 2. 이 3. 략 4. 약 5. 률 6. 율 7. 력 8. 력

Section A-10
Exercise 3
1. b, c 2. a, b 3. b, c 4. a, b 5. a, c

Exercise 4
1. 간 2. 감 3. 단/담 (The two can sound the same before 배 because ㄴ can be pronounced ㅁ in this context. However, only 담 matches the English translation provided.) 4. 단 5. 인 6. 임 7. 몇 8. 몇

Section A-11
Exercise 4
1. c 2. b 3. c 4. b 5. c 6. a

Exercise 5
1. [웬닐] 2. [심능] 3. [꼰니피] 4. [나문니피] 5. [생년필] 6. [암닐] 7. [뒨닐] 8. [옌닐] 9. [전철력] 10. [칠류]

Section A-12
Section A-12.1

Exercise 3
1. 겁보 2. 맛있다 3. 다섯권 4. 약속 5. 꽃집

Exercise 4
1. 잡비 2. 악기 3. 찾자 4. 맛있다

Exercise 5
1. 잡비 2. 갔다 3. 맛이다 4. 백원 5. 악기 6. 이 속 7. 찾자

Section A-12.2
Exercise 2
1. a: [N], b: [T] 2. a: [N], b: [T] 3. a: [T], b: [N] 4. a: [N], b: [T] 5. a: [N], b: [T] 6. a: [T], b: [N] 7. a: [T], b: [N]

Exercise 3
1. a 2. b 3. a 4. b 5. b 6. c 7. a 8. a

Exercise 6
1. [T] 2. [T] 3. [N] 4. [T] 5. [N] 6. [T] 7. [N] 8. [T]

Section A-13
Exercise 2
1. b 2. a 3. c

Exercise 3
1. 다 2. 닷 3. 빗 4. 비

Section A-14
Exercise 2
1. [D] 2. [D] 3. [S] 4. [D] 5. [S] 6. [S] 7. [S]

Exercise 3
1. [ㄷ]   2. [ㅊ]   3. [ㅈ]   4. [ㄷ]   5. [ㅈ]   6. [ㅈ]   7. [ㅊ]   8. [ㅌ]   9. [ㅌ]
10. [ㅊ]

Exercise 5
1. 붙   2. 부/붙 (The two have the same pronunciation in this context. However, only 부 matches the English translation provided.)   3. 혔   4. 혔   5. 혔

Section A-15
Exercise 2
1. [N]   2. [W]   3. [N]   4. [W]   5. [W]   6. [W]   7. [W]   8. [W]

Exercise 3
1. b, c   2. b, c   3. a, b

Practice: Prosody

Section P-2
Exercise 1
1. 와요   2. 일하러   3. 저녁에

Exercise 2
1. [학]   2. [월]   3. [노]   4. [했]

Exercise 3
1. B$_1$ 2. B$_2$ 3. B$_1$ 4. B$_2$ 5. B$_1$

Exercise 4
1. B$_2$ (for 'Are you going somewhere?'); B$_1$ (for 'Where are you going?')
2. B$_2$ (for 'Is someone coming?'); B$_1$ (for 'Who's coming?')
3. B$_2$ (for 'Did you see it sometime?'); B$_1$ (for 'When did you see it?')
4. B$_1$ (for 'How many times did you see it?')
5. B$_1$ (for 'What are you doing?')

Section P-3
Exercise 2
1. both rising   2. both falling/flat   3. prolonged rising; falling/flat
4. both rising   5. prolonged rising; falling/flat   6. both rising
7. prolonged rising; falling/flat   8. both rising   9. both falling/flat

Exercise 3
1. Are you coming to the party?   2. Please come to the party.
3. Are you making a phone call?   4. Please call.   5. I've been to Korea.
6. Have you been to Korea?   7. Please come sometime.   8. When are you coming?

Exercise 4
1. [S] ('I've seen that movie several times.')
2. [Y/N] ('Have you seen that movie several times?')
3. [Wh] ('How many times have you seen that movie?')
4. [S/P] ('I'm going somewhere today./Let's go somewhere today.')
5. [Wh] ('Where are you going today?')
6. [Y/N] ('Are you going somewhere today?')
7. [Y/N] ('Is someone coming tomorrow?')

8. [Wh] ('Who's coming tomorrow?')
9. [S] ('Someone's coming tomorrow.')

Exercise 5

A: 안녕하세요?	falling/flat
어디 가세요?	rising
B: 네, 볼 일이 좀 있어서요.	falling/flat
A: 어디 가시는데요?	rising
B: 학교에를 좀 가려구요.	falling/flat
A: 오늘 일요일인데...	falling/flat
누구 만나세요?	rising
B: 네, 누구 좀 만나려고요.	falling/flat
A: 누굴요?	rising
B: 친구 좀 만나려고요.	falling/flat
그럼, 저 먼저 가 볼게요.	falling/flat
A: 네, 그럼 안녕히 가세요.	falling/flat
B: 네, 안녕히 가세요.	falling/flat
또 뵈요.	falling/flat

Section P-4

Exercise 2

1. B₁ (for 'I bet that person is going to the party with us.')   2. B₂ (for 'I wish that person had gone to the party with us.')   3. B₁ (for 'I wish he'd sit down.')   4. B₂ (for 'Why don't you have a seat?')

Exercise 3

A: 안녕하세요?	falling/flat
날씨가 꽤 추운데요.	dramatic
B: 네, 정말 추워요.	falling/flat
어, 눈온다!	dramatic
밖에 눈 와요!	dramatic
A: 와, 정말 첫눈이네요!	dramatic
그런데, 우리 뭐 시킬까요?	rising
B: 전 냉커피로 할게요.	falling/flat
A: 여기 냉커피 하나하고	
인삼차 하나 주세요.	falling/flat
B: 아, 춥다!	dramatic
찬 걸 마시니까 더 춥네요.	falling/flat
A: 그렇죠?	rising
뜨거운 걸 시키시지.	falling/flat

Exercise 4

A: 나 여자친구 생겼다!	rising
B: 정말?	rising
예뻐?	rising
A: 끝내 줘.	dramatic
얼마나 예쁜데.	dramatic
B: 와, 부럽다!	dramatic
나도 네 친구 하나 소개시켜 주라.	falling/flat

A: 말만 해.   falling/flat
어떤 타입을 좋아하는데?   rising
B: 난 이해심 많은 남자가 좋더라.   falling/flat
A: 그래?   rising
내 여자친구는 이해심도 많다.   rising
B: 야, 자랑 좀 그만해.   falling/flat
근데, 나 언제 소개시켜 줄 거야? rising
A: 이리 오기로 돼 있어, 이미.   falling/flat
한 한 시간이면 될걸.   rising
B: 그래?   rising
어, 옷 좀 예쁘게 입고 나올 걸.   falling/flat
미리 얘기 좀 해 주지.   falling/flat

Section P-5
Exercise 2
1. a   2. a   3. b   4. a   5. b

Exercise 3
1. 매운 음식은/ 못 먹어요./
2. 내일부터는/ 저녁 먹기 전에/ 30분씩/ 운동하려고 해요./
3. 어제는/ 너무 피곤해서/ 저녁도 안 먹은 채/ 그냥 잠이 들었어요./
4. 지금은/ 전화받기가 어려우니/ 메시지를 남겨 주시면/
   감사하겠습니다./
5. 처음에/ 미국에 왔을때는/ 영어가 많이 서툴었는데/ 이제/ 꽤/
   능숙해졌어요./
6. 이번 일요일에/ 친구들하고/ 등산을 가기로 했는데/
   갑자기 일이 생겨서/ 못 갈 것 같아요./

Exercise 4
　작년/ 8월 말에 시작된/ 나의 대학 생활은/ 정말/ 값지고도/
소중합니다./ 비록/ 1년이 안된/ 짧은 기간이지만/ 그동안 나는/
너무나 많은 것을 배우고/ 체험하고/ 또 느꼈습니다./ 부모님으로부터
떨어져/ 자립이 무엇인가도/ 알게 되었습니다./
　개성있고 멋진/ 나의 사랑하는 친구들과의 시간들은/ 대학 1년 생활
중 얻은/ 가장 큰 선물이었습니다./ 그리고/ 이제는 제법 졸지 않고/
꾸준히 공부하는 법도/ 터득하게 되었습니다./
　부모님 품밖에* 나와/ 빨래와 요리도/ 스스로 할 수 있게 되었으며/
학교 단체에서 여는/ 여러 행사에도 참여했고/ 대학생활의 첫
목적이라고도 할 수 있는/ 지식을 넓히게 되었습니다./
　그러나/ 대학생활 중/ 반성하고/ 고쳐야 할 점도 많았습니다./ 갑자기
얻어진 자유 탓인지/ 정신적으로 많이/ 느슨해져 있었던 것 같습니다./
이제 3년 이상 남은 대학 생활,/ 나는 이 길고도/ 짧은 시간동안/
최선을 다해/ 내 생애 최고의/ 가장 값진 시간을/ 보내려고 합니다./

*The speaker on the CD inadvertently read this item as 품밖에서.

List of Practice Exercises

(by section number)

Vowels

Consonants

Adjustments

Prosody

Index of Topics

Lightning Source UK Ltd.
Milton Keynes UK
UKHW020828111120
373193UK00005B/212